Site Divine
An Alternate Method of Site Analysis

written by C. *Lanfranco*

This book is dedicated to Karen Quiana
All hail the Mighty 'Q'

The creation of this book stands as a testament to many people. I would first like to thank Mr. Herbert Muschamp, whose lecture at Cornell in the fall of 1996 gave me the first seed of an idea. My deepest gratitude goes out to Karen Quiana who encouraged the planting and nurturing of my idea when it was but a seedling. As well, I would like to thank Cornell's Professor Peter Trowbridge, whose single-handed support and dedication led to the foundations of my design education. Further thanks are given to UCLA's Chair of Architecture, Sylvia Lavin, for accepting me into her program and allowing me to continue my design education.

I would also like to thank Zoë Lonergan whose gifted design skills helped make this book possible and for her support throughout the last push towards completion. My deepest appreciation must also be given to the brilliant brain storming of Lisa Mann, a true creative force unparalleled in our time. In addition, I would like to thank all of the individuals who granted me interviews on the site, especially the modest Chris Gagosz, whose words show his deep understanding of the world. Thanks to my mother Johanna and sisters Katerina and Andrea for believing in me. Finally, I would like to thank Jennie Wilbur, who is without a doubt one of the best young editors in America today. Without her, there would be little more than ink on paper...with her, I offer you this book.

introduction

The modern scientific forms of site analysis practiced by the majority of architects, landscape architects, and others henceforth referred to as designers, are clearly explained in various text books. These texts, ranging from elementary planning textbooks, environmental textbooks, to engineering books, explain the scientific methods of site analysis clearly and in depth. Yet one fundamentally important aspect of site analysis, the examination of the sensual or intuitive nature of the site, lacks discussion in present site analysis and design guidelines. The elements of site analysis that are often overlooked in our present reductionistic site analyses are those categories that are based upon the divine, the sensuous, and the sublime characteristics of the site. As a foundation to a new spiritual structure of design, this book will examine the search for the divine within the site. This search will re-introduce ancient techniques of site analysis that existed before the purely scientific analyses that designers presently undertake. This book proposes that by examining ancient methods of divination, the contemporary designer can attain valuable additional perspectives after examining the site. In conclusion, this book will argue that site analysis practiced by both our academic and professional communities needs to re-discover the subjective aspects of site analysis.

As currently practiced, the sensual, intuitive, and even spiritual aspects of site analysis are abstract and often misunderstood elements of the site analysis process. The genius loci, or spirit of the place is nothing more than an abstractual component of the site analysis process when compared to the hard and rigid elements that are argued to be 'more real,' or 'more applicable.' Designers should be encouraged to examine each of the elements of a site, examining all aspects of reality in the world regardless of the spiritual structure or moral foundations that presently dictate and direct their designs. A complete site analysis will challenge designers to examine more than the sphere of mere physical existence, and will lead them to a deeper, even spiritual understanding of the site. Just as people are awed and moved by things very different from the 'hard' facts and numbers of final designs, so too should designers actively search for an understanding of the site that will better enable such an appreciation. As it is something from within the sublime nature of design that moves people, successful designers will begin with a search for the divine of the site within their own design disciplines. In the end, an investigation of site analysis that leads to an understanding of the complete nature of the site will lead to an examination of the future of design. If this book is to successfully examine both the past and the future of the site divine, a new form of design will emerge.

This book is organized into three parts. One portion consists of six chapters that rediscovers ancient ways of examining and understanding the site while the second portion examines a specific Case Study and the final portion concludes with a new contemporary design methodology based upon these ancient ways of site analysis. As part of methodological portion of the book, the first chapter discusses the importance of site analysis in the design process, and examines the present state of site analysis in our contemporary society. Chapter Two argues that a new perspective regarding site analysis is needed, and that this new perspective would result in a new type of site design. In Chapter Three, site divination is introduced as a starting point for a different approach to site examination. Chapter Four examines a form of divination that is directly related to the site and is generally referred to as geomancy. In this chapter, three ancient forms of geomancy are discussed, augury and extispicy as practiced by the ancient Romans and Greeks, and vastu as practiced by the ancient Southeast Asians. Chapter Five examines feng shui, and Chapter Six examines dowsing as another form of geomancy. After Chapter Six, the Case Study of a site located in Toronto, Canada is presented. This Case Study attempts to apply some of the above-referenced forms of site analysis to a specific site. After completing a scientific site analysis, people who claim either a geomantic expertise or who are active inhabitants of the site are interviewed. These interviews provide a deeper insight, into not only the site itself, but also into the quality of geomantic expertise that is available to assist designers in unconventional forms of site analysis.

Following the site specific analysis in the Case Study section, Chapter Seven attempts to find modern parallels to the philosophical underpinnings of divination in the Gaia concept. Chapter Eight suggests ways in which the Gaia concept can influence our methods of design, and Chapter Nine concludes the book by offering some tenets, that are applicable to design and that embrace the concepts of both divination and Gaia. Throughout the book, words are both introduced and used in unique ways, and to assist in understanding these words, please refer to the glossary that is located at the end.

Part One   chapter one *the analysis of site*

Consult the genius of the place in all:
That tells the waters to rise or fall;
Or helps the ambitious hill the heaven to scale,
Or scoops in circling theaters the vale,
Calls in the country, catches opening glades,
Joins willing woods, and varies from shades to shades;
Now breaks, or now directs the intending lines;
Paints, as you plant, and, as you work, it designs.

"Epistle to Lord Burlington" by Alexander Pope

The site is alive. This view is the key to the analysis of any site, and designs will ultimately fail if the site is seen as a tabula rasa upon which elements can be indiscriminately inscribed. To successfully understand the site, designers must search for the spirit of this living place.

The site is our environment. To design within it, it must be analyzed. The examination of what exists before realizing a design is an essential part of design. This analysis is nota singular act, but rather a process for understanding the systems that most affect eventual designs. Commonly, this analysis is termed 'site analysis.' Site analysis reflects upon the structures of power and upon the values within which a site exists. Because the site is a living community, all site analyses must by necessity consider their occupants. Site analysis should have two elements: one oriented to human purposes, the other to the site itself as an ongoing natural process. All sites are composed of distinct elements above, below, and on the ground surface. Each of these elements are interrelated, whether they remain static in this relationship or are constantly changing. A complete analysis of any site will show us that each site is unique. Understanding this singularity imposes limitations, yet offers new possibilities for all designs. The key to both understanding the site, as well as creating a connection to the site lies in the devotion of time and effort to site analysis. This is the search

Detecting hidden springs
Leon Battista Alberti
The Architecture of
Leon Battista Alberti
plate 66, 1755

for the 'spirit of place.' According to the famous architectural theorist Leon Battista Alberti:

The region must be examined carefully; clues to its character must be sought in its most hidden places and figures, for site interpretation involves detection. Observing obscure signs of underground water, for example, involves lying with one's chin on the ground in the early morning in order to catch sight of vapor wisps rising into the air. Every circumstance must be weighed and the most occult tokens must be taken into account. Obviously signs are helpful, but insufficient; things taken normally unseen, like the entrails of an animal, should be examined. To be investigated also were local produce, the longevity of inhabitants, and the character of infants (because every native abnormality demonstrates a topographical defect). Disease and privation are place bound. Also indicative are the way local trees bend, the shape of native animals and the finish of nearby old buildings. Detecting character involves hermeneutic comprehension.

Site analysis informs design, therefore the analysis of site is the most important prelude to successful design. A complete site analysis, one that inventories the pressures and forces in the space, informs the designer about the site and its context, enabling her to respond to these conditions and their contexts when developing a design. A thorough site analysis ensures that designers will make their decisions deliberately and thoughtfully resulting in designs that are intentional, not accidental. The designer's approach to the site determines the way they will structure their designs into the site. Successful site analysis must immerse the designer into the site and allow her to develop an acute sense of awareness regarding the site. Successful site analysis investigates the past, the present, and the future conditions of the site. Regardless of the future the designer may envision for the site, site analysis will enable the designer to clearly understand the site's past and present, and thereby foresee changes or adaptations likely to occur in the site's future. To have predictive capabilities, site analysis must be seen as a continuous process, where site analysis includes potential conditions as well as the ones presently observed on the site. Site analysis should teach designers something about the nature of the site's internal functional and systemic requirements, as well as its relationship to its external environment. To achieve this, designers must actively define their scope of site analysis and make decisions as to the extent to which they will address the various elements of the site.

Successful site analysis records both objective and subjective information. Objective information is information that is both quantitative and independently verifiable Subjective information includes the sensory aspects of the site that are not quantitative, and require designers to express individual opinions about the quality of the various characteristics of the site. Typical examples include views, odors, noises and social values about the site. Atypical examples might include the quality of ch'i or sh'a, the spiritual nature of the site, or its relationship to the five basic elements of the earth. Since objective information informs designers differently from subjective information, there should be extreme care taken in the designer's valuation of this information, for both are fundamental to the experience of the site. As such, any cataloguing of a site includes not only the physical elements of the site but also the sensuous nature of it, in both its tangible and intangible features. A competent and complete site analysis requires a careful analysis of the site as an ongoing social and ecological system. Any analysis of these site factors, both objective and subjective, should separate transitory or disappearing features from more permanent or emergent ones, thereby classifying the aspects of the site that are unchanging regardless of the design intervention and those that are likely to change through the designs. This classification of information according to permanence and stability may provide a sequence of attention to further inform the design process. Priority may be given to elements most affected by designs and likewise to those elements that would affect potential designs the most.

Besides knowing as much as they can about the site's character and the various influences on it, designers must also understand how the site affects its main participants and likewise how these participants affect the site. These participants include the environment as a greater entity in itself, the users, the clients, the non-using public and finally, the designers themselves. To further understand these roles, it is important to realize that while the client may be the privileged participant in the design process and its impact on the site, they are not necessarily the participants most affected by resulting designs. Contrary to the chain of command dictated by clients, designers are responsible for incorporating the concerns and desires of all of the participants of a site. Designers must understand for whom the site is being designed and must define what each of their roles will be in creating a design. It is important to complete any site analysis at the beginning of the design stage, thereby creating design concepts that are not only compatible with the site, but also originally based upon the site. In an attempt to create something that accurately relates to both the site and its many participants, designers should carefully examine the totality of the site.

To fully understand all site information, there must be an understanding of how long the site as an event occurs. Questions such as how the site changes over relative time periods will help to explain the site's relationship to time. As designs occupy the site, there must be an attempt made to have those designs respond to the relevant temporal conditions that may exist throughout their life spans. In this temporal examination, as designers considers their design as part of a continuous time line, it is important to attempt to predict not only the future that will exist within the site as dictated by the design, but also what has or is in the process of occurring at other similar sites. Successful site analysis will examine what exists on the site and what is lacking from the site. If important site characteristics exist on contextually or geographically similar sites do not exist on the site under investigation, it is important to understand why the site under analysis is lacking the characteristics that are present elsewhere. If a site under analysis is not compared to other contextually similar sites, important defining characteristics of the site may be overlooked due to the fact that it may be their absence that makes the site so unique. For example, an urban site that has had a complete absence of criminal activity can only be discovered when compared to other contextually similar urban sites that have greater levels of criminal activity.

In the end, a defined site is not something given, but is instead something invented. Sites are not only a collection of clinical, scientific facts, they are also potential places whose definitions are created by the structures that use them. The site is where the ever changing, both visible and invisible spatial characters of a society overlap and fold into one another. In the same way, the task of site analysis is to find those characteristics of place whose ideas and experiences are both permanent and transient, spatially and culturally derived. As such, successful site analysis transcends the spiritual structure that dominates it at any given moment. A complete understanding of the site is not limited by the Procrustean principles of market capitalism, nor by the directives of scientism that dominate modern design's understanding of the site. The site's continued presence, regardless of its presently imposed definition, is fundamental to its understanding. In the end, site analysis creates not only the definition for the land within which a design is integrated, it creates the method of investigation that will influence the rest of the design process. A new method of investigation and the definition of the site will change the designer's fundamental relationship towards the land. When the perceived reality of the site changes, the relative reality of design will similarly change. When the most elementary forms of space and time are seen in a new light, designers can discover a new sense of the space that exists around them. A new understanding of site analysis is the beginning of an entirely new perspective on site design.

19
site divine
the analysis of site

chapter two *a new perspective on site design*

"What is the use of a house if you haven't a tolerable planet to put it on?"

Henry David Thoreau

With a new perspective on site analysis, the fundamental precepts of modern design will necessarily change. The key to understanding any design precept is to first understand its spiritual structure. What is the spiritual structure that drives modern design, and what are the architectural images that express and reinforce the values of modern design? A fundamental characteristic of modern design has been an uncontrollable expansion of the built environment. Such expansionism is fundamental to modern design intentions and symbolizes the values held by the dominant capitalist society. The form of the built environment physically represents the reigning ideology of the society. It clearly proclaims what is valued and what is devalued. The modernistic heritage represents a repudiation of the site, and fundamental to this heritage is a pervasive rejection of the influences of the site itself. Many site designers of our modern period envision the site as inert and passive, as an empty stage upon which to impose their designs. These unexamined images of modernity must be scrutinized. Designers stand at the crossroads of cultural change and what is needed now is a new perspective of design that will acknowledge and respond to change that privileges the site. Any new design paradigm must require designers to understand and respect the site. The problems created by the uncontrolled expansion of the built environment cannot be solved at the same level of awareness that created them. New

21

site divine
*a new perspective
on site design*

levels of awareness must be introduced to evaluate previously held assumptions that encourages unsustainable methods of design based upon materialism and expansionism. Given that inevitability, design must remake itself.

Design is a balance between functional purpose, technical execution, and artistic expression. Design is born of the constant tension between rational features, particularly represented by its technical composition and partially represented by its utility, as well as its emotional or sensual qualities. Society's system of values dictates these relationships. Above all it is the compositional language of the design of the land and all its structures that generates an understanding of what a society does or does not stand for; what it values or does not value. Design responds to intimations of worth, through a systematic allocation of finite space in accordance to society's own doctrine. The design of the land represents the ultimate valuation of a society, it is the most intensive and comprehensive way of physically articulating value. Design constantly evokes the value system that erected it. As we live, see, hear, feel, and therefore design by our basic values, design becomes an accurate symbol of the time and spirituality that produced it. Presently, Modernist design theory dominates the formation of our visual environment; it delineates the cities, the countryside, and the gardens; it defines the individuals' position in it and gives character and scale to the whole of the inhabited world.

Every architectural style began with a change in the spiritual belief system, just as any kind of spiritual change initiates a new style. As the old order of Modernism is found unresponsive to issues incorporating the site, designers searching for new design paradigms will replace their dominant consciousness and reconsider their values, faith, and focus. As design occupies a point of significant leverage as the collective symbolism most clearly rooted in the values of a society, designers should become the leaders in embarking on the journey to the establishment of new styles.

The present modern consciousness that engulfs us all is based upon the doctrine of scientism. In scientism, scientific opinion is accepted as fact, even if it means denying one's own personal experiences. In the dominant modern consciousness, personal experiences, shaded and colored by deeply held personal values, are not confirmable experiences, and are therefore not considered valid experiences upon which to based reality. If scientific opinion and personal experience should conflict, modern consciousness, based upon the doctrine of scientism, demands that the personal experience be disregarded or amended to conform to standard scientific precedent. In essence, these demands of modern consciousness are no different than the monotheistic insistence that there be only one God. Both of these examples show that personal experience must conform to the governing spiritual structure, but in truth we all know that personal experience is unpredictable and does not conform to any governing doctrine.

Besides being a secular practice designed to provide specific answers to limited questions, scientific faith is also the spiritual doctrine of Modernism and the generator of the modern design movement. Through modern design, scientism has given birth to a new world. The crisis of modern design is, therefore, the crisis posed by modern science beyond a method of inquiry to a theology. Scientism has become the spiritual structure for our lives. Through a new understanding of site analysis, design will find itself in a search for a worthy successor to a scientific consciousness without abandoning the virtues of science itself.

While there is much that is noble in striving for clarity and objective truth, a spiritual structure based on scientism is significantly flawed. The problem with a design paradigm that is governed by scientism is its unwavering reliance on methodological doubt, which is the deliberate suspension of judgment in the face of insufficient evidence. Scientific philosophers accept only what the objective evidence warrants, even if that means discounting that which is true. The central doctrine of methodological doubt is critical objectivity, which is a highly regarded skill in contemporary society. We share most of the values that a science generated objective consciousness has instilled in us. We should, however, recognize that belief without knowledge found beyond objective evidence — through subjective hunches, poetic suggestions, or even sheer delight — is a possibility. What is so advantageous about an objective consciousness that it merits losing the possibility of believing beyond evidence, thereby ignoring beauty or even truth itself? The modern heritage of the world has designated objective consciousness as the highest authority not only in explicitly scientific contexts but in modern design as well. In today's modernistic heritage, design is committed to the ideals of objectivity, where design's duty is to obey no final authority but critical objectivity. Modernity has made objective consciousness the functioning foundation of our present architectural doctrine.

René Descartes explained a vital distinction required by objective consciousness: the primary versus the secondary qualities of observations. The primary qualities of observation are quantitative, public, and confirmable, while the secondary qualities are sensorial, private, and therefore transitive. Descartes argued that the real world, the objectively true world, is made up of what exists apart from the private irrelevancies of subjectivity. What is real is the measurable, the material. What is suspect and relative is the qualitative, the private, and the

23

site divine
a new perspective
on site design

merely mental. Descartes urged modern thinkers to understand the whole by dividing the problem, and analyzing it in terms of its smallest components. The objective truth will become clear when these elements, together with the quantifiable laws of their combination, are known. Everything is composed in aggregate of parts that have laws of their own, by virtue of which the larger wholes are constructed. The basic reality is the part. The compound object is a derivative result of many different parts working together according to their individual laws.

In this reductionist world view, the cell is more basic than the living being, a molecule is more basic than the cell, the atom is even more basic than the molecule. Architecturally speaking, the city is more basic than the planet, the neighborhood more basic than the city, and the individual building more basic than the neighborhood. The more basic the element, the more real it is. These familiar ideas of reductionism conspire to make the smallest particles the most important of the material realities, and makes their properties the fundamental basis of the universe. Reductive analysis, implicit in objective consciousness, claims to be exhaustive and complete, and therein lies its mistake. Reductive forms of analysis are not exhaustive and complete, but only starting points from which more complex and uncertain forms of analysis must depart.

To trace the impact of scientism on our history of design is to examine how this phenomenon has manifested its most basic traits in the gardens, buildings, and cities of the modern world. First, an essential trait of objective consciousness as we have seen is its requirement that belief be strictly tied to objective evidence. What is primary for providing objective evidence are aspects of reality that can be checked by others and that allow precise, quantitative measurements. What is merely personal or private is unconfirmable, unmeasurable, and secondary for social purposes. This means that the design of strip malls, urban plazas, and corporate skyscrapers no longer incorporate site issues governed by sensuous or spiritual concerns. These designs are accountable only to the quantifiable needs of the design itself, and not to the demands of the site. The parking lot must hold ten thousand cars, the skyscraper must contain fifteen thousand workers, and the highway must find the shortest distance between two points. Modern design governed by a reductionist approach to the site is only concerned with surface issues and never touches upon the spiritual nature of the land. By basing its theoretical foundations on such reductionism, modern design has clearly alienated humanity from the site.

In modern design, what really counts is the countable — the measurable, the tangible, the material. The consciousness of modern design can be measured with money, size, and efficiency. "More, bigger, taller and faster" are the transcendent design values and they have bred design professionals that have rejected the whispered words of the land and therefore led to the pervasive expansion of the modern world. Aesthetic considerations in the heritage of modern design have become incorporated into the beauty of economic ones. Wherever material and quantifiable values are threatened by merely subjective and qualitative concerns, the majority of builders and their professional designers recoil and reject the subjective concerns. Obsessive material consumption, adulation of growth, and pervasive expansionism are not the only social consequences of the modern spirituality. Reductionistic objectivity is the basis of our alienation from subjective qualities in the site and all they provide for human life.

Thus, at last, if the aesthetic qualities of the sound of the wind in the forest and the colors of a rainbow must be credited to the human mind, and not to the objective world, we find their experiences without value in our society. The thrilling dissonance of crashing waves or the subtle beauty of the tulip is not a thing of value in the objective world. Since "beauty is in the eye of the beholder," not within the realm of quantification itself, all the qualities of the world that are unquantifiable are devoid of value. A design paradigm based on a new understanding of site analysis must work to change this; between mere theory and human experience, designers must learn to understand and incorporate their experiences. Theoretical abstraction must give way to concrete experience, even when the concrete experience is only personal and unquantifiable.

Ironically, the seeds for the new paradigm of design and site analysis will come from the extremes of reductionism. At these extremes of reductionism, it is as if scientism is approaching a point where it has begun to eat its own tail. Initially, according to Newtonian physics, all observable events of the universe are predictable once their causality is understood. However, at the beginning of this century the study of atoms forced physicists into several conceptual revolutions that clearly reveal the limitations of this worldly view. The relativity theory and atomic physics shattered the principal canons of the mechanical world view by revealing the idea that matter consists almost entirely of empty space. When physicists investigated the atomic and subatomic realms, they were confronted with the limitations of their ideas and were forced to radically change many of their assumptions of reality. This was rewarded by deeper insights into the nature of matter and of the human mind. Quantum physicists suggested, among other things, that the very act of observation changes the reality of the object or event observed. "Fundamentally, the observer creates reality by observing it," asserted Niels Bohr and Albert Einstein, a statement

25

site divine
*a new perspective
on site design*

that remains the mainstay of our present understanding of reality. Quantum physics suggested that in altering intention, the object is altered. In so doing, one creates the desired result. In other words, we each see the reality we intend to see, with intention being the key.

Thus, the universe is no longer considered a machine that is made up of a multitude of separate objects, but instead is viewed as a network of indivisible dynamic relationships. Modern physics and the manifestation of extreme specialization of the rational human mind has created a transition enabling the search for new consciousness regarding both design and the site. The two foundations of 20th century physics, Einstein's theory of relativity and the quantum theories, have forced physicists to view the world in a way similar to how a diviner might view it. It is in these parallels between modern physics and ancient mysticism that the future of site analysis and design will emerge.

Physics serves as a useful lesson for design. Like physicists, designers must be challenged to modify or even abandon their accepted concepts of reality in this expanded realm of understanding. One of the major lessons that Western Society has been forced to accept in this century is that all ideas and theories used to describe nature are limited. Designers must come to the understanding that there is no complete and definite description of reality, that there are only approximations of the true nature of things.

Modern design has dangerously alienated itself from the natural environment on which we all ultimately depend for life. Modern designers are alienated not merely because they deny the intrinsic values of the site, nor merely because they are obsessed with material growth and therefore heedless of the expansionism they spread. Rather, modern designers are alienated because they do not think, feel, or perceive holistically from the site through to the design. Their reductionist assumptions and exclusively analytical logic have discarded the realities of the site. Chief Seattle of the Duwamish Tribe clearly understood this in 1855 when he said:

"*We know the white man does not understand our ways. One portion of land is the same to him as the next. His appetite will devour the earth and leave behind only a desert. Man did not weave the web of life; he is merely a strand in it. Whatever he does to the web, he does to himself.*"

The built environment that surrounds us exhibits deep-seated disregard for the site and its subjective traits. The spiritual flaws in objective consciousness have lead to materialism, excessive consumption, obsessive growth, expansionism, and anthropocentric insensitivity to nature. Ingrained in the modern subconscious is the belief that the rise of civilization is matched by an accompanying increase in intelligence. This is a deeply held implicit faith. In considering this belief, the discovery that relevant methods of inquiry may have existed in antiquity is an unpleasant thought to those who have a vested interest in progressivism. For many, the study of geomancy and site divination is regarded as a plot to undermine the fabric of modern design, which is exactly what it is.

To discover a new design paradigm calls for a critical interpretation of site and design subjectivity. The spiritual structure of any new design paradigm must embrace antianthropocentric and antilogocentric discourses. What we need is a new way of thinking about the site that does not assume real and unreal, material and immaterial dichotomies. In this new method of analysis, a site must be considered in a spiritual structure that rejects the split between body and subject, or site and design. This demands a thinking about design that is not an act of construction or deconstruction, but is rather a process of generation. Challenging reductionistic dichotomies is fundamental to a new spiritual structure, allowing us to stop seeing site and design as isolated elements in design. Designers need to realize that they are not separate from nature, that designs and sites integrated into our social and ecological systems are a vital part of our lives.

Site analysis and design can examine the work of the ancients to create a framework of methodologies applicable to the present. Constructing that framework involves examining the various systems of site analysis that have existed through time. The focus must be on methodologies that are site-based. This examination must attempt to examine the physical, the social, and the cultural site, however these may be defined. The answer lies in site divination. The divination system used by the Romans and Greeks for city planning was based upon the occupation of site by animals and the pattern of the sun. This system, known as Augury, was fundamental to the ancient settling of lands captured by Rome. Augury is a form of geomancing, which has in itself many related disciplines, each of which relate to in-depth analysis of the site. Systems of site divination formed a method of site analysis that existed before the widespread use of the written word. Oral traditions were used to teach designers how to read a site, how to experience the site, and how to make judgments regarding design. While some of the ancient suggestions were simply practical knowledge, some ritualistic devices allowed the diviner to look beyond herself to see the will of the spirits on a site. Even if there is a moment when the oral tradition of

27

site divine
a new perspective
on site design

divination breaks down and becomes worthless to the present state of design, it is the responsibility of designers, in the wake of their modernistic heritage, to examine site divination and decide for themselves where that moment may lie.

In the end, the discussion found in this book will act as a test, and will suggest types of divination systems that could aid in ways of better understanding the site. These methodologies drive the format of this discussion, where their applicability to the site itself is the constant. This examination will in the end be based upon the experiential order of the site, and will deal with the sensory experience, and the interpretation of the site as valuable forms of subjective information. This discussion will not attempt to compare the various methodologies, but instead will try to merge the concepts of site divination to form a method of contemporary site design and a collection of knowledge, based on this study, that can critically ascertain how to imagine site analysis in the present world of design.

Divination assumes that there is a combination of physical things, the known and the unknown, the sensory and the acute, the measurable and the immeasurable. Contemporary site designs that include the myriad qualities of divination will allow designers to develop strategies that embrace the site as a whole. It is to be hoped that an approach to the site will emerge from this discussion to allow site divination to be useful to contemporary designers, enabling them with new knowledge about the site and thereby opening up new venues of experience. If designers understood site analysis to include these experiential methodologies, that understanding would be enough to begin dissolving the modern heritage of the repudiation of the site.

Contrary to the particulate approach of modern design where it is possible to isolate parts of the world from the universe and use them without concern for the possible consequences, site divination is an ancient philosophy that envisions the world as a holistic continuum in which each part is related to and responsible for the others. The reductionist mores of modernism have allowed us to dismiss these ancient ideas, and to instead concentrate on the cost effective expansionism that is increasingly covering our planet. The final intention of site design should be to establish balance in design by modifying human activity to ensure respect for the site. When the site and design dichotomy is overcome, the forces of destruction and construction become harmonized. This striving for balance conceives of the world holistically and creates a continuum in which all acts and modes of existence are linked. In this system, any isolated act will necessarily have an effect upon the entire continuum of the design and the site.

Resisting any critical inquiry into the expansionism and materialism of contemporary design, modern designers hold their impressive achievements as proof that objective thought and scientism are the only roads to a successful system of design. As such, other modes of design consciousness are relegated to the status of superstition and discounted by the modernistic orthodoxy. Regardless of the achievements of modernism, the continued desacralization of the world demands that designers examine site divination. Although often dismissed as mere superstition, divination consists of ancient methodologies that provide for a successful form of design critical of modernism and its spiritual values. Running counter to the dialectical materialism of the modern age, the spiritual nature of divination strikes a chord with those critical of the modernistic triumph. That the site was once examined with a reality beyond the physical realm needs to be considered. These considerations must return to the thinking of designers if they are to create and live in environments that respect and nurture the totality of the site.

The rise of the scientific method and rationalism in design has been systematic. Today, divination and geomancy are alien to modern modes of design. This has lead to an increasing global homogeneity in design, as cultures succumb to the rationalism of reductionistic design. Today, the average designer in the western world is so far removed from a world where divination was an everyday occurrence that it is difficult to envision geomancy as an integral or even peripheral part of design. One of the reason divination is rejected as a methodology consistent with the modern sense of design is that designers do not know enough about it. Divination is not a part of normal, everyday life and is, therefore, suspect. The real problem, however, is that fundamental structures of modernity demand the acceptance of confirmable, and thus normal experiences as the only credible experience. This state of disbelief radically estranges designers from fully understanding both the site and their final designs. Though there are notable exceptions, such as the open-ended, dynamic designs of George Hargreaves, the majority of modern designers do not see with the lively, wayward eye of the diviner, which allows itself to be seduced by what is charming, dramatic, or awesome—and to remain there, entranced. It seeks a neutral eye, an impersonal eye, a scientific eye in effect, the eyes of the normal wherein reality is reflected without emotional distortion, based in the conceptual realm of factuality.

29

site divine
a new perspective
on site design

There are three types of experiences. Some experiences are true because a person has experienced them. Some experiences are true because everyone seems to agree that they are true. Then again, some experiences are insoluble and cannot be solved by any stretch of the imagination. Actively disbelieving is a belief system much like any other; you have faith in the fact that something does not exist or is not valid. That faith is the indefensible belief in an untested hypothesis. People who think of themselves as modern, rational, or scientific are most likely to fall into this intellectual trap. The designer who claims to be modern must be proficient in the highest degree, for unless she can atone by creative ability for her break with ancient tradition, she is merely disloyal to the past. It is sheer arrogance to look upon the denial of the past as the basis for the consciousness of the present.

Many designers afflicted with the modern reductionistic cognitive system will develop ways of interpreting the claims of divination as being without value, thus neutralizing the implicit threat to their own modernity. This is the result of fearful insecurity, rather than confident knowledge. A true believer of modernity will examine a challenging belief system before rejecting it. Designers should be cautious before dismissing divinatory ideas as inconsequential or misguided primitive attempts of site analysis, for divination is founded upon a millennium of observations of life processes and the relationships between humans and their environment. From these observations, diviners have developed a descriptive vocabulary for a myriad of subtle environmental patterns, a vocabulary presently available to modern design but that is not used due to its emphasis on reductionism. In the end, this discussion on divination is all about differences in philosophy and design processes, not about differences between modern civilization and primitivism. Though the belief in divination is one of the most long-lived of ancient beliefs, divination is as applicable today as it was in antiquity. Ancient peoples believed that they were capable of creating situations in which they could use the forces of nature to their benefit. Diviners expressed their doctrines with concepts describing — through stories and poems — their natural world and inspired the search for the divine as an integral part of the design process. While presently modern designers approach most matters with systematic assurance because of their scientific association, in antiquity design and its impact of peoples lives was looked upon with extreme insecurity. To embrace divination is to embrace this insecure and unpredictable world that never ensures a constant and stable outcome.

Contemporary forms of site divination are needed in order for our society to move towards a spiritual structure that is not governed by a doctrine placed upon it by conceptual hierarchies. Through the spiritual structure of divination, all site design can grow from the site. It can understand the meaning and importance of every part of design. By listening to their hearts, their own intuition, and the site, designers can attempt to restore health and harmony to their designs. This is not an easy task, and it cannot be expected that any single generation of designers will complete the construction of this new spiritual structure. In time, all design could occur within a deeper understanding of the universe. Contrary to the reductionistic desire of scientism, in order for design to understand the universe, design will have to understand the 'Gestalt' of the universe. When the Gestalt of the universe is understood, then design will be ensured a place within the whole. At that point, dignity and respect will replace the physical world of disrespect within which we now live. When designers sculpt designs that honor themselves as well as the Earth, then we will know the new spiritual structure.

site divine
a new perspective
on site design

chapter three *an introduction to divination*

"Is it not written in your law? I have said, 'You are Gods'."

John 10:34

Designers have lost their intimate connection to the Earth. By embracing modernism, designers have lost the innate human ability to be close to nature. Before the days of modernism, designers conceived of mystical relationships between themselves and their environment, and believing that the future was orderly, shaped their designs and their destinies accordingly. Today, however, designers seek to dominate the environment with increasing ferocity and have lost the power to make their designs speak about their environment and the future. Most modern designers would dismiss the concept of harmony with the natural environment as needlessly sentimental, and at odds with modernism's philosophy of dominion over the natural world. However, the finest emotion of humankind is the mystical emotion of harmony rather than domination. In this emotion lies the aspiration of all true art and all true design. To believe that what is unknowable and impenetrable for us exists and manifests itself as the highest wisdom and the most radiant beauty is the core of the true mystical sentiment. This spiritual aspiration, to search for the radiance of the unknowable and design with respect to such wisdom, is the strongest and noblest driving force behind design. The loss of these divinatory rituals in the design process has led to designs that tend to disregard the earth.

Design can only maintain its roots and connections to the Earth if the modern world we live in also strives to sustain its spiritual roots and connection to the Earth. The search for a new spiritual structure for design will also suggest a new spiritual structure for the modern world. To search for a new spiritual structure of design, it is appropriate to begin by examining the oldest of spiritual disciplines, divinations. Divination was the basis of ancient spiritual structures relied upon to interpret omens, elicit meaning, and to provide guidance. Ancient societies believed that it was safest and most rational to live in a world patterned on the forces of the Earth's spirits or genius loci. Site divination was a means by which to comprehend the intrinsic connection between these forces, the earth, its people, and the universe as a whole. Divination was also a method by which events were interpreted or explained as prognostication, prediction, or intuition. A more holistic approach is to view divination as the art of investigating the life force of the universe, and as an attempt to understand the relationship of that force to all things living.

The application of divination to design and site analysis attempts to create harmony between the site and the design. Many cultures have developed methods of place-making, and have derived remarkably similar observations and precepts. Interestingly, the common theme underlying the many varieties of divination is that holistic design systems are dependent on peace, health, and prosperity. This suggests that humankind can gain greater fulfillment from life when it builds in harmony with nature. Generally, the different divinatory practices are not contradictory; in fact, there are significant similarities among the various forms of divination.

In present Western cultures, divination has dramatically changed. Modern diviners, attempting to explain their work in reductionistic terms, often attempt to present a level of objectivity under the guise of pseudo-scientism. Regardless of the validity of modern divination, in every culture traces of ancient diviners' methods remain enshrined in folk sayings. A familiar example occurs each February in the United States, when the appearance of a groundhog prognosticates the approach of spring. Though not often acknowledged, divination remains a part of modern life, affecting each of us at many levels, from the interpretations of our dreams, to the belief in our weekly horoscopes. The reason that design must examine ancient forms of divination as opposed to modern forms of divination is that these other forms of divination have forgotten much of their ritualistic origins, in an attempt to maintain their pseudo-scientism.

The reason modern divination has attempted to cloak itself in pseudo-scientism, is due to its exorcism from the spiritual realm, after the unification of spirituality into mono-theistic religions. Early in its conception, the Christian Church believed incorrectly that divination was nothing more than the illicit foretelling of the future, and divination was decried as an illicit form of spirituality.

"There shall not be found among you any one that maketh his son or his daughter to pass through the fire, or that useth divination, or an observer of times, or an enchanter, or a witch, or a charmer, or a consulter with familiar spirits, or a wizard, or a necromancer. For all that do these things are an abomination unto the Lord." Deuteronomy XVIII:10-12

In complex liturgical discussions, the Church argued that in understanding the divine, some part of the future was understood as well. This understanding was thought sinful because the future is only known in three ways: through God, in its causes, and as it unfolds. The causes of the future are likewise only known in three ways. First, the future is known with certainty when one considers the causes, such as the coming of an eclipse. Second, the future is known by a kind of conjecture such as the coming of rains and droughts and their affects on the lands. Finally, there are events that occur by chance that cannot be known from a consideration of their cause, because their causes have no relationship to the future event. The Church argued that people could not intuitively consider the environment in a predictive manner except when they are present to God, who alone in His eternity sees the future as though it were the present. The Bible states this position: "Show the things that are to come hereafter, and we shall know that ye are gods" (Is. XLI:23).

In this view, to know the future by any means except divine revelation is to usurp the power that belongs to God alone. For this reason, Isidore says: "They are called diviners, as though they were full of God. For they pretend to be filled with the Godhead, and by a deceitful fraud they forecast the future to men" (Etym. VIII:9).

Accordingly, the Church argues, it is not divination if a person understands occurrences in the environment that happen by necessity, for the future can be understood by human reason. Even if one knows of future things through divine revelation, one does not divine, but rather receives something divine from the singular authority of God. God is clearly against anyone who follows spiritists or mediums, and according to the Bible, anyone who practices divination will be cut off. "I will set my face against the person who turns to mediums and spirits to prostitute himself by following them, and I will cut him off from his people" (Lev. XX:6). A person is said to divine when he usurps God to himself, unduly foretelling divine events. The power of divination belongs to only God, and therefore to divine or to practice divination is to sin. According to the Church, humans have no institution for the knowledge of the divine. Consultation about the divine exists only accompanying religious matters. "Do not turn to mediums or spiritists; do not seek them out to be defiled by them. I am the Lord your God" (Lev XIX:31).

While the Church views divination as an undue usurpation of divine power, the scientific communities argue that the foreknowledge of future events is possible after establishing patterns of repetition and causal relationships, and therefore does not pertain to divination or the divine. During the period of Enlightenment, it was widely held that there was an irreconcilable conflict between knowledge and belief. The opinion prevailed among advanced minds that belief should be replaced by knowledge; belief that did not rest on knowledge was superstition, and as such had to be opposed. Following the spiritual exorcism by the mono-theistic religions, divination began to cloak its spiritual rituals in the guise of scientism and attempted to prove itself as knowledge-based as opposed to belief-based. But just as design is based upon a system of beliefs, so too is divination fundamentally a system providing for intuitive methodologies. To cultivate a new understanding of the site based upon intuitive methodologies, designers must look to the ancient origins of spirituality in divination.

There are three common types of divination: the ecstatic, the inductive, and the interpretative. The ecstatic diviner contacts the spirits of the inner world to elicit answers to her questions, while the inductive diviner observes natural events, such as the direction of the wind, the fall of the leaves, or the shadows of the sun and interprets these events according to ancient precepts. Finally, the interpretative diviner uses a combination of both the ecstatic and inductive methods. Just as scientism reflects the modern spiritual structure of our society, these methods of divination reflect upon the spiritual structure of many past societies.

The broadest form of inductive divination is geomancy, which is loosely defined as the art of harmonizing humans with the natural world. Geomancy attempts to make clear the connections between the Earth and humankind. Geomancy is concerned with the propagation of fertility, the sources of water, and the positioning of light. Many aspects of geomancy appear to simply be practical advice to ensure a favorable water supply or adequate sunshine, but to regard divination and geomancy as primitive forms of city planning or farm management is to simplify their major intents, and underestimate their potential analytical contributions. In divination, the world is considered a continuum in which all acts, natural and supernatural, conscious and unconscious, are linked. As such, any mistake along that continuum brings on unforeseen consequences that may result in tragic destruction. For the ancients, therefore, divination provided a methodology that was preventive in its intent.

Any design is an intervention in a site. There are spiritual risks in this fact and therefore certain precautions should be followed. Divination attempts to determine these risks and suggests possible precautions or remedies. Its methods for responding to mute spirits and a silent planet shows a sensitivity that is a welcomed addition to modern design practice. History shows that divination was fundamental in both guiding and maintaining spiritual and environmental values. Throughout history, site divination has wrestled with moral dilemmas about humankind's interaction with the Earth, and has offered modes of conduct that could ultimately provide a new methodology in addressing the site. Site divination may also help to develop a new spiritually aware system of design. Divination is an attempt to communicate with our world that is imbued with holiness, and helps lead us to the way in which we are to peacefully coexist. In designing from the site, designers should not seek to escape the Earth, but should instead attempt to engage the world and all beings in it with a sense of awe, wonder, respect, and compassion. Overall, divination works best in conjunction with a philosophical framework and shared spiritual values. By combining the methodologies of site divination and the spiritual concerns of ancient societies with modern environmental and social concerns, divination can make significant contributions to the emerging paradigms of design.

Discovering the Earth Energies

Through divination, ancient cultures developed an understanding of the complex energy patterns emitted from the earth, encouraging them to approach the site with the recognition that the whole of the world is united. The understanding of these subtle energy fields was an integral part of their design methods. The ancient Greeks called this energy 'pneuma', the Romans termed it 'spiritus', and the ancient Chinese referred to it as 'ch'i'. With the advance of modern science, one would likely believe that divination's claim as to the presence of some sort of surrounding energy force has finally been relegated to mere superstition, but upon closer examination we can see that science supports rather than refutes the theory of an ever present energy. It is only recently with further investigations in super-string theories that science has uncovered the fact that things that were once thought to be solid masses are, in reality, merely vibrations or waves of energy. While this is relatively new to science, it is arguably not new to humankind. Since all matter is consequently made up of energy, can one truly refute the idea that diviners can sense this energy?

For thousands of years, the ancients have regarded energy as the thread that binds all things together. Modern designers have lost the understanding of site energy. The site and its inherent energy are no longer integral parts of modern design. Understanding the different forms of divination could help designers understand this energy, and with that understanding hopefully view the world and the impact of their designs on it differently. When lands are designed with an acute awareness of the interconnectivity of each aspect of the planet, it will herald a different perspective of design, and we will gain a much better idea of how to live on this planet.

Today, a branch of modern science known as geobiology dedicates itself to an investigation of the principles on which these energies are based. In the early 1970's, physicist Ernst Hartmann developed the Lobe Antenna to identify what he believed was a system of energy fields that emanate from the earth's surface and circumscribe our globe. Though significant questions about his scientific methodologies abound, his theories provide a fascinating bridge from the ancient conception of such energy. Hartmann claimed that lines of energy comprise a grid that can be found at 2 meter intervals in the north-south direction, at 2.5 meter intervals in the east-west direction, and that these energy intervals exist throughout the globe. Two decades of research on these Bio-Electro Magnetic fields suggested to Hartmann that the energy grids may consist of up to twenty different forms of energy radiating from the surface of the Earth. Of those twenty grid forms, four are thought vital for human development: the First and Second Global Grids, and the First and Second Diagonal Grids. The First Global Grid, oriented to the cardinal directions at a 2 meter by 2.5 meter interval, is said to affect the formation of human bones. The Second Global Grid is also oriented to the cardinal directions at an interval of 15 meters by 20 meters. This grid is said to affect the human nervous system. The First Diagonal Grid is located at a 45 degree angle to the Global Grids, occurs at an interval of 3 meters by 3.5 meters and is said to affect the growth of cells. The last of the vital grids is the Second Global Diagonal which has the same orientation as the First Global Diagonal, but with 15 meter by 20 meter intervals. This gird is said to affect cerebral functions of humans. Hartmann theorizes that the Bio-Electric Magnetic grids affect the electromagnetic fields of the body. He also suggested that while the cause of these Bio-Electro Magnetic fields is primarily a natural phenomenon, humans and their accompanying modern technology seem to affect the grids through electricity, television, radio, and telephone transmissions. Regardless of the validity of Hartmann's claims, it is a proven fact that people are constantly inundated by energy radiation from modern technologies and those emitted from the earth. However we may look at it, we are immersed in the energy fields of the planet, both those controlled by us and those that we have yet to discover.

Recent ideas in theoretical physics concerning the implications of quantum theories and theories of relativity suggest that both matter and thought are merely tiny explosions in a vast sea of energy filling the whole of cosmic space. The properties of thought waves may not be vastly different from the properties of the electromagnetic fields that surround all matter. An observation that offers possible connections between ch'i, dowsing energy, and Bio-Electro Magnetic energy is the belief that the Earth is a living organism and not an inanimate mass of water and minerals. Under this belief, it might be possible that the earth energies are properties of both Earth's matter and its thoughts. Feng shui is based upon the idea that ch'i is a vital energy that connects all living objects. In connecting the earth and ourselves, this idea alludes to a planet that is alive, just as we are. Plato, the ancient Greek philosopher, provides an early definition of the earth as a living, divine being: "Gaia. This world is in truth a living creature endowed with soul life and reason." Basilius Valentinus provides a later definition of the living being called Gaia. "The Earth is not a dead body, but is inhabited by a spirit that is its life and soul. All created things, minerals included, draw their strength from the earth spirit. The spirit is life, it is nourished by the stars, and it gives nourishment to all the living things it shelters in its womb." Aldo Leopold, a founder of the modern environmental movement, coined the modern version of this world view, couched in the terms of environmental and ecological science. "Land is not merely soil; it is a fountain of energy flowing through a circuit of soils, plants, and animals. A thing is right when it tends to preserve the integrity, stability, and beauty of the biotic community. It is wrong when it tends otherwise." In his book The Ages Of Gaia : A Biography of Our Living Earth, modern biologist James Lovelock reexamined this reasoning, arguing that the planet is indeed one interdependent, homeostatic system.

The Gaia hypothesis suggests a model for our return to a holistic mode of design, armed this time with a precise repertoire of disciplined site analysis and ancient divinatory methodologies. Just as divination is based upon the notion that the Earth and its inhabitants are intimately linked into a complex web, so too is the modern idea of Gaia. Divination, geomancy, and the Gaia hypothesis stand as strong models for a reemerging consciousness to instruct the complexity of holistic design intentions. In the last decade, a number of

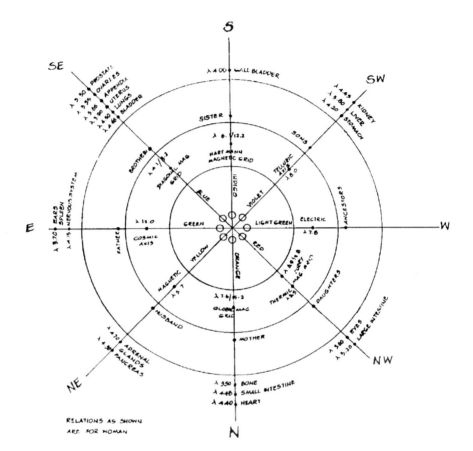

The Human Systems
affected by Energy Fields

interdisciplinary thinkers have developed what they term "the new paradigm." In books such as Peter Russell's The Awakening Earth: The Global Brain, he argues that the old paradigm dominated by Cartesian logic and Newtonian physics no longer encompasses society's values. It is not that science and technology are wrong, but that a paradigm that is dominated by scientific thinking is biased. Russell argues that we need to balance rational knowing with intuitive wisdom. Systems of divination such as geomancy and feng shui are visions of the tangible methodologies beyond this new shift in paradigm.

Yin and Yang, ancient symbols of interdependence, demonstrate that just where a thing is greatest, its opposite will emerge. A touch of white is contained at the center of black. Similarly, in the heart of modern physics, the seed of a new paradigm of design emerges. With this in mind, it is in the confidence we have in our understanding of evolution due to reductionist thinking that has prepared us to examine the chaos and complexity of the complex system we call Life. When we see the Earth as living, we can begin to understand how consciousness relates to physical processes. When dowsers or feng-shui masters analyze a site, perhaps they are able to read the earth's energy patterns. The search for and understanding of these various energies may lead designers to a new spiritual structure, thereby resulting in a new way of envisioning design. What must be learned from all diviners is that the search for the divine is in itself the objective. The truth appears to come not from the answers that we may encounter, but from the process of the search.

chapter four *geomantic site divination*

"Know thyself and you will know the Universe"

Plato

Geomancy attempts to reveal the spirit of the Earth through its elemental spirits and is therefore the form of divination specifically related to the understanding of earthly things. Geomancy literally means "divination of the earth." The word geomancy itself comes from the Greek words Ge, Gaia, which means Mother Earth and from manteia, the Greek word for divination. Geomancers are ritualistic diviners searching for the spiritual nature of the Earth through the examination of the Earth itself. Geomancers are often described as being 'psycho-spiritual' in nature. Geomancers attempt to respond to subtle energies from the Earth that have physiological effects on biological systems that may influence, for example, a plants' growth pattern, a bird's nesting preferences, or a human's emotional or physical health.

In the practice of geomancy, the geomancer evaluates a site's dominant patterns and features with regard to a holistic understanding of space and time based on an Earth-cosmos connection. Geomancy stems from a profound understanding of the Earth's natural elements and cycles. There are two distinct yet related forms of geomancy: oracular geomancy, which deals with prediction, and locational geomancy, the art of placement. In the Western hemisphere, locational geomancy includes the practice of augury in Greek, Etruscan, and Roman societies, while in the East there are several related forms, the most

site divine
geomantic site
divination

important of which are vastuvidya or vastu which is practiced in India, and feng shui, a form of geomancy prevalent in China.

Geomancy attempts to uncover the innate character of a place. The earth energies present are powerful indicators of this character. In addition to the earth energies, the accumulated psycho-spiritual residue of people who have passed through the place and remain as place-memories, or memories that reside in a place as opposed to a person, may also be perceived by geomancers. Geomantic principles stipulate that most of us are responsive to these subtle external stimuli. Geomancy suggests that when the web of earth energies is traumatized or inharmonious, the energy or spirits of a place will exist in a state of trauma. Reversing trauma in the site is part of the process of bringing a space into health. Geomancy creates a method of examination that embraces our environment as living, dynamic, and responsive. Geomancy can assist us in understanding the indivisibility of ourselves and our environment, allowing us to act accordingly. Geomancy offers us a way to relate to our environment. When geomancy and divination are part of our patterns of design, we will have begun to embrace a new spiritual structure for our society.

History

For a deeper understanding of geomantic ritual, one must examine the history of Roman religious rituals, for the Romans connected technology, civilization and the land with divine rituals more so than any other state that also employed divination. The Roman ritual books on divination were divided into two portions: the tragetic books that dealt with reading omens and appeasing the gods and the dead, and the rulings books that contained the collection of codified ritual rulings that were used as precedents, as well as instruction about the interpretation of natural forces such as lightning and thunder. The ancient lexicographer Festus explained that these ancient books, the tragetic and the ruling books, "set out the rules for the rites by which towns are founded, temples and shrines consecrated, and walls hallowed."

In ancient Roman culture, the natural scientist and the diviner coexisted, both possessing a distinct realm of influence. The natural scientist focused on explaining the causes of events. The diviner, on the other hand, deciphered the meaning behind the events. Natural science was not blasphemous as some of the Greeks had argued previously, nor divination irrational as is argued today.

In approaching any site, ancient town planners first considered it on spiritual terms. To the ancient designer, the advantages of a particular site were deemed direct and arbitrary gifts of the gods. Drawing wisdom from the omphalos, the divine center of the Earth and the site of divine power, geomantic divination would suggest to the designer the will of the gods. The omphalos was the theological foundation of the ancient roman divination system of augury. Originally this word referred to the Omphalos at Delphi, the seat of the oracle of Apollo and the center of the Greek world. In legend, the site was divined by Zeus who sent out two swans to locate the Earth's true center. One bird was released to the west, and the other to the east; their paths crossed at Delphi and the omphalos was then set. The word 'omphalos,' meaning 'navel,' was eventually applied to any divined center. The omphalos legend emphasized the imposition of order and the fixing of divine energies to a specific point. Once restricted to a specific site, the energy could then be tapped and channeled. The omphalos provided the diviner with a link between Earth and Heaven. To the individual, the omphalos was the place where he or she existed at any given time; it was the place from which the observed world originated. As the spirit is located in the center of body, so too is the world's spirit located at a central fixed point. Both the spirit of the body and the omphalos act as pivots around which everything revolves. These centers remain fixed while all else moves, stable in the circling of the heavens and in the cycle of time.

Oracles in particular have always been associated with sites where, due to the presence of the omphalos, humans believed they could hear the voice of their planet. The original voices of the omphalos were feminine, and were therefore believed to have deep connections with the rhythms of the planet. Archeological records show that certain locations were favored in distant times for their connection with these goddesses. With the passage of time and the introduction of new spiritual structures, these locations were incorporated into the new spiritual structures, in essence providing a continuum to the traditional view of the Earth, architecturally traced through each civilization into the past.

Although practical and utilitarian design considerations were current enough in Vitruvius's time, such as the suggestion that an ideal site should be situated away from the hot sea air and away from marshes, as the location of Rome illustrates, they were not often applied in practice. At the time of Vitruvius, the Greeks had only recently revolutionized site design. In the fifth century B.C., when Hippocrates formulated his ideas of siting in rational, rather than to spiritual terms, his ideas were seen as eccentric and blasphemous. Contrary to the suggestions of Vitruvius who emphasized the progressive development of a sensible planning method, the Romans never forgot the obscure magical and religious rituals that most contemporary designers find unattractive, unedifying, and most often irrelevant. For the Romans, favorable physical conditions

The Omphalos
from Delphi

were an indication of the good will of the gods, and were therefore more easily obtained if harmony between the design and the site was established. Ancient designers trusted the unpredictable but divine power of the gods over the imperfect rules of science. The task of selecting a site was a serious matter on which the whole fate of the people depended, and the final decision was always left to the gods.

Augury

To determine the will of the gods in regarding site selections and the process of designing, the Roman state employed diviners known as augurs. It was the augur's duty to evaluate each site where the empire of Rome was intent on building. As part of his examination of a site, the augur began by selecting a place with an unobstructed view of the intended site, where the augur prepared for his divination. To begin, the augur recited a prayer to announce his intentions to the gods, then he named an omen, and finally orally described his field of view. When the named omen appeared, the augur decided whether it was an appropriate time to do a reading. If the omen suggested that it was an appropriate time to designate a site, the augur, his head veiled, drew figures in the air with a curved staff called a lituus. These figures represented the great temple of the sky condensed into the ideal form of the augur's diagram, and then projected onto the site before him. The purpose of these drawings in the air was to establish the order of the sky and the earth, with the augur at its omphalos. With the diagrams establishing the order of the sky and the land, the augur called upon the landmarks that bounded the site, pointing to them with his staff. As the augur named each boundary, the site became bounded and contained by these incantations, drawing a magical net around the landmarks named. It was this naming that fixed the boundaries of the site, both in Roman law and in the eyes of the gods.

This initial construction of boundaries, the enclosure of hitherto open space, was also believed to be necessary to placate or neutralize the guardian spirits of the place that would otherwise punish humankind for restricting their liberties. During the augur's fixing of the boundaries, interference with the original condition of the land was kept as minimal as possible so that its natural attributes might be permitted to function unhindered. In addition, this use of ritual in the founding of boundaries was specially contrived to exclude undesirable forces and entities. Consequently, the crossing of any sacred boundary without authorization was an act that desecrated a place's sanctity, destroying its shield

47

site divine
geomantic site
divination

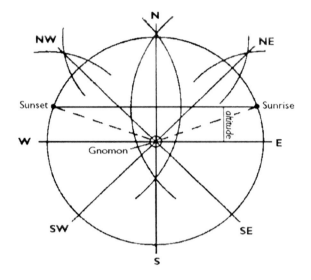

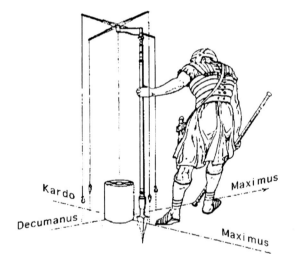

The calculation
template for using the
gnomon to determine
the cardinal directions
and the altitude of
the gnomon. Where
r = the radius, and
G = the height of the
gnomon, and both
are equal

Drawing by
P. Frigerio, 'Antichi
Istrumenti Technici'

spiritually, if not physically, and therefore permitting entry to the unwanted entities. Such an act could only be expiated by death to the offender.

[The calculation template for using the gnomon to determine the cardinal directions and the altitude of the gnomon. Where r = the radius, and G = the height of the gnomon, and both are equal]

When the boundaries were set, the augur then established the cardinal directions. Just as humans interpret the world in relation to the orientation of their body: in front, behind, left, and right, the establishment of the four cardinal directions was the foremost responsibility of the augur. The orientation of the individual was reflected on the planetary level by the four cardinal directions that were structured by the two poles of the axis upon which the earth rotates, north and south, and the directions of the rising and setting sun, east and west. To find the exact cardinal directions, the augur used a stick called a gnomon. This simple instrument was thrust into the ground, casting a shadow whose length and position indicated the cardinal directions, the time of the day, the season of the year and, given reliable calibrations, the latitude of the site itself. The length of the shadow and the time of day could also indicate, through its variance, the season. Set at a level place at sunrise, a circle was drawn around the gnomon, with its radius equal to the length of the stick. The points where the shadow of the gnomon touched the circle at sunrise and sunset marked east and west. The line that passed perpendicular to these two points, connecting the base of the gnomon to the circle, was the north to south axis. Finally, the augur drew a quartered circle on the ground, which represented the earth, the four cardinal directions and, by extension the site. This was the final mark of the augur. In many cultures, these four directions were each assigned a specific spirit, regent, power, angel, or god. Based upon the heritage of the omphalos, these four directions remain the foundation of site divination, and become the basis for any geomantic design of the land.

Extispicy

Extispicy, or the reading of animals' entrails, was another common form of geomancy practiced during the Greek, Roman and Etruscan empires. Circero, who was himself an official Roman augur, proclaimed in his book On Divination that "the whole Etruscan nation has gone stark mad on the subject of entrails." In extispicy, the entrails, and in particular the liver of a sacrificial animal, were opened and inspected. A haruspex, or liver-diviner, made predictions and reached

The final mark of the
augur dictating the
cardinal directions

An Etruscan liver
model made
from bronze

decisions on the basis of what the gods had 'written' in the entrails. While most of modern society views such practices as not only unscientific but possibly satanic, they were quite respected by the ancient empires and were considered one of the most reliable means of understanding the will of the gods.

The death of animals in site divination is not in itself significant, since they were not simply sacrificial offerings to the god, in search of appeasement or promise fulfillment. Extispicy was a way of assuring the quality of the lands through the sanctioned tools of the gods. While sheep were the most common sacrificial animal, lambs and oxen were also used. The liver was the main organ examined in this form of divination, as it was thought to be the seat of the animal's soul. The premise of extispicy was that any animal consecrated to the gods became a mirror of the site at the moment of sacrifice. The scarring and markings of the sheep's liver as a result of its sensitivity to internal diseases corresponded to the health of the site. If a liver was found to be black, it was thought that the site's spirits were evil, and therefore dangerously destructive. If the liver was found to be red and reflective like a mirror, then the site was a healthy site, and its use was thought sanctioned by the gods.

Although there are few surviving documents that describe the actual rules and procedures of entrail reading, there are many visual references in ancient arts and statuary. Two important surviving liver models provide us with a vague understanding of the process of extispicy. One Etruscan model, made of bronze, is an abstract representation of the liver of a sheep. The liver is divided into sixteen compartments, each containing a name of one of the sixteen Etruscan gods of the sky. The augur's division of the sky and the earth into four regions corresponds to the haruspex's division of the liver, both of which refer to an abstract representation of the world. The other model, made of terracotta, is a more realistic representation of a sheep's liver. In this model, tiny holes signify locations in the liver that corresponded to generalized information about a site, and wooden pegs were used to indicate the locations of marks found on the liver. From these locations, the health of a specific site could be read.

In addition to the liver, the intestines were also important to extispicy. The intestines were called the 'great palace' of the body. A lamb's intestines, when laid out for inspection, formed a spiraling labyrinth, and the arcs of the intestine were examined for inflammation, discoloration, and infection, such as is found in gastric-enteritis. When both the liver and the intestines were examined together, the liver and the intestines represented an abstraction of the universe, with the liver representing the signs from the heavens and the intestines representing the signs from the underworlds. Mostly, the haruspex

understood that unfavorable signs in the intestines and liver were due to disease, and understood that these inauspicious signs of disease were therefore related to the unwholesomeness of the environment. Thus, extispicy was used to indicate whether to move on to healthier pastures when grazing, or to discourage building on a certain site.

In times of social crises the haruspex also looked for signs of broader social implication in the entrails. To do this, they looked for fissures, abscesses or protrusions in the guts, most often searching for a part called the 'head,' 'lobe,' or 'finger,' all of which likely referred to the gall bladder. To the haruspex the gall bladder is shaped like a tetrahedron, a shape considered significant by the Pythagoreans and the Platonists, who believed it represented the element of fire. The absence of the gall bladder was a dreadful sign as it indicated a future without the balance of natures main elements, with fire the most likely of the elements to be out of balance resulting in the destruction associated with uncontrolled fire. The gall bladder is said to have been absent in important entrail readings before the deaths of both Alexander the Great and Julius Ceasar.

The early tradition of entrail divination is preserved in the text of Vitruvius, who believed that the choice of a sound site was a necessary prerequisite to both designing and building. Though Vitruvius was a rationalist compared to his peers, he was most insistent that the examination of animal livers should not be neglected. In On Architecture, he outlines his firm belief that the ritual of extispicy was essential in the design of towns, temples, and other buildings of virtue:

"Our ancestors," he said, "sacrificed some of the cattle that fed off the land and examined their livers If the livers of the first victims were dark and abnormal, they sacrificed others to see whether the peculiarities were due to disease or to their food. They never began building in a given place until they had made several such examinations." (O.A. 1.4.9)

Thus for Vitruvius, a city was to be sited only where animals lived in good health:

"If, however, they found the [blood and liver] faulty, by analogy they judged that the supply of food and water which was to be found in these places would be pestilential in the case of human bodies."(O.A. 1.4.9)

This practice and symbolism of extispicy rested on three principles: 1) that the liver or intestines indicated the fitness of ill-health of the whole of the animal, 2) that the health of an animal was reflective of land that it lived on, and 3) that there was a connection between the health of the animals and the health of the people. Later, as the sacrificial element began to lose favor under the growth of Christianity, a modified version of extispicy was used extensively in rural areas. Domestic animals such as sheeps or goats were herded onto prospective building sites, and the location of any structure was dictated by where the animal chose to bed down and sleep.

53

site divine
*geomantic site
divination*

Vastu

Another important geomantic tradition practiced in the Indian subconti-nent, reaching its zenith during the Gupta period during the 6th century AD is outlined in the Vastushasta texts. The Vastushasta texts deal with an entire range of building-related subjects, such as soil testing techniques, solar and lunar orientation, measurement and proportion, and divination associated with the design of buildings. This ethos of vastu was rooted in brahmanical ideas centered on cosmology, the theory of creation, space-time dynamics, and humankind's place in nature. In these ancient design texts, architecture was presented as a concrete translation of brahmanical precepts and included each

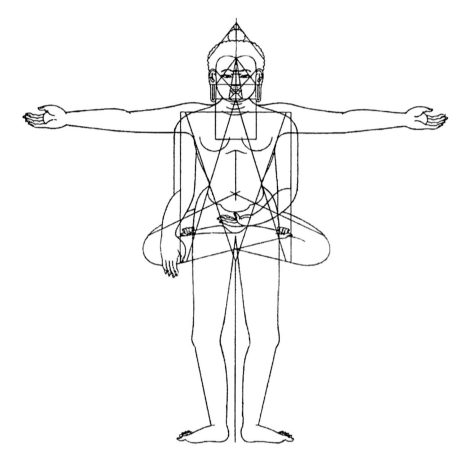

The perfection of
the Universal Being.
Only the Universal
Being is perfect
in proportion
and symmetry

of the scientific disciplines, or vidyas, within its fold. Mathematics, philosophy, geology, astrology, divination, semantics of form, myths, and narratives each formed an integral part of the art of design. To achieve perfection in design, each of the vidyas were woven together into one seamless disciplineto create a holistic matrix of design knowledge. This design knowledge based on integrating each of the vidyas was called Vastu. Traditionally each of the interrelated variables of design such as siting, orientation, proportion, and decoration were shaped and regulated by the spirits of the Earth, called the vasturpurusha, as well as by the laws governing these vasturpurusha.

In vastu, the site becomes defined as the place where the living being resides. The tenets of vastu therefore considered design a spiritual act and attempted to link the private and public, and sacred and secular realms of life. The private expression of a home, if built according to the brahamanical principles, would enrich public life by bringing prosperity and contentment. The Vastushasta texts are a record of oral traditions that were in ancient times best known to the masons or sthapatis, and served to maintain the brahmanical design standards. These canons were considered cohesive yet flexible enough to provide for design variation, enabling vastu to remain relevant and useful for centuries.

According to the Hindu principles upon which vastu is based, the cosmos is a manifestation of a singular transcendent, animating principle. The one, undivided principle is known variously as Brahman, or Purushna. This principle, which contains the universe in its womb in potential form, is the beginning of all spatial dimension and temporal duration. The sacred cosmos manifests itself in the form of a mandala, a perfect universal being spread across the known universe. The perfection of this being is seen in its perfect proportions and symmetry. As this perfect form projects itself from the center of the universe to the periphery, the mandala maps out space in a graded hierarchical order. As the space evolves into worlds, it gives rise to five elements, earth, water, fire, air and sky, and the five senses. Whatever lies outside the periphery of the mandala symbolizes the zone of chaos and anti-life; whatever lies within the boundaries is part of the integral unity of life. In this drama of creation, the relationship between the zone of chaos and the zone of life is always changing, the sacred space of life is visualized as expanding horizontally and vertically. This notion links space to time, time and space become inseparable. Where there is space, there is time and as time expands, space expands. In vastu, every act of design must be based upon an understand of this expanding nature of both space and time. The only element of the undivided principle that is ever fixed in vastu is

55

site divine
geomantic site
divination

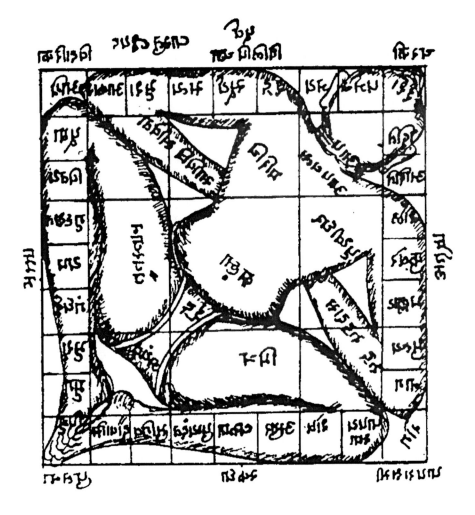

An ancient mandala
with the names and
hierarchy of the gods
and demi-gods

the center, and therefore the center is always the most important starting point in looking at any space.

The space-time continuum is a central feature of Indian geomantic design thought. Both the metaphysical and the physical are not at variance. In the grand design of creation, everything from the cosmic to the microcosmic is united along a single thread. In this traditional ethos space, time, site, building, the cosmos, and nature exist only in the spiritual realm. The Vastushastras claim that only the individual who has experienced the unbroken totality represented through the harmonic convergence of space and time is complete, and only then may affect the structure of the cosmos through their designs. To experience the unbroken totality the Vastushastras suggests that one must be at rest with oneself to be complete. When the spiritual structures of life are fragmented, existing without reference to the sensibilities of the earth and rhythm of the cosmos, people become fractured from their roots. When fractured from their roots, people are incomplete and are therefore not at rest with themselves. This connection between the sensibilities of the earth and the rhythms of the cosmos and the act of designing is the fundamental ethos of Vastu, and gives us a vision of a wholeness possible in design.

The most potent design mechanism that embodied these 'cosmic' principles is the mandala, whose sacredness and special significance are stressed in the Vastushastras texts. A metaphorical diagram of ritual significance, the mandala provided a descriptive analysis of the site for design. Its physical representation, is in actuality, a linear computation that governs the rhythm, design, orientation, and structural synthesis of a site. The mandala is made up of a grid of squares. The square is used because under Vastu it is seen as the most fundamental form in architecture, and when oriented to the four cardinal directions, it take chaos and creates comprehensible space, and therefore is looked upon as the all-encompassing symbol of the world. In the square frames of the mandala, the square in the center is presided over by the Supreme Principle known as the Brahma Sthana, the supreme throne of the principal deity. Encircling it are a number of smaller square called padas, these are seats presided over by a hierarchy of lesser deities. Around the border of the mandala are thirty-two divinities that preside over the solstitial and equinoctial points. The eight cardinal directions are presided over by the eight planets, as Pluto had not yet been discovered. In this way, the mandala represented both the sacred space and the cyclic movement of time within the cosmos. The mandala image suggests a contained and ordered cosmos. The boundaries of the site define the conse-crated area. The periphery is a ubiquitous universal space, the inner center, a

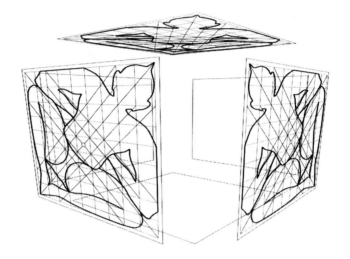

The mapping of the
mandala into the
third dimension.

Ayadi-sadvarge: 6 x
(aya) = Remainder aya
= X(hasta) + Y(angula)
Mandala = 9(R.aya) x
9(R.aya)

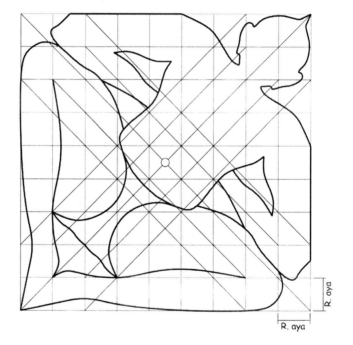

R. aya

R. aya

contained space, unified and flexible. Between the center and the periphery lie the structures that define and enclose the space.

To understand a site, it is marked out on the spreading body of the mandala. A site design governed by the mandala creates a sacred center from which design will evolve naturally. The basic application of the mandala lies in the ritual of pada vinyasa — of dividing the site into a uniform grid. For this purpose, the mandala is traced unto the ground by making deep marks in the earth. The process of drawing onto the ground prepares the mind of the diviner to determine the relative proportions of the different parts of the site. The most important area laid out on the 'site-mandala' is the invisible center, the residence of Brahma. Reminiscent of the omphalos, Brahma occupies the center of the mandala with his navel or the nabhi. What the heart is to the body, this center is to site: the meeting point of all energies on the land that appear as an invisible vertical column, or Linga, a luminous shaft of energy rising from the ground. This invisible cylinder of luminosity is also called the Brahma Nala.

Vastu reflects macro-micro correspondence of the world. Every object, thought, and action radiates some kind of magnetic or elemental force that must be combined in perfect harmony if they are to act favorable upon each other. As a result, vastu developed complex formulae to compute the size of the mandala squares. The most widely used formula in vastu is called ayadisadvarge, or the series of six computations on the aya, or 'course.' These computations determine the auspicious design solutions and site proportions of the mandala. The aya formula is derived from the doctrine of remainder or residue. According to this doctrine, a design must conform to a perfect form. The realities of the world, however, are grounded in imperfection. Absolute perfection is the central feature of the Supreme Principle that governs the cosmos. Therefore, an iota of imperfection must exist in all objects of creation. This rationale is simple, for if all objects of creation were perfect, they would not exist as they do, but would instead disappear into the Supreme, who is the personification of perfection, as the color white would disappear into whiteness. This view is also reflected in the notion of sacred time. If there was no residue left in time, the time-cycle would come to a stop. Hence, the doctrine of remainder suggests that there is always a remainder of time units that become the seed of the next time cycle. The remainder contains the germ of continuity and gives impetus to the ever-revolving wheel of time. It is for this reason that the designers working under vastu principles employ only the remainder result of the computation. Any new creation will be created by the residue of previous creations. Thus, in working out auspicious design calculations, the main concern is with the remainder, as it

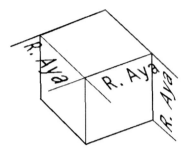

Gabhagriha

This conceptual
diagram suggests the
search for fusion
ecstacy with the union
of space based upon
the perfect being.

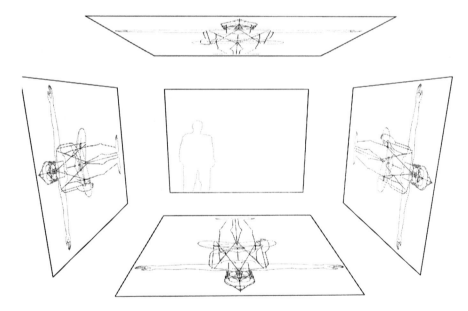

is the sum that will provide for the creation of the mandala and provide for all the auspicious design solutions. For example to find an aya, take an important site dimension, multiply it by eight, and then divide the product by twelve. The remainder sum in this case is technically one of the six aya. Similarly, another aya might be found if one took the circumference of the site and multiplied it by nine and divided it by seven. These ayas become the proportional basis of the mandala grid. Although these calculations may seem arbitrary, it is the designer's task to determine the figures that would be used to find the aya. Here, the numbers eight or nine represents the planets, twelve, the months, and seven, the days of the week. As a result of the work of the designer, who may spend years searching for the appropriate aya, the aya became the determining horizontal and vertical unit of design. The final aya is often anthropometric, based upon multiples of the angula (finger), and the hasta (hand). The aya multiplied by itself creates the fundamental unit of primary space called the garbhagriha, a cube that encloses the primary energy of the site. Thus, with the doctrine of remainder and the aya, and the creation of the garbhagriha cube, vastu architecture becomes a system of enclosure capable of containing the unique vibrant energy of a site as perceived by the designer. The successful creation of the garbhagriha necessitates that the designer create designs in her likeness on the site that reflect her feelings about the site in a manifested form.

Augury, extispicy, and vastu all attempted to create designs that were capable of evoking in the individual a deeper awareness of divine beginnings. For the ancients, the mere ability to respond to nature or other arts as designers was not considered sufficient. It was essential that designers experience and form an understanding of the purity of a site's essence, and create places that were endowed with the same quality as was contained in that experience. Such a work, created from the essence of the designer's being, would arouse an observer to a state of profound awareness. In ancient Indian thought, this response was known as fusion ecstasy. It was only through the act of remaining pure and receptive to the site that a designer could hope to evoke this ecstasy in the beholder. The skill and training of the designer are thus directed towards the creation of the tangible form for the Divine Being, and to house it in a space that would reflect the Universal Reality. In these traditions, the creation of the primary space, or the garbhagriha, is an expression of the endless energy of the earth. If it is one of the goals of design to liberate humankind from the bondage of the isolated self, and allow it to merge with an understanding of the universe, the search for the divine is fundamental to design.

chapter five *feng shui*

Feng shui is the ancient Chinese discipline of manipulating the invisible and subtle energies of the cosmos, termed ch'i, to create harmony between humankind and its environment. Feng shui is often translated as 'wind and water,' but there is no exact Western equivalent for the expression. 'Feng' is described as an invisible stream of energy over one's head, while 'shui' is associated with the energy moving under one's feet. Together, these earthly energies are the result of cosmic ch'i. Feng shui is founded on two basic components: one is its metaphysical cosmological basis centered on the ancient Chinese philosophical and religious beliefs such as the yin-yang principle, ch'i, and the five elements. The other component of feng shui is its practical pursuit of harmonious relationships between humankind and nature. Feng shui is the art of adapting the signs of celestial yin and yang to the residence of the living and the dead so as to harmonize all humans with the cosmic breath — ch'i. One principle of traditional Chinese philosophy that is fundamental to feng shui is that the universe is a living organism. All parts of nature are intricately linked by ch'i in a symbiotic relationship, and humans are integral components in this living organism. Ultimately, feng shui is based on the Chinese understanding that a balanced environment brings peace of mind, good health, long life, and ultimately happiness.

The Chinese symbol
for Feng-Shui

Even though we can find traces of several ancient Chinese sciences in feng shui, including chan hou which centers upon the analysis of atmospherics, ch'ih yin, which deals with the detection and analysis of sound in nature, and feng ch'iao, which is known as the science of winds, there are also many feng shui suggestions don't seem to have a scientific basis. They do, however, appeal to an aesthetic culture that was found throughout ancient China. In this way, feng shui became a design template used to foster a sense of commitment to environmental harmony.

Overall, the imperative of a feng shui was not to follow the rule of science, but to provide a design template that would enhance the environment instead of harming or depleting it. Both within the realm of the ancient sciences and the art of design, feng shui attempts to harmonize with nature rather than disrupt it. Included in feng shui's design template is the requirement that environmental changes be planned and executed carefully. Indiscriminately altering the balance of nature can trigger a series of events that may lead to unpredictable and even destructive results.

Through observations over many hundreds of years, the ancient Chinese began to see a link between humankind and the landscape, and came to the realization that some natural surroundings seemed more prosperous than others. The practice of feng shui grew out of these observations, believing one's fate was inextricably bound to the whims and cycles of the Heavens and the Earth. When the environment was healthy, its people prospered, but when the balance was destroyed, people suffered. As people began to understand that they shared their fate with the Earth, they came to respect the environment in which they lived. Thus, they took great care in locating, orienting, and designing their dwellings. Through feng shui, people sought to harmonize their relationship with the environment to improve their fortunes.

Spiritually, feng shui is an attempt to communicate with the Earth. By understanding patterns of ch'i, feng shui attempts to tap the resources and power of the planet and the cosmos. Feng shui covers a vast area of human endeavors. Along with directing the destinies of both families and individuals, it also deals with the welfare of entire countries and its ruling dynasties. While feng shui is highly personalized depending on individual needs and desires, feng shui believers argue that the aggregate effect of disharmony between themselves and their lands will lead to disruptions nationwide. While to most people feng shui is shrouded in mystery, its cultural heritage is still evident throughout much of modern Asia. Often feng shui's design suggestions seem to parallel modern ideas of science and principles of good design. At other times, however, logical

explanations for feng shui's interpretations fall short. With an approach that is both knowledgeable and intuitive, feng shui encompasses both ru-shr, the worldly, rational, and logical, and chu-shr, the transcendent, irrational, and illogical. The term consistently used in place of feng shui in ancient Chinese texts is 'dili,' that literally translates to mean land patterns or geography. This suggests that feng shui was originally based on the study of the land and the patterns found on it, both natural and artificial. Later, as the principles of feng shui became more structured, magnetism was introduced as fundamental to feng shui's methodology. The ancients believed that the Earth's magnetic fields affected ch'i, which in turn affected human wellbeing as much as the surrounding land patterns. It is important, therefore, to consider the orientation, layout, and siting of a building with reference to the surrounding environment, both natural and built, as well as the magnetic variations that exist through a site. Designs must be sited so that they are in harmony with the surrounding structures, natural elements, and the cardinal directions — North, East, South, and West. Therefore, in summary, when evaluating the flow of ch'i or the 'cosmic breath of life' of a site a designer using feng shui methodologies considers four factors: the surrounding land patterns, the site's dominant orientation, the site's magnetic reading, and the mutual influences of the five elements—fire, water, wood, metal, and earth—upon each location,

Fundamental to the Chinese approach to design is the fact that the world is in a perpetual state of constant cyclical change. Feng shui maintains that every design must articulate the understanding that the universe is in constant flux. The future is never static, but instead is based on eternal regenerative change. All human designs and creations must float along the ebb and flow of nature. According to the Confucian and Taoist religions, when the great extreme Tai Ji came into being at the beginning of all existence, it produced complementary opposites, yin and yang. Yin, translated as the shaded, north side of a hill, controls heaven and all things positive, active, masculine, hard, moving and living. Yang, on the other hand, is the sunny, south side of a hill that controls the Earth and all things negative, passive, feminine, soft, still, and non-living. Yang is shown as a solid, single, continuous line, while yin is portrayed as a broken line in two distinct pieces. During the creation process, yang and yin gave birth to the four primary symbols: greater yang, greater yin, lesser yang, and lesser yin. To these primary symbols, the line of either yin or yang was added to create the eight trigrams. These trigrams relate to the eight directions of space and form the foundation to the orientation of place in Feng Shui.

In the ancient Chinese belief-system, the eternal changes of existence are ascribed to the waxing and waning of the relative qualities of yang and yin. Any circumstance contains a balance of these qualities that can be determined by consulting the I-Ching, which is a text indicating the changing balances of yang and yin. The I-Ching's explanation of the seasonal cycles clearly demonstrates this interplay of yang and yin. In winter, the I-Ching states that the influence of yin is at its maximum, with yang at its minimum. In spring, yang and yin are equal, with yang increasing its influence and with yin fading. In summer, yang is at its maximum and yin is at its minimum, while autumn finds yang and yin in balance once again, but with yang waning and yin waxing. Finally, as the cycle is completed, yin is again at its maximum influence during the following winter. According to the I-Ching, the principle of yin and yang may also be applied to the daily cycles. As the Chinese symbol for existence, the yin-yang depicts this essential unity of all time. The dark yin has within it a seed of light yang, while the light yang contains a seed of dark yin.

Ch'i

Related to their cyclical understanding of the universe, the Chinese believe that the universe continues to evolve under a series of repeating patterns. The

sun rises and sets each day, just as the cycle of seasons forms the different climates of the year. Plants and animals grow and die accordingly. The Chinese believe that this universal cycle was based on the waxing and waning of yin and yang, resulting in the generation and disintegration of ch'i. Ch'i is the vital force that breathes life into plants and animals, inflates the Earth to form mountains, and carries water through the Earth's rivers and oceans. Ch'i is the life essence and the motivating force behind everything. It animates all things. Without ch'i, trees would not blossom, rivers would not flow, people would not exist. While all things — hills, streams, trees, humans, stones — inhale ch'i, they also exhale it, thus affecting one another. Just as the cosmos is in a constant state of flux, the flow of ch'i is never static but is constantly changing. Thus, a site with a beneficial flow of ch'i does not necessarily always remain so. The disruption of ch'i is greatest when yin and yang are in discord, and when sh'a, the opposite of ch'i, dominates the landscape. Whereas ch'i is said to be the breath of health and life, sh'a is said to be the breath of sickness and death. In feng shui's advocacy of balance and harmony, there exists a proper relationship between the buildings and land, and, by extension, humans, nature, and ch'i.

According to feng shui, people are sensitive to the ch'i of their environment. Atmospheric ch'i shapes human ch'i, just as human ch'i can affect atmospheric ch'i. When ch'i is forced far away from the earth's surface, water does not flow, pollution and sickness thrive, and bad luck abounds, thereby creating sick, unlucky people who in turn emit sh'a. A primary intention of feng shui is to maintain a smooth current of ch'i to a person and to divert harmful sh'a. Ch'i should bubble effortlessly through a site, without becoming trapped in any enclosed area where it could become stagnant and consequently disappear. It is unwise for ch'i to flow through the site without being able to pass on its revitalizing forces; as in a corridor or pathway that runs straight through a site without allowing the ch'i to permeate the rest of the area.

The Compass School and the Form School

To understand the flow of ch'i, which is undetectable to human senses, a designer trained in feng shui studies landscape forms through the form school, as well as compass orientation in the compass school. The form school of feng shui is based upon the effects that ch'i has on landscape shapes and forms. The form school emphasizes land formation and terrain, believing these forms are a result of ch'i passing through the terrain and surroundings. The compass school, based on the ritual significance of the compass points (ideas that have been enshrined in the Sacred Book of Rites), emphasizes the location of the planets and the trigrams regarding the site, and the generation and destruction by the five elements as a method to understand the flow of ch'i. To find additional ways of understanding ch'i, modern schools of feng shui have begun to incorporate astrology and fate calculation based on numerology into their basic understanding and application of feng shui.

In the form school, when a designer examines a site to find its potential qualities, the first step is to look at the surrounding landscape. On each site there are special topographical features, either natural or artificial, that are reflective by the historical effects of ch'i. As a result of the molding influences of wind and water, the forms of hills and the directions of watercourses are the most important elements of the landscape. The height and form of each building and the orientation of roads and bridges are also potent factors to consider. In the form school, a feng shui trained designer interprets the landscape and examines a site by focusing on shapes that suggest animals or specific objects. The form school suggests that these metaphorical masses are endowed with the attributes of the creatures they resemble, and the surrounding environment therefore takes on a metaphorical quality. The main feature of the landscape, known as the dragon is focused on extensively, for it is through the dragon that the ch'i is thought to touch the Earth. The dragon could take the shape of

Ancient Chinese scroll depicting both the compass school and the form school working is unison. Notice the use of a measurement staff to assist in reading land forms by the form school practitioners.

a prominent hill, a mountain, or, in an urban context, a skyscraper or tower. Once the dragon is identified, various parts of the dragon are distinguished, such as its head, body, or limbs. The area that exists under the protective eye of the dragon is thought to be prosperous, for this is the area that a dragon is thought most protective of. The protective Nine Dragon mountains to the north of Hong Kong are believed to be the result of an incredible amount of ch'i historically located there and are often credited for the prosperity of the city. The area situated under a dragon's open mouth is not prosperous, for this is the area from which the dragon wishes to eat. If a part of the dragon is cut or separated from the rest of the dragon, every part of the site affected by the dragon suffers, as a wounded dragon possesses unhealthy ch'i. In addition to the dragon, various other creatures are often associated with landforms they most resemble . In understanding the creatures impact on a site, feng shui encourages its believers to understand that while life imitates nature, likewise nature imitates life; for example a dog mound may guard, and a tiger hill may threaten.

Having taken into account the surrounding environment, the compass school dictates that the designer committed to incorporating feng shui concerns measure the cardinal relationships found in the site. Crucial to this idea is the Lo P'an, or 'net-plate,' which is a saucer shaped compass in a square base with two cross-threads used to examine cardinal relationships in the site. While the traditional European compass point refers to a particular direction, the Chinese compass bearing refers to a segment of the circle, not to a specific point on its circumference. The Lo P'an compass is divided into twelve sections at intervals of thirty degrees and has a number of 'rings' divided according to different classifications. To use this Chinese compass, the bearings of significant landscape formations are taken and used to determine how each formation may affect the flow of ch'i through the site. The five rings of the compass indicate different characteristics of the site.

(1) The first ring, or the 'outer-heaven ring', governs the potency of the ch'i flow, while (2) the second 'Earth ring' is used to divine the pulse of the ch'i by locating the veins and arteries of the Earth ch'i. (3) The middle ring, or 'main plate' is to be used to discover the influence of the heavenly ch'i and earthly ch'i on the site. (4) The fourth ring of the common Lo P'an indicated the orientations of the eight trigrams, and (5) the final and smallest ring indicated the cardinal directions. By observing the site and its environment through the Lo P'an, feng shui determines the best orientation of any design.

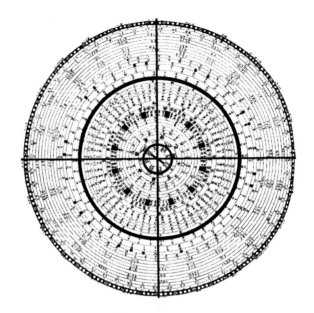

A traditional Lo P'an

The Five Elements

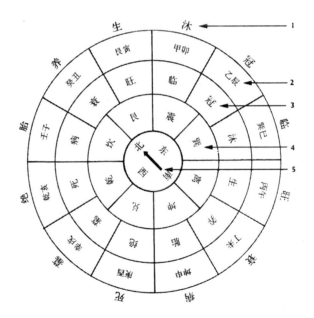

Five Elements

The Five Elements, or wu-hsing, are also fundamental in determining the cyclical presence of ch'i. The Five Elements refer to mutually dependent points in continual flux, and are the symbols of ch'i symbiotic correlation. These five elements are Wood, Fire, Earth, Metal, and Water. Divided into productive or destructive cycles, the Five Elements are used to illustrate both the animating character and the repetitive patterns of changes in ch'i. Wu-hsing can be translated as follows: the Chinese character wu is the cardinal number five, while the character hsing means mobility: to do, to act, to walk, to travel. Hsing can also be taken to mean process, conduct, behavior, or way. Wu-hsing, therefore, is known as the 'Five Elements of Time,' or the 'Five Elements.' Wu-hsing is also sometimes translated as the 'Five Agents,' 'Five Forces,' 'Five Qualities,' or 'Five Properties,' which are simply variations on the same theme. The Five Elements are the five basic categories under which ch'i evolves into the next cyclic stage.

While understanding the Five Elements is the most difficult part of feng shui, it is important to be familiar with the underlying philosophy behind the Five Elements as they are essential to a complete understanding of ch'i. Four of these five elements relate to the cardinal points, with the last element located at the center. The four cardinal points are in turn related to the four seasons, each of which has its own symbolic color and shape. There exist two main cyclic relationships among the Five Elements. The creation cycle, referred to as the 'Former Heaven' sequence, is based on the yang aspect of the elements. Wood burns, giving rise to Fire, which thereby results in ash or Earth that contains veins of Metal, from which springs Water that nourishes vegetation and produces Wood. The destructive cycle, or the 'Later Heaven,' portrays the yin aspect of the elements. Each element in turn destroys another. Wood, which represents all vegetation, swallows, covers and binds the Earth, which then muddies and pollutes Water, that extinguishes Fire melting Metal that chops down Wood. Thus the Five Element doctrine consists of two fundamental principles: The Five Elements produce one another, and the Five Elements destroy one another.

• *Wood*, representing all growing, vegetative life, is the element related to spring, the beginning of the year. As such, wood flourishes in spring, retires in summer, is imprisoned in the sixth month, perishes in autumn, and helps in winter. Wood is the sunrise from the East, and its color is blue-green, like the color of all plants as well as the color of the Great Sea to the east of China. The shape associated with wood is a tall and narrow cylinder, like the trunk

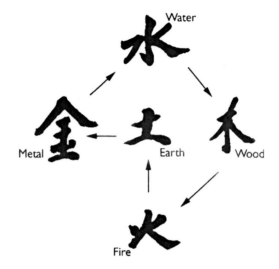

Creative Order :
Wood, Fire, Earth,
Metal, Water, Wood

Destructive Order :
Wood, Earth, Water,
Fire, Metal, Wood

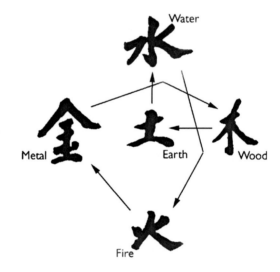

of a tree. Wood is ruled by Jupiter. In creation, Wood produces Fire, and in destruction, Wood destroys the Earth.

• *Fire* is the heat of the sun in the summer. As such, fire helps in the spring, flourishes in summer, retires in the sixth month, is imprisoned in autumn, and dies in winter. Fire is the element of midday, the South, animal life, and the color red. Its symbolic shape is pyramidal, similar to the sharp points of flames. Fire is ruled by Mars. Fire produces Earth but destroys Metal.

• *Earth* is at the center, and as such is not associated with any direction. Earth dies in spring, helps in summer, flourishes in the sixth month, retires in autumn, and is imprisoned in winter. Since it is the center, it is symbolized by shapes that have no third dimension. It is represented by the shapelessness of flat, and its color is that of all the browns of the earth. The Earth represents stability, and is ruled by Saturn. Earth produces Metal, and destroys Water.

• *Metal* is the element of autumn, and as such, Metal is imprisoned in spring, dies in summer, helps in the sixth month, flourishes in autumn, and retires in winter. Metal signifies all weapons and tools that are fabricated, and represents the minerals. The color of Metal is silver or white. Metal is the sun setting in the West, like the snow tipped mountains of the Himalayan mountains west of China. Metal is represented as a sphere, much like the moon. Metal is ruled by Venus. Metal produces water, and metal destroys wood.

• Finally, the element *Water* represents all vapor. It is the element of winter, and as such, water retires in spring, is imprisoned in summer, dies in the sixth month, helps in autumn, and flourishes in winter. Water is the night, the cold winds from the North, and the color black. Water represents fluidity, and is represented by shapes that are irregular and lack form. Water is ruled by Mercury. Water produces Wood destroying all fire.

From the Former Heaven and the Later Heaven sequences, secondary sequences are derived:

• *Wood,* the producer of Fire, is the destroyer of Earth, a friend to Metal, and neutral to Water.

- *Fire,* the producer of Earth, is the destroyer of Metal, a friend to Water, and neutral to Wood.

- *Earth* the producer of Metal, is the destroyer of Water, a friend to Wood, and neutral to Fire.

- *Metal* the producer of Water, is the destroyer of Wood, a friend to Fire, and neutral to Earth.

- *Water* the producer of Wood, is the destroyer of Fire, a friend to Earth, and neutral to Metal.

To aid in one's understanding of ch'i, the main characteristics of a site are classified according to the Five Elements. Once all the characteristics of the site are classified, the elements are examined for balance. When the elements are out of balance, the potential for the destruction of ch'i is greater. For example, if on a site there are many pointy towers made out of metal, such as transmission towers, and if the designer felt that the shape of the towers is more dominant in the site's character then the material of the towers, then this would indicate an abundance of the Fire element. If there is an abundance of the Fire element on a site, situating any building towards the South is unwise. Such a building may aggravate the fire element, suggesting great destruction of the metal element. This cycle of destruction would necessarily lead to a decrease in the flow of ch'i. To intervene between the Fire and Metal elements, both Earth and Wood are needed to turn the potentially destructive situation created by these elements into one that is productive. The house should therefore face towards the easterly direction to favor the Wood element. On the other hand, if the material of the towers has a more dominant effect on the site than the shape, then the towers might be classified as Metal elements, and the resulting recommendation for situating a building would therefore be completely different. Understanding the relationships among the five elements is the most difficult task of a designer using feng shui. The reason the five elements are such difficult aspects of feng shui to master it that is that it is the designer who must make the final, crucial decision as to which dominant characteristics inform the classification of the Elements. Feng shui dictates that most designers spend years mastering the unique characteristics of each of the five elements to understand their relationship to one another.

Practical Aspects of Feng Shui

While feng-shui is thousands of years old and steeped in both complicated and esoteric rules, it contains many suggestions that for the ancient Chinese were practical knowledge. Feng shui's precepts for the ideal building form are closely tied to China's geography and climate. Many of the practical suggestions in feng shui are based upon measures used to counteract the patterns of historical disasters in China. To the north and west, Central China is flanked by mountain ranges. Most rivers originate in the West, run east through the agricultural regions, and finally drain into the eastern seas. Chilling winds blow from the northwest while the southeast wind brings in warm, moist air. One of the most basic principles of feng shui is the situation of the door of a house to the South, because in China not only is the North the precinct of cold winds, but it was also the direction from which the marauding Mongolians came. Also, a building must not open to the rising sun of the East, for it is from the East that the flooding Yellow River flowed. Given these conditions, it is no surprise that feng shui suggests that the ideal building must have the most protection from the northern and eastern elevations. The southwest should be open to capture light, warmth, and the summer breeze. Additionally, a northwest to southeast site orientation is superior as it conforms with the location of the Gates to Heaven. Conversely, entrances in the northeast to southwest are to be avoided, for these directions lead to the Gates of Hell and The Gates of Illness, harbingers of ill fortune.

Over time, the ancient Chinese determined that a house was ideally sited halfway up a hill on the north side of the river, facing south to receive the optimal amount of sun. It was in this position that the home was most protected from harsh winds, and floods, while retaining optimal access to water for crops. Thus, feng shui suggests that there must be a protective mountain, hill, or higher ground at the back of the building to shield it from dangerous natural forces. In such surroundings it was easiest to survive: rice, vegetables, and fruit trees grew under an unhindered sun, cattle grazed on lush grass, and the home stayed relatively warm in the winter months. Feng shui principles add that to take the ultimate advantage of the vital ch'i on any site, a home should be built between two hills of unequal size, with a river running along one side of the structure, turning in front of the building and then disappearing. Such a home will receive the maximum amount of sunlight, is shielded from the chilly, health-sapping north wind, and has a good supply of water for drinking and cleaning. The environment proved comfortable and harmonious, and helped inhabitants to survive and prosper.

Ancient geomantic suggestion as explained by a feng shui master

While ch'i is the advantageous cosmic breath, there are also dangerous forms of energies emitted from the Earth. This energy, known as sh'a, is roughly considered the opposite of ch'i, and is indicated by irregular and unhealthy forms of the Earth. Where ch'i promotes health, sh'a creates an unhealthy environment that fosters illness. When designing according to feng shui, sh'a must necessarily be considered, for example if there are unnatural shapes and odd angles pointing at a site, a planned building must be situated so that the flow of sh'a from these shapes cannot penetrate into the building through doorways or windows. Sometimes feng shui rules if not executed correctly can actual increase the exposure to sh'a. For example, feng shui suggests placing the main entrance of a building nearest to a road, thereby encouraging the maximum exposure to ch'i, and increasing its accessibility to the building. On the other hand, feng shui warns that care must be taken to ensure that there is no road directly aligned with an entrance, for this situation creates dangerous exposure to sh'a. To reduce the exposure a building has to sh'a and because sh'a only travels in straight lines and is unable to turn corners, feng shui suggests that curving paths be used to maximize the proximity of entrances to flowing ch'i while reducing the direct flow of sh'a.

In addition to the rule that major entrances must be given a clear view to receive the maximum beneficial ch'i, other feng shui rules are summarized as follows. If in its optimum orientation an entrance faces a temple or church, it is better to adjust the orientation slightly to the East or West, for it is believed that a house of God exerts too powerful an influence on any building directly opposite it. Too much light signifies too much yang, thereby creating too much exposure and invasion and not enough privacy, while too much darkness indicates excess yin, consequently producing too much mystery. Good sound insulation is also important, as noise reduces ch'i by creating undesirable vibrations. The land must be sloping and well drained, and the depth of the site must be greater than its width. The best sites are those where dragon and tiger forms create a horseshoe in the landscape, with the dragon in the East and the tiger in the West, where the point of transition between the dragon and the tiger becomes the point of the greatest concentration of beneficial ch'i. Boldly rising formations are termed yang formations while gentle, undulating elevations are termed yin. On a site where yang characteristics prevail, the spot possessing yin characteristics stands out as propitious. To encourage the maximum concentration of the beneficial ch'i on the site, the ideal proportion of yang and yin is three-fifths yang and two-fifths yin. Triangular sites are ill-omened as they are strange shapes that attract sh'a. The necessary components for a beneficial landscape are water, plants, and earth. For each of these components should exist on the site in meandering and undulating forms, so as to reduce the amount of sh'a entering the site and to retain the maximum amount of ch'i.

Avoid sites surrounded by high boundaries that restrict views of the horizon, as well as houses located directly over wells and water veins. If one side of a site is too low, plant trees to raise the height. If a neighbor builds a home higher than the other houses in the neighborhood, feng shui suggests adding to the height of the rest of the homes in the neighborhood so that the view of the stars is not obstructed. In properties that back onto a river, the entrance must be at the rear to allow the ch'i to gain its necessary entrance. If the ground slopes upward from the front of a building, then again the entrance should be at the rear. A large tree immediately opposite the front door is ill-omened, as it deflects the entrance of ch'i. The vitality of ch'i is best conserved in a gently meandering stream, while a pool of water or fishpond is especially useful to conserve ch'i. Alter a stream or river to give it bends and curves, but do not make the bends too sharp or the ch'i will 'run off' and dissipate. As with all the other suggestions, most of the practical advice suggested by feng shui stems from China's unique cultural heritage. For a nation of rice cultivators, the value of a meandering river, in the last example of a feng shui rule, is an agricultural blessing, providing better irrigation and a more fertile silt than a straight rushing torrent. Such conditions produce larger crops, providing a family with better health and greater prosperity.

While feng shui emphasizes combining the practical and spiritual qualities of a site, to design according to feng shui is not to simply correctly place a design, but is rather an attempt to understand all of the elements of a site and through that understanding gain knowledge as to where an appropriate design belongs. This ideal holds the key to understanding feng shui's vision of the world. To design according to feng shui is to become aware of the flow of ch'i in a place and to encourage as well as respect that flow. Feng shui is not a philosophy of inactivity, of humbly letting nature take its course. Feng shui is instead a doctrine of intervention, seeking an aesthetic harmony between humanity and the environment. By examining the ch'i of a site, feng shui attempts to harmonize nature and culture, encouraging designers to concern themselves with both the visible and the invisible elements of a site. Through ch'i, feng shui attempts to provide a way to grasp the less visible, though no less significant, forces in the landscape, and provides a method of contemplation to understand the elemental forces that influence any site. In feng shui's methodology, site analysis and design become a ritualistic and devotional process, divining the spirit of place in the hope of generating appropriate designs.

Modern Feng Shui and Its Problems

Though feng shui is presently the most widely practiced method of holistic design, the present new-age version of interior design and self improvement is vastly different from ancient feng shui . True feng shui is a codified and traditional spiritual system of indigenous knowledge expressed in philosophical terms, and expanded to the ritual of systematic analysis used to investigate the site before the act of designing.

Contrary to ideas espoused by modern proponents of feng shui, there are no simple solutions to be found in classical feng shui that can be universally applied to a wide variety of sites. Classical feng shui centers upon extensive site observation and analysis. The authentic approach applies the form school, the compass school and the Five Elements to each site individually to understand the flow of ch'i and to arrive at auspicious and appropriate designs. It is not uncommon to see literature offering standard solutions, but these approaches suggest only an oversimplified interpretation of feng shui. Many of these approaches omit the Five Elements due to their ambiguity and complexity, and thereby eliminate a crucial variable in determining the flow of ch'i.

This simplification has led to the corruption of classical feng shui. Feng shui today concerns absurd notions of interior decoration, the use of charms and talismans, and unrelated ideas of personal spiritual improvement. Being most fundamentally a method of site analysis, feng shui cannot be applied to interiors, at least not in its traditional sense. Feng shui can open the mind and train the eye, leading to a sense of balance, harmony, and order. This aesthetic understanding can be reflected in the placement of objects in interiors, or by a general awareness of space and circulation, but fundamentally this is not what traditional feng shui is about. Color and light are similarly important in the classification of the Five Elements, but to focus solely on color coordination is to move away from the essence of what feng shui truly is. Feng shui uses extensive observations to discover the divine nature of a site by estimating the flow of ch'i through that site. It is important to remember that feng shui originated in an agricultural society and is founded on concern for environmental health and well-being. To design a site in harmony with forces seen and unseen, tangible and intangible, is the true goal of feng shui.

Instead of examining the surrounding forms, magnetic readings, and the balance of the Five Elements on a site to judge the flow of ch'i, modern feng shui practitioners use a standard diagnostic formula based on eight 'life stations.' To get an instant feng shui reading, an octagonal diagram called an 'energy template' representing these 'life stations' is superimposed on the site, with the template aligned with the North. This instant feng shui reading determines which 'life stations,' or aspects of a person's life, are not being supported by ch'i in proposed designs. When the template is used and a necessary part is missing due to the building's design, crystals, wind chimes, or mirrors are often used to activate the flow of ch'i. The ancient Chinese did believe that mirrors could render solid matter transparent, and thereby the mirrors implied a higher, more rarefied plane of existence visible only through their portals. Thus mirrors, regarded as doors to the world beyond, were sometimes used to encourage the flow of ch'i, or to redirect harmful sh'a. The mirrors most often used in Feng Shui rites possessed octagonal frames based on the trigrams of the yang and yin forms, and were either concave or convex to either better dissipate or to better collect energy flows. Wind chimes were sometimes used to warn of passing sh'a, and were historically hung at the corner of temple eaves in the belief that they would dispel any evil spirits. Many modern feng shui practitioners, however, have a tendency to overuse both mirrors and chimes, creating a generic panacea and essentially overvaluing their historically marginal use. True feng shui concerned itself little with the use of mirrors and chimes, but rather focused on the process of site evaluation and design.

As shown in the indepth examination of feng shui in this chapter, the modern versions of feng shui do relate to the historical feng shui in a marginal way, but modern feng shui is evolving into something significantly different. Contrary to many modern claims regarding the origins of feng shui, authentic feng shui is not related to any religious belief. Feng shui was instead conceived as an ancient combination of site analysis and natural science. Authentic practitioners, employing the ancient principles of keen observation based upon the surrounding land forms, the compass readings, and the interaction of the Five Elements understand that the environment affects an individual, but that the path towards improving a design is a result of the harmonization of the natural forces of a site. Contrary to modern feng shui, ancient feng shui does not seek a simple solution. True feng shui instructs designers that to understand the divine cosmic breath ch'i is to carefully analyze the site, for it is only from the patterns in the site that the patterns of ch'i emerge. Under feng shui, to understand the site is not a simple proposition, and accompanying that is the idea that there are no simple solutions to questions posed by the site, only solutions as complex as the site itself.

83
site divine
feng shui

chapter six *dowsing*

Dowsing is a form of geomancy. It attempts to read the energies of the Earth with a mandate to dictate design in accordance to those energy flows, and is closely related to augury, extispicy, vastu, and feng shui. In all forms of geomancy there are similarities that suggest that they are based upon common ideals. While these ideals not only provide designers with concrete methodologies that can be applied to all design processes, they also hint at a greater potential for design. Geomancy and other similar forms of divination can allow designers to understand the concept of site and its importance in a new and special way. Dowsing, having much in common with feng shui, provides an alternative method of site analysis that could help to reconnect designers to the land. As with all forms of geomancy, using dowsing alone to understand the nature of a site is as ineffectual as using only scientific site analysis to understand a site. Dowsing, along with feng shui and other forms of geomancy, must recognize its common ancestry and unite with scientific site analysis to provide a new method for designers to understand the site. Following post-modernism with its embrace of multiple perceptions of reality, designers need to understand that dowsing and feng shui provide a valued perspective that has been recently missing from design and its relationship to the site.

Dowsing as a
respectable practice in
the nineteenth century

Although the exact origins of dowsing are uncertain, in the Tassilin-Ajjer caves in southeastern Algeria there are 8,000 year old pictoglyphs depicting a group of people watching an individual who is holding what appears to be a divining rod. Various ancient figures are credited with inventing or introducing dowsing tools to humans, including the Egyptian god Thoth and the Greek inventor Daedalus, who are credited with inventing the plumb bob and the pendulum respectively, both of which are dowsing instruments. The earliest known dowser was Emperor Yu, who practiced in the third millennium B.C. In the Freer Gallery in Washington, D.C. there is a Han Dynasty bas-relief of Emperor Yu with the following inscription: "Emperor Yu of the Hsia Dynasty was a master of the science of the earth and in those matters concerning water veins and springs; he was well acquainted with the Yin principle and when required, built dams."

The art of dowsing claims to be less spiritual than the other forms of geomancy already discussed. Since the Middle Ages, diviners using dowsing have attempted to present their work as scientific and completely analytical. Before the condemnation by the Christian Church, dowsing was often said to be simply a 'prosthesis' that helped diviners focus and read their body signals as dictated by the Trinity of the Father, Son, and Holy Ghost. During that time, diviners claimed that their bodies where responding to the subtle signals of God. The Church, however, argued that dowsing was a form of divination, and as such the work of the Devil. Since that time, the geomantic practice of dowsing has shrouded itself in pseudo-science.

Although the Bible severely censures dowsers and diviners, it does tell of Moses finding water with the use of his magical rod: "Thou shalt smite the rock, and there shall come water out of it, that the people may drink." (Exodus XVII:5-6) "Take the rod . . . and speak ye unto the rock . . . and it shall give forth water." (Numbers XX:9-11) Martin Luther denounced dowsing in 1528 A.D. as the work of the Devil. Early priests argued that dowsing threatened established religions because it attempted to allow laypersons to demonstrate a spiritual knowledge directly, bypassing the priesthood. However, since settlements were continually dependent upon clean water supplies and dowsing seemed able to repeatedly provide clean water when needed, the church was never able to exterminate the practice of water dowsing. Another kind of dowsing that was not suppressed by the Church was written about by the sixteenth-century magician Georgius Agricola. In 1556, in De Re Metallica , Agricola described how at that time German prospectors in the Harz region were using forked twigs to find underground veins of metal.

The employment of various rods for divination purposes goes back to the time of ancient Greeks and Egyptians. While most of the dowsing rods were used in the search for water and minerals, some of these rods were thought able to detect guilt and magic. During the Holy Inquisition, a decree was issued against the use of divining rods for deciding between guilt and innocence in criminal trials. Throughout the seventeenth century, non-trial related dowsing became more widespread over England and the entire European continent, and became a topic of violent controversy among scientists. In the eighteenth century, during the supposed Age of Enlightenment, people decided that the now common act of dowsing was a respectable practice, and was no longer associated with the Devil.

Dowsing was commonly accepted in Europe while America was being settled. Sixteenth and seventeenth century treatises and coins depict the diviner at work with dowsing instruments. Dowsing skills came with the colonists to the New World and are said to have been a significant means of locating water wells. The American Society of Dowsers (ASD) late Secretary Raymond Willey said of colonial America, "the dowser was a respected member of the community and it was commonly said that a man undertaking to dig a well without consulting a dowser was a fool." The use of dowsing apparently persisted until the end of the last century, when scientific technology began to exert its influence on our culture and as dowsing was seen as scientifically unprovable. Also, as communities constructed municipal water systems and began to rely less on individual water wells, dowsing became marginalized to rural areas where water wells were still necessary.

After World War II, expansion in suburban building brought urgent calls for new water sources. As the quiet, country dowser received nationwide attention through a new national media, people also began to believe that this searching tool could be applied to a wider range of needs. Currently, dowsing is used in an attempt to locate a wide range of elements, including water, metal ores, oil and gas deposits, lost articles, archeological sites and artifacts, criminals, missing persons, and downed aircraft.

There are four basic types of dowsing tools: Y-rods, pendulums, L-rods, and bobbers. The most familiar of the basic dowsing tool types is the Y-rod, or forked stick. Traditionally the Y-rod is cut from an apple or willow tree, although today many diviners use plastic rods because these rods are less likely to break under the constant twisting created by the downward pull of the rod. The forked stick is held in both hands with the diviner's thumbs pointed outwards, and with the stem of the 'Y' pointing outwards. This is termed the search position. The tip of the rod then points down sharply as the dowsing rod is held is over the target. The pendulum, also known as a plumb bob, can be any well-balanced weight positioned on the end of a thread or light chain. Each diviner establishes her own code to interpret the movements of the pendulum. For example, a back and forth movement might instruct a diviner to move forward, where a circular motion might indicate that the diviner should stop and stand still. The L-rods are comprised of two rods held much like pistols were held by the old cowboys. When the diviner stands over a target, the rods swing around, indicating some presence. L-rods are commonly used by those interested in earth energies such as electro-magnetic fields. The fourth dowsing tool used by diviners is the bobber. The bobber is a long flexible pole that bobs up and down like a fishing pole catching a fish when the target is reached. The bobber is used primarily by oil dowsers, who often call themselves 'doodlebugs.' While these are the four basic types of tools, many dowsers create their own unique rods that they believe work better than other more conventional rods. The instruments of dowsing are nearly limitless and underscore the fact that the divining power of dowsing is not derived from the dowsing tool used.

While only field dowsing maintains a direct connection to the actual site, the American Society of Dowsers (ASD) recognizes four distinct methods of dowsing. Field dowsing is the most traditional form of dowsing which involves directly investigating a site. This is termed "witching the area." The other methods of dowsing are remote, map, and information dowsing. In remote dowsing, the diviner uses trigger devices such as a lost person's article of clothing, and then attempts to locate the target from a distance as far as several miles away. Remote dowsers believe that they have to be in the vicinity of a site, but not directly on the site to successfully dowse a site. With map dowsing, the diviner uses a pendulum to locate targets such as wells or mineral deposits on a map. These diviners claim that there are no distance limits here, since the they attempt to locate their targets from thousands of miles away. Information dowsing allows the diviner to obtain information on any subject without space or time limits. A large number of general descriptions of the various dowsing methods have been published in books designed for popular reading. Christopher Bird's excellent book titled The Divining Hand contains in-depth examination of the many different types of dowsing.

Even though all four methods of dowsing are presently acceptable according to the American Society of Dowsers, the practice of field dowsing offers the only real opportunity for designers interested in investigating different perspectives of site analysis. Field dowsing is the only form of dowsing that

Dowsing for metal
as illustrated in
De Re Metallica

is directly related to the site and issues concerning site analysis. Through field dowsing there is the possibility of occupying a site in ways that sites are not presently occupied and thereby increasing a designer's understanding of the site. Field dowsing is also the only form of dowsing that is supported by a variety of pseudo-scientific theories that may help frame the phenomena as more relevant to site analysis — from an innate sensitivity to energy radiation to presently unknown geo-physical phenomena. Field dowsers often claim that they possess a natural sensitivity to either the Earth's magnetism, water radiation, or some other natural phenomenon. They believe their dowsing tools enables them to focus and identify the Earth's energy fields, enabling them to find water or other elements related to the Earth. As water flows through underground streams, field dowsers claim it creates a subtle energy field several feet wide that rises vertically above the water course and exerts a subtle effect on people either physically, mentally, or spiritually. Some diviners claim that the energy feels faintly warm and fuzzy and explain that the energy undulates with a directional pull, that acts as series of flowing ripples that give off an impulse, which in turn initiate involuntary muscular contractions which causes the dowsing instruments to move. Other dowsers claim to feel a calming energy that causes their muscle to relax, instead of contract.

Some dowsing practitioners claim that they experience a variety of physical sensations, such as a tingling or shivering of the skin, or a trembling and unpleasant sensation in the stomach. The possible reasons cited for these reactions include gravitational, magnetic, electric, electromagnetic, radioactive, seismic, geothermal, cosmic, or geochemical fields. Of these, magnetic, electric, and electromagnetic fields seem the most likely possibilities. A simple science experiment can explain why these energy fields offer the greatest possibilities. It is widely understood that moving water can cause electricity to flow. For example, water moving down a wire will move enough electrons to flash a small neon bulb that requires over 68 volts. Moving water underground could be associated with electric flow in a similar way. Any time electricity flows through a conductor, it creates an electromagnetic field. These electro-magnetic fields could then be picked up by the internal sensors of anyone who has been made aware of them. Like the eye that can differentiate between forms, shades, and colors, humans may be able to differentiate between patterns of electromagnetic energy fields from different sources. Therefore, the diviner trained in the techniques of dowsing could, in theory, obtain information about the existence of moving underground water by transferring this information from the subconscious to the conscious mind with the help of dowsing devices.

At the other end of the spectrum is the argument that dowsing is entirely psychic, and that the art of dowsing can only be explained by extrasensory perception. To justify their findings, these diviners argue that we are all psychic, and that the degree to which we are psychic depends only upon the development of our intuitive skills. Perhaps dowsing succeeds by accessing the extrasensory perception of our subconscious mind and having it respond by muscular contractions. The response may take the form of a tingle in the fingers or in the palm of the hand. The response may be in the form of a body signal, like a muscle twitch, or a pain. It may be pictures formed in the mind, or an inner-knowing that could be extrasensory in nature. Dowsing may simply be a more sophisticated method of using our natural instinctual abilities. If the diviner has access to this subconscious and is able to access it with a dowsing device, he or she could receive unique information directly related to questions concerning the site. The dowsing instrument might allow the diviner to tap into the subconscious selectively and obtain information regarding a site.

Regardless of what the diviner experiences, the movement of the dowsing rods, sometimes violent enough to peel bark from a Y-stick, is clearly initiated by muscular action. The material the rod is made of does not matter, since the rod is simply acting as a mechanical amplifier of small muscle movements. Whether it be a forked willow stick or a bent coat hanger, dowsing may provide a way for humans to attempt, through their subconscious states of awareness, to understand the patterns of the earth. There is no consensus on how diviners using dowsing tools detect these natural energies, and there likely never will be. Just as with all geomancy, dowsing is an extremely individual experience, with each diviner both experiencing and believing something slightly different.

In the face of all of the supporting theories on dowsing, scientific testing also consistently disproves diviners' claim that dowsing is a natural or learned sensitivity to some physical phenomenon. Careful examination of diviners' dowsing claims and results, which are frequently contradictory, reveals that there is no factual basis for concluding that dowsing represents a response to any physical phenomenon. For example, controlled tests conducted by famous psychic debunker James Randi in the Skeptical Inquirer yielded no evidence that people practicing dowsing have a unique ability to find water. Says Randi, "the sad fact is that dowsers are no better at finding water than anyone else. Drill a well almost anywhere in an area where water is geologically possible, and you will find it." While many scientists have attempted to understand the physical basis of dowsing that links the rod in the diviner's hand to earth energy phenomena, no one has yet successfully explained, nor completely discredited dowsing's success. Apart from its convoluted history, the fact that dowsing has persisted for so long is clearly its major defense.

Dowsing is likely a complex reaction to the energies of the earth. Whereas diviners trained in feng shui attempt to discern the energies of the earth through applied methodologies, diviners using dowsing attempt to uncover the earth's energies by being acutely aware of their bodies' reactions to the land. The diviner experienced in dowsing is likely endowed with a subconscious cognitive faculty that results in unconscious muscular reactions when encountering different earth energies. This reaction may be the result of a myriad of energies in nature. The movement of the rods is caused by the amplification of small involuntary muscular contractions resulting from stimulation of the central nervous system, perhaps by stimulation of the brain or spinal column. Dowsing survives today because its use and value does not depend on scientists' inability to explain its successes and continued existence. Increasingly, as dowsing's cloak of pseudo-science has been torn away, diviners using dowsing skills have begun returning to their pre-scientific heritage. Modern diviners using dowsing have become less interested in the theories behind dowsing, and more interested in the results that are achieved. Unfortunately, however, modern dowsing, with its increasing emphasis on information dowsing, is losing its heritage of site analysis upon which it is founded. With an increasing emphasis on the other forms of dowsing, field dowsing is becoming less prevalent, and dowsing is losing its historical association with the land and the geomantic heritage upon which it was originally founded.

Dowsing Guidelines

Dowsing methods and interpretations are completely subjective and individual processes. Their success depends on the techniques developed by the diviners themselves. According to dowsing literature, since most people are intuitively aware of their environment, most people also have the innate ability to dowse but simply have not tried it. Designers attempting dowsing may nevertheless have to practice for a time before they manifest what dowsers believe is an inherent talent.

New diviners interested in dowsing techniques are often encouraged to use one of the basic divining rods: the pendulum, L-rods, Y-rod, or the bobber as explained in detail in Appendix One. As with all human skills, aptitude will vary among different dowsing practitioners and students. As diviners develop confidence in the dowsing reaction, they also develop selectivity in understanding the subtle differences between various reactions. With practice and patience, experienced dowsers believe that both the tangible and the intangible can be dowsed. Experienced diviners remind people attempting to dowse for the first time to believe in their mind that dowsing works, and that the dowsing instrument will respond. It is also important to remember not to preconceive any answer, as the conscious mind easily overrides the subconscious, and the dowsing response will agree with any preconception.

When attempting to analyze a site using dowsing skills, diviners begin by using their chosen tool in the search position. From this position, a diviner keeps his or her mind focused on potential questions he or she may have regarding the site, or keep it blank. If the diviner covers too much ground or passes over a known target without result, they might try another tool. Diviners suggest that it is best to begin analyzing a site by looking for flowing, underground veins of water. Diviners begin by focusing on a need, asking for a 'vein of water, less than fifty feet in depth, which flows uninterrupted at the rate of five gallons a minute or more.' Marking the spot where a dowsing reaction occurs, the diviner then approaches it from the opposite direction. If the second reaction does not coincide with the first reaction, the diviner may try several times again. If the second reaction remains the same on subsequent attempts, the midpoint between the first and second reaction is a good place to suggest that there is a vein of water.

After finding the tool that works best and provides consistent reactions, diviners interested in dowsing must begin to develop the art of dowsing. As mentioned previously, there are at least two schools of thought on the mental approach to dowsing. One says that the mind should be emptied, rendered blank, to become a nirvana of nothingness. The other group holds that concentration on the object of the search is the key to success. Both groups agree that it is extremely important to ask the right question, as the subconscious is very literal. It observes and stores information and delivers exactly what is asked for to the conscious. A student of dowsing must be clear in their mind what they wish to divine. The most difficult thing for a student of dowsing to learn is to not preconceive. If a diviner already believes that they know the answer, the dowsing rod will simply agree with them, rather then lead them to a greater awareness of their subconscious and intuitive reactions to the site. The conscious mind has been in control for so long that it automatically tries to figure out the answer to every question that it is asked. Preconception and reasoning will be responsible for most of the beginning dowser's mistakes. Experienced diviners stress that much practice is necessary to achieve results that will assist inexperienced diviners and designers in finding new perspectives in understanding the site.

In many ways dowsing provides designers with an opportunity to engage in a ritual that focuses all of the senses on the study of the land. By bringing a stick or rod to a site and spending time focusing on specific site-related questions designers will ensure a physical presence on the site that they are presently neglecting. Though it may seem unprofessional or awkward to bring a dowsing instrument to a site and attempt to divine, dowsing might be described as a form of active concentration that attempts to engage the senses in an intuitive analysis of the site. Arguably dowsing is nothing more than a natural tool that may enable designers to focus on what they already perceive but simply have not bothered to pay attention to before. Dowsing is a ritual that provides an entrance into the abstract world of feeling and intuition concerning a specific site. Similarly, when designers begin sketching rough ideas for new designs, the paper and the pencil become tools that focus the designer on a specific realm. In this realm of concentration, forms and shapes begin to develop. It is at this point that the beginning seeds of the design begin to grow. The rod, y-stick, pendulum, and bobber are related tools that can allow designers to receive similar seeds of conception regarding the living and sacred nature of the site.

site divine
dowsing

Part Two   case study *site*

The following case study examines a site located in Toronto, Canada, called the Summerhill Lands, using standard reductionist methods of site analysis as well as contemporary but lesser known or used methods of site investigation. This case study is an attempt to examine divination methods in a contemporary light. The following section is an in-depth examination of one distinct site. Hopefully, this examination will show both the commonalties as well as the differences between the different methods of divination, along with contemporary methods of site analysis and investigation. In the end, the readers of this investigation will have been able to participate in an attempt to apply some of the suggestions from the earlier sections of this book to an actual site. Together we will have examined the Summerhill Lands from various perspectives, and these perspectives will hopefully provide us with greater insight into this site in particular. However some of the perspectives, will provide us with lesser insight, showing us the precarious nature of site divination and the necessity to constant evaluation of the information presented to us, as opposed to the acceptance of everything as equally valid. Among diviners there will be both areas of agreement and areas of disagreement regarding the analysis of the site, and it is in this that the reader must take an active role in placing value on the comments of the various diviners. It is the author's hope that the following section can

97
site divine
case study
site

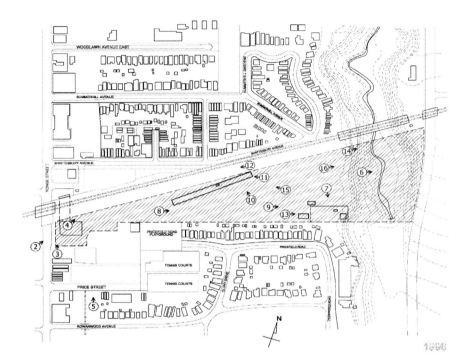

Summerhill site with
numbered locations
of photographs on
following pages

provide new perspectives on how to perceive, analyze, or even inhabit a site. This examination is an attempt to achieve a sense of the site through many varied methods of thought. As we examine both site analysis and site divination, we find that site analysis methodologies are culturally specific rather than environmentally specific. In this case, the site acts as the common thread that ties each of the analysis methodologies together.

In our present world, it is no longer sufficient to perform site analysis with the intention of obtaining functional, working designs. After modernism and its scientific heritage, that endeavor is a given. The designs that are created and the analyses that are performed must fundamentally fulfill the requirements of successful function. Additionally, as expressed throughout this book, designers must seek new ways of understanding the site that are not limited by questions of functionality. Herein are presented eleven people, who either through their training, their experiences in life, or their use of the site claim the potential to tell us some of the secrets that lay buried in the Summerhill Lands. The seers have been split into two groups, those who are professional diviners, and who claim a heightened awareness to all lands, and those that are users of the site, whose relationship to it therefore provides them with heightened awareness to the site. Though the users claim no professional status as diviners, their ideas and perspectives on the site overlap with those of the diviners in often surprising ways. The transcripts of the participants are presented from the author's site visit between March and May 1997.

The following transcripts provide an in-depth examination of a singular process of investigation. An attempt is made to understand the wholeness and totality of the site. This search reveals a dynamic and vibrant array of opinions and beliefs, some surprisingly complementary, and others in complete disunion. The examination of the site begins with a standardized contemporary site analysis, and the following information is intended to provide both a reference point to all the information that follows, and to allow the reader to begin engaging in a critique of the 'objective' nature of the information presented. From there, eleven participants are introduced whose perspectives of the site are each in themselves unique, as we are presented with information that is outside of the general boundaries of contemporary site analysis. Every attempt was made to locate persons who mirrored the diviners discussed in the previous chapters. Unfortunately, many practices of divination are so obscure to modern society that the ancient practices have been lost, and the remaining practitioners are representative of a small segment of society. Of the eleven participants in this site analysis, seven are diviners, and four are users of the site. The diviners are

2: Summerhill
Station and
parking lot

3: Summerhill Station
Clocktower. Yonge
Street overpass can be
seen on the left side of
the photo

4: The CPR right-of-
way (looking north).
The northern
boundary of the site
is seen in the lower
right hand side
of the photo

people who have trained and studied their craft in an attempt to hone their intuitive skills to investigate society, its lands, and its people. These are people who have embraced the suggestions of divination, and though they may not be direct descendants of ancient diviners, or even practice the rituals in accordance with these ancient beliefs, they are diviners nonetheless. Of the seven diviners, four are broadly characterized as diviners practicing divination. These include an urban shaman, a psychic with second sight, a bioenergetics counselor, and a witch. The remaining three diviners consist of a feng shui master and two dowsers, each of whom are more closely related to the ancient diviners as discussed previously. The final four participants are users of the site who, in discussing their feelings about this land, clearly show us that everyone is, to some extent, spiritually aware of their surroundings. In all, the revelations about the site are often surprising, and contain many references to the divine nature of the land as well as to their own personal methods of divination.

Before reading the following perspectives, it is important to understand that even though there are statements that can be judged to be correct and statements that can be judged as false, each perspective is valuable in itself. The following participants provide insight about the site that would otherwise never have been heard. Regardless of what the participants said, their stories build together to fulfill a search that is essential for design. In their voices are the beginnings of the divine future of design.

The methodology used in bringing the diviners to the site was identical in all cases. None of the persons interviewed were paid for their services, and it was made clear to each of them that their comments would be documented to form an integral part of this discussion of site analysis and divination. The author explained to the diviners that there was no relevant design for them to examine and, as such, there was no programmatic discussion of the site. Their task was to explain what they thought was significant about the site on the particular day that they examined it. The location of the site was not kept a secret, as the meetings were usually arranged a week or more prior. In such, the diviners had ample opportunity to research the site on their own. This opportunity was not something that was suggested or encouraged, but the possibility nevertheless existed. I allowed the diviners the ability to set the pace, as well as the tone of the discussion. If questions were asked by the diviners, the response was noncommittal, which allowed each individual to examine the site using only their own abilities. Finally, site examinations lasted as long as the diviners wished them to last.

5: The Toronto
Transit Commission
subway tunnel

6: The land drops off
steeply on the east
side of the site. This
ravine begins to form
the Vale of Avoca

7: The Balfour
Junction Transmission
Station located on the
southeast edge
of the site

8: Paved entrance
into the center of the
site (looking east)

In the following section, the evaluation of the comments of the various participants is left to the reader. It is the reader's prerogative to examine what each person said about the site, and to then determine whether their views hold any validity. This examination will only present what has been said, and will exempt itself from passing judgment, for everything that is said that stems from the site is important and must not be dismissed.

Presently, the Summerhill Lands have been dramatically altered. After remaining under used and at various times abandoned for its entire existence within the downtown core of Toronto, it was ultimately folded into the surrounding urban fabric. For the last twenty years, extreme developmental pressures were stifled by the surrounding community that overwhelmingly rejected various proposals. The construction on the new Summerhill Lands began shortly after the last site visits recorded herein. Considering the perspectives given by the various diviners and users, some readers may now wonder what became of the site, and how designers have applied their belief structures to this land. That answer will not be given herein, for the exact nature of the final designs were not known when the author last left the site. The only indication of what was to come for the Summerhill Lands can be seen in the picture that ends this book.

Summerhill Case Study

The case study site is located in Toronto, Ontario, Canada. Referred to as the Summerhill Lands, or the North Toronto Railway Lands, the site is located near the Yonge and Summerhill subway stations. The entire site is a 17.76 acre block of land on the east side of Yonge Street between Shaftesbury Avenue and Price Street (figure 1). It straddles a 68.5 foot wide Canadian Pacific Railway (CPR) right-of-way, centered on a pair of tracks that run in an east to west direction with a grade separation at Yonge Street. This right-of-way is one of the busiest in Ontario, with more than forty-five train passings per day. The total area of the active right-of-way within the Summerhill site is 1.61 acres.

The portion of the site that is located north of the railway is triangular in shape and covers 2.4 acres, with 1070 feet of frontage on Shaftesbury Avenue, and 155 feet of frontage on Yonge Street. A surface parking lot was operated on that portion of the site that fronts onto Shaftesbury Avenue. A brewer's retail store with ancillary parking is located on the portion with immediate frontage on Yonge Street, and is served by an access corridor situated north of the CPR overpass. This smaller portion of the site was considered secondary to the investigations on the southern portion of the site.

9: Looking east
towards the
hydroelectric towers

10: East end of
storage building

11: Closeup of
storage building

12: The railroad tracks
with the clock tower
in the
background

The portion of the site south of the CPR right-of-way is the main focus of this case study. It has an irregular shape and covers approximately 13.5 acres. This parcel has 260 feet of frontage on Yonge Street. One access point from Yonge Street presently serves the surface parking lot to the south of the historic train station, now used by the Liquor Control Board of Ontario as a liquor store. The case study area extends eastward from Yonge Street for or 1590 feet, to the top of the Vale of Avoca and Balfour Park. Just east of the liquor store the site is mostly vacant, but is used for vehicle storage by various owners. Continuing east, three buildings remain in use as furniture storage, which were originally used to serve a spur line that traversed the site. East of the Summerhill site, an unopened road allowance extends southeasterly to Mount Pleasant Road. This road allowance is owned by the City of Toronto and effectively separated a 0.19 acre triangle from the remaining land to the west. The policy of the City has been that unopened road allowances in the ravine areas remain permanently unopened. In the south-east corner of the site, an Ontario Hydro-Electric substation is located.

A very prominent feature along Yonge Street in this location is the CPR overpass, which effectively disrupts conventional uses and building patterns. The structure of the historic train station extends north below the full width of the railway right-of-way. The station's westerly wall, whose openings are boarded up, forms part of the Yonge Street underpass. The subway runs in a north to south direction just east of the former train station. At the time of the subway construction, a "roughed-in" connection was provided to the train station from the southerly end of the Summerhill subway station platform. Currently, the only existing subway exit is located on the north side of Shaftesbury Avenue, directly across from the northern part of the case site.

A 6-story commercial structure was erected in 1985 at the southeast corner of Yonge Street and Shaftesbury Avenue. Across from this structure, in the north-easterly portion of this intersection, a mixed commercial residential complex is located. To the east of the Summerhill subway station structure on Shaftesbury Avenue there is a series of row houses, some of which are used for residential purposes, others for business administrative offices. The site is bordered on the east by the Vale of Avoca, which is part of the Balfour Ravine system. Along the south runs Price Street, which is characterized on both sides by a number of low-rise office buildings. On the northeast corner of Price and Yonge Streets there are low density commercial office buildings with retail uses at grade. Price Street is somewhat unusual in that it is a cul-de-sual with abutting low density commercial use instead of low density residential use as occurs with other

13: Closeup of a concrete garage adjacent to the hydroelectric towers

14: Homeless man's shelter in the wooded portion of the site (east side)

15: Grove of trees located in the center of the site, with the storage buildings in the background

16: A well-traveled path through the wooded area of the site

Opposite: **Station view**

streets in this area. Located at the end of the cul-de-sac and east of Price Street is the Toronto Lawn and Tennis Club, a legal non-conforming use for many years that buffers the residential neighborhood of north Rosedale to the east. Pricefield Playground, a local park at the west end of Pricefield Road, also acts as a buffer for the North Rosedale Neighborhood, a well-established and wealthy low-density residential neighborhood. The existing Pricefield Playground is approximately 4210 square meters in size and is located at the south edge of the site with access off Pricefield Road. The existing playground facilities, including play equipment and a baseball backstop, are well used by area residents.

On the western side, the site boundary runs along Yonge Street, a metropolitan arterial road, that is characterized by low-rise development with retail and service commercial uses at grade, and office or residential uses above. Building height along this portion of Yonge Street ranges between 3 and 4 stories. Storefronts are generally narrow and well defined, or, in the case of newer and larger buildings such as those located on the former Ports Hotel site, the facade has been divided at street level into smaller individual bays.

As is characteristic elsewhere along Yonge Street, the streets east and west of Yonge Street are often off-set intersections. Examples of the off-set intersections include Shaftesbury and Birch Avenues, and Marlborough and Price Streets. Thus, Yonge Street buildings provide street-end views from residential neighborhoods.

History of the Station
A distinctive urban feature and landmark in this area is the former train station and its clock tower, which are designated historical landmarks. The Summerhill Station, also known as the North Toronto station, is familiar as the 'Yonge Street Liquor Store, 'which was originally an active railway station with a tower modeled on the Campanile of St. Mark's Square in Venice, Italy (figure 2). In the nineteenth century, Toronto was crossed by several railway lines and dotted with numerous stations. The most important line led along the waterfront to the old Union Station. The smaller stations of Toronto disappeared in the early years of this century with the construction of the new Union Station. The Summerhill Station was to be phased out in the early 1900's along with the other smaller stations, but this was postponed due to long delays that occurred in the building the new Union Station. In 1912, to provide a better setting for the services connecting Toronto to Montreal and Ottawa, the CPR moved these services to the Summerhill Station. The North Toronto Railway Station site was bought from Royal Trust on October 26, 1910, after Royal Trust originally purchased the site from Mrs. Alexandra Schofield on November 20,1909.

Station view

The Summerhill Station was part of a whole scheme of track elevation across the north end of the city, which involved raising the tracks for about four miles, and thereby eliminating all grade crossings. Originally, the Ontario and Quebec Railway laid the North Toronto subdivision down in 1883, which was subsequently leased to CPR. As early as 1883, the City of Toronto ordered the CPR to make a grade separation at Yonge Street, but the CPR decided that gates would not be financially practical. To create the subway at Yonge Street for the new station, the track was elevated for three to four miles, which effectively resulted in the elimination of all level crossings including those found at Avenue Road and Spadina Road. On May 26, 1914, the Yonge Street level crossing was abandoned. The North Toronto line has been used for a number of years as a freight cut off between Leaside Junction and west Toronto, from where the main line ran down to Union Station and the lower part of the city. Originally, the Leaside to west Toronto line was the only entrance into Toronto for the Ontario-Quebec Railway, which was absorbed by CPR in its early days. Subsequently, a connection was built from the Leaside Junction to connect Union Station, and all passenger trains from the east were run through Union Station. While CPR built the station, the Canadian Northern Railway (CNR) was a joint tenant, which used the station for most, if not all of its Toronto passenger service While CPR used the North Toronto Station for only certain trains, maintaining their connection with Union Station. Both railways also felt that the rapid growth of the city northwards made a centrally located station more essential than the downtown Union Station.

North of the station, the CPR once maintained a small hotel known as the 'Ports of Call.' Although the original Summerhill Station was built because of the delays in the completion of Union Station and therefore was not grand enough to be an important city terminal, the station was in no sense a temporary facility. In 1914 the CPR commissioned Darling and Pearson, one of the principal architectural firms in Canada, to design a new passenger station, and their work, both in quality and character, places the station among the most important railway stations built in North America in the first two decades of the twentieth century. The design they produced was a miniature station with no provisions for freight. The architectural design of the North Toronto CPR Station blended the classical features, scale, and axial planning associated with the Beaux Arts Styling with traditional Canadian material, such as Tyndall limestone from the west. Wherever possible, all materials and labor employed in the construction of the building was carried out by Toronto firms of Canadian or British origin.

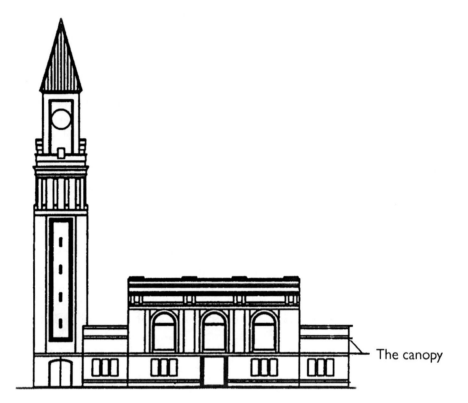

Train station elevation

The canopy

The Summerhill Station is organized with a rectangular 3-story pavilion waiting room flanked by lower wings, set back from Yonge Street to face south and linked to a 140-foot clock tower (figure 3). The clock tower was intended to function as a landmark that would locate the station on the skyline of the city. Oriented south towards the central core of the city, the station is set in a plaza. The present parking lot in front of the building was, in 1916, the work-yard of a manufacturer of cemetery monuments. The facade — in mottled beige Tyndall limestone imported from Manitoba, with some cast-stone detailing on granite bases — is shadowed by a deep canopy that shelters the main entrance and the side vestibule in the base of the tower. Above the canopy rise three 2-story arched windows, flanked by wide pilaster-like panels on which hang stone-carved railway crests draped with swags. A simplified frieze, cornice, and parapet extends around the building, emphasizing the pavilion's blockish shape. The roof consists of two parts, the main roof, which is flat and can be accessed from the tracks, and a canopy roof. The main roof is composed of flat tile steel arches, while the canopy consists of steel frames supported by diagonal tie rods clad in copper. The outside perimeter is lit by Marquis lighting fixtures that are cast iron fascia in creek key patterns. The tower roof is copper clad, with a spire and wood finial The main waiting room is 70 feet wide and 51 feet deep, and fills most of the building; faced with marble, it is flooded with light through the large south windows. Occupying the lower east wing are the ladies' waiting room, the smoking room, and the lavatories; to the west are the ticket offices.

Arriving passengers entered the station through the main doors into the waiting room and, after buying tickets, passed straight through a wide corridor, called the midway, that ran under the tracks. Passengers arriving by train came down the stairs from the tracks to the midway and, without entering the waiting room, turned sharply right into the 'concourse.' The baggage room that ran under the tracks parallel to the midway opened into the concourse and onto the outside driveway, permitting passengers to collect their luggage before exiting through the vestibule under the clock tower to the waiting taxis or cars, or loading it directly into their vehicles in the driveway. For both types of traffic, the large forecourt front of the station allowed parking and turning as it does today for the LCBO. This separation of traffic was one of the most interesting elements found in stations of this period, and a similar rational arrangement was provided in the original plans for Toronto's Union Station.

The clock tower remains the most impressive feature of the design. It is typical of the lavish gestures made by both Beaux Arts and Edwardian Baroque

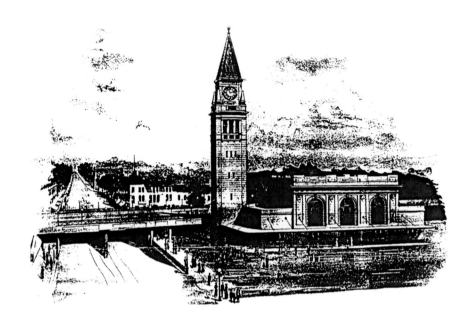

Darling and Pearson
Architects Rendering
1914-6 North Toronto
Station. Canadian
Pacific Railway

architects in an attempt to make buildings of importance that stood out as landmarks in the streetscape and on the skyline according to the 'City Beautiful' movement popular at the time. The clock tower has four 8-foot dials. The complete system of electric clocks were supplied and installed by British manufacturers. The clocks, located not only on the tower, but throughout the building, were controlled by a master clock that was synchronized daily from the CPR's chief time station in Montreal.

The design of the tower pays homage to the tower of E.J. Lennox at Toronto's Old City Hall, but it is from the Campanile of St. Marks that a majority of the design precedent came. One of the most important towers in the world, the St. Mark's Campanile had recently collapsed in 1902. The Campanile disaster and its subsequent rebuilding entered into the public's imagination, while its form was commemorated by several replicas in North America. The most prominent of these, the tower added to the Customs House in Boston in 1910, may also have influenced the choice of prototype for the station. While the Summerhill tower is neither the closest nor the tallest replication, it had the advantage of being placed in a neighborhood dominated by smaller buildings, and therefore presented itself as relatively quite tall. Today, the tower still functions as a landmark in the section of the city below the St. Clair Avenue Hill, especially when seen from the east across the trees of the Rosedale neighborhood.

Delayed due to a widening dispute over Yonge Street between the City and CPR, and disregarding the fact that the clock tower was only three-quarters complete, the corner stone was laid on the ninth of September, 1915, and the station was opened on the fourteenth of June, 1916. CPR put a large timetable and advertisement in the Toronto newspapers announcing the grand opening of the station. Through newspaper articles, Mayor Tommy Church extended an invitation to the citizens of Toronto to attend a grand opening from 8:00 p.m. to 10:00 p.m. After a dinner at the National Club, Mayor Church, speaking from a dais erected in the main waiting room, declared the station open. At 10:00 p.m. the North Toronto Limited, Number 24 bound for Montreal was the first official passenger train to leave the North Toronto Railway Station. Among the destinations for Number 24 were sleeper cars for Ottawa, with stops in Peterborough, Bobcaygeon, Lindsay, Port Hope, Streetsville, and Teeswater, and a final stop in Montreal.

The North Toronto station was one of the few large scale projects that was completed in Toronto during the First World War. Until Union Station opened in 1927, the North Toronto Station provided the most elegant and aesthetically satisfying gateway into Toronto. After Union Station was opened, however, problems making connections between the two stations decreased the importance of the North Toronto Station. After 1929 it was closed, to be reopened shortly afterwards as a liquor retail store under the management of the Liquor Control Board of Ontario. The station was shortly reopened in 1939 to welcome trains carrying King George VI and Queen Elizabeth during their Royal Tour of 1939.

Presently, the main sales area of the liquor store occupies the waiting hall. The original space, with its beautiful windows and marble designs, has been obscured by a dropped ceiling and masked walls. The building envelope and the tower have fortunately defied the alterations of the interior space. Originally, there were also inverted umbrella roofs extending along 360 feet of rail platform, protecting access to the spiral stairways and elevators. The interior grand hall is completely hidden behind a dropped ceiling, and the marble has been removed from the north wall. The two side wings also have a dropped ceiling, and the west ticket wickets are now concealed behind a false wall. The original clock broke down during World War II and disappeared sometime between 1948 and 1950.

Canadian Pacific Rail and the Toronto Transit Commission Subway.
The CPR right-of-way traverses the site and divides it into a small northerly and larger southerly parcel (figure 4). The existing legal right-of-way width of the Canadian Pacific North Toronto subdivision line in this area varies from 19 meters east of Balfour Park, to 30 meters through the park, and 21 meters between the park and Yonge Street. However, the actual space taken up by the trackage is significantly less, and ranges from 10-12 meters. In 1985, an average of 46 trains per day were observed heading in both directions of this right-of-way. These train movements were evenly distributed over the 24 hours of the day. The majority of trains using the railway line carried freight, sometimes including hazardous goods. Over the past few years, a number of sidings that were located on the site have been removed. The existing rail bridge over Balfour Park is about 13.5 meters wide and 24 meters high. This is space enough for three tracks, but only the two mainlines presently cross the bridge, since the third track (siding) was removed recently. The Balfour Park Bridge is 115.3 meters long. A separate bridge 31 meters long crosses over Mt. Pleasant Road for automobile traffic. Near Summerhill Gardens and for 3/4 of a block west, the tracks are less than 1 meter above the grade of Shaftesbury Avenue. To the South, the nearest residential parcels are on Pricefield Road and, due to the

natural slope of the land, these parcels are 1.5 meters below the railway elevation. West of Ottawa Street, the railway tracks are on a 0.5% upgrade towards Yonge Street, while Shaftesbury Avenue gently declines towards Yonge Street. The railroad embankment thus increases from about 1 meter high at Ottawa Street to about 4 meters at Yonge Street.

A 1985 noise and vibration study undertaken by the City Public Works Department concluded that within 100 meters of the railway tracks, 80% of the residents claimed to be bothered by the vibrations, and 86% were bothered by noise. CPR's policy is to discourage any residential use immediately next to its right-of-way, but in cases where residential uses are permitted in such locations, dwellings are to be set back a minimum of 30 meters from the railway right-of-way and are also separated by berms, fencing and sound barriers.

In addition to the CPR, the Toronto Transit Commission subway tunnel is a physical constraint to any development of the site (figure 5). The TTC's subway tunnel runs in a north and south direction immediately east of the former train station building. The width of the subway easement is approximately 70 feet between Shaftesbury Avenue and the south wall of the former train station. Further south, its width narrows to about 35 feet. The subway tunnel precludes the construction of any below grade structures within the alignment of the tunnel.

Topography, Vegetation and Soil, Air Qualities

The case study site consists of relatively flat land which gently slopes to the south. Immediately east of the site, the land drops off steeply to form the Vale of Avoca. Slope stability has been a considerable problem at the east end of the site for some time. Numerous pathways are located in this section, which have been detrimental to vegetation growth and conductive to rapid surface erosion (figure 6). Along the south side of Shaftesbury Avenue, twenty-two deciduous trees with intermittent shrubbery, owned by the City, form a visual buffer against the railway tracks during the summer months. South of the tracks, wild tree stands and dense shrubbery cover the eastern most portion of the site, and the rail dependent uses ceased to exist on the site. Due to regular maintenance of area trees, the wild tree stand is composed of mostly pioneer species of weedy varieties. There are very few mature trees in that portion of the site.

Soil quality testing was carried out on the Summerhill Lands in September, 1989, by Trow, Dames, and Moore Geotechnical Ltd. as reported in their Phase Environmental Audit. These tests included geotechnical sampling, bulk soil and leachate analysis, groundwater quality sampling, groundwater level monitoring,

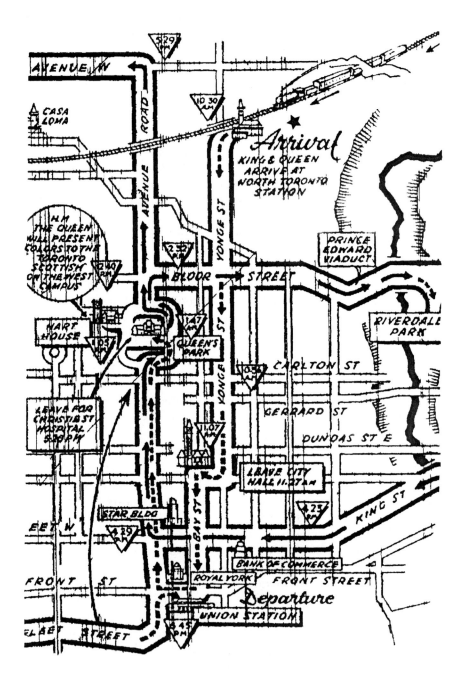

King George VI
and Queen Elizabeth
Royal Tour of 1939.
Star marks
the location of the
Summerhill site

methane gas monitoring, and an electromagnetic survey to locate underground tanks. Results indicate that levels exceeding the guidelines for parkland use were present throughout the site. Based upon historical analysis, support testing, and site inspections, the contaminated soil was localized, and appeared in specific locations where past land uses may have resulted in contamination of the soil. These uses included coal, fuel oil, chemical, and general storage facilities, metal processing facilities, and service and garage uses. Analyses of soil samples collected on the site indicated the presence of oil, grease, and hydrocarbon contamination at borehole locations. In addition, the soil was found to have ammonia and hydrocarbon odors in some areas. Soil samples also indicate the presence of between 0.5 and 2.0 meters of fill material under the surface at the eastern end of the site. This fill consisted of materials such as asphalt, concrete, rubber, metal, bricks, and tires. Groundwater samples were analyzed for inorganic and organic compounds, and contained concentrations of several metals that were above drinking water guideline. Two boreholes on the east side of the site found concentrations of metals, suspended solids and phenols which exceeded the Metro Sewer Use By-law and also indicated concentrations of volatile organic compounds in excess of acceptable Ministry of Environment levels for groundwater. These concentrations may have represented normal background concentrations on the site. Oil filled equipment and underground cables at the adjacent Balfour Junction Transmission Station were tested and were found not to contain PCBs.

The winds most often come from a westerly direction. Because of the absence of local industrial sources, the majority of air pollution is related to Yonge Street and the CPR line. The Yonge Street and the CPR line that traverses the site, are sources of contaminated and nuisance dust, diesel, odor, transportation related emissions, and volatile vapors. 1991 air quality figures compiled by Rowan, Williams, Davies and Irwin Consulting Engineers and Microclimate Specialist indicated that only two pollutants regularly exceeded the provincial criteria. These pollutants are total suspended particulate matter (TSP) and ozone (O3). Dustfall levels have also exceeded provincial criteria. Diesel odors exceeded the 50% detection limit, as well as the 20% annoyance limits during high traffic days.

Electric and Magnetic Fields
Overhead transmission lines that formerly traversed the property were relocated underground and offsite. The Ontario Hydro's Balfour Junction, which joins the underground cables to the suspended transmission line traversing the

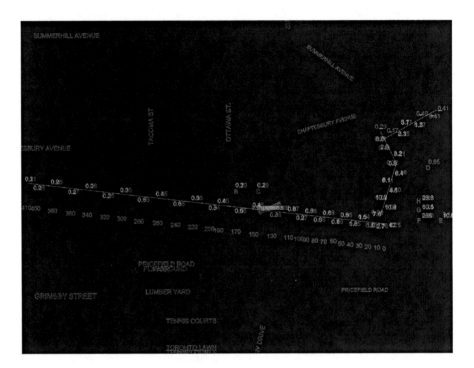

Electromagnetic
readings

ravine, abuts the southeast corner of the property. This junction represents a source of electric and magnetic fields similar to the previously existing overhead transmission lines. The measurements of the electrical and magnetic fields were performed by Ontario Hydro's Community Relations Department, Design and Development Division - Transmission section, and measurements were taken at the site surrounding the Balfour Junction Transmission Station (figure 7). Measurements were taken at several individual locations, as well as along several cross-sections of the property in an attempt to give a representative summary of the distribution of electric and magnetic fields present. In several locations, an electrical field measurement is absent due to the presence of trees, high shrubs, and weeds that have a shielding effect on electric fields. These trees and shrubs do not influence magnetic fields. Electric fields were measured using a Denometer. When measuring electric fields, the operator held the meter at the end of an insulated rod to minimize disturbance by their body. Magnetic fields were measured using an ELF Field Strength survey meter. All electric and magnetic field measurements were taken at a height of one meter. The electric field strength is given in terms of rms (root mean square) values and in units of volt per meter (V/m). The magnetic field is also reported in terms of rms values. The units used in the microtesla (uT) which is equal to 10 milligauss (mG). The results are shown in Figures 18 & 19.

Floor Area Ratio

The Rosedale Official Plan Part II, approved by the Ontario Municipal Board in 1975, covers the portion of the site south of the CPR tracks. West of the Pricefield Playground between Yonge Street and Price Street, the land is designated as "Special Commerce Area A." This designation permits a maximum density of two and a half times the area of the lot for residential use, or commercial and mixed commercial residential uses up to a maximum density of 3 times the are of the lot, provided the residential component does not exceed a density of 2.5. The portion of the site north and east of Pricefield Playground is designated as "Special Commercial Area B," where residential uses are permitted at a maximum density of 1.35 times the area of the lot.

Noise

According to the environmental noise consultants Valcoustics Canada, daytime sound exposures were around 70 to 80 dBA. The vibration measurements of the CPR trains were taken 30 meters from the railway right-of-way, corresponding to the closest proposed residential building face setbacks. Whistle

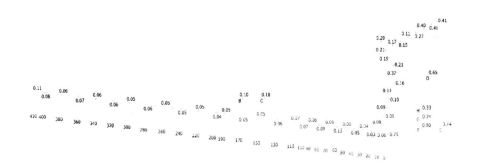

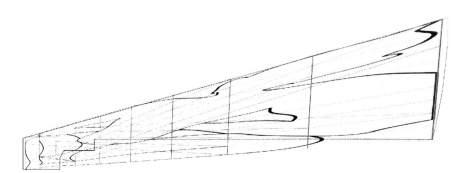

Site model for electric
and magnetic
field values

Mandala overlaid
onto Summerhill site

signals are prohibited approaching all public crossings at grade on the North Toronto Subdivision, but may be used in dangerous situations when a suitable warning would be required.

Rail Traffic

The North Toronto Subdivision is classified as a Principal Main Line, and the Summerhill Station is classified as starting point 0,0.

As observed on the site by the author:

1. *Number of freight trains (0700-2300): 22 trains*

Number of local switchers (0700-2300): 10 trains

1a. *Number of freight trains (2300-0700) : 17 trains*

Number of local switchers (2300-0700): 3 trains

2. *Average number of cars per train: 60 freight, 25 switchers*

Number of locomotives per train : 3-4 freight, 1-2 switchers

3. *Recent annual total freight (1993): 224,159 cars*

The track gradient is 0.53% falling to the west. This gradient bottoms out at Summerhill Avenue and begins climbing from 0.192% to 0.5% and levels off at Yonge Street. A 3 degree curve is present just before the bridge, east of Summerhill Avenue.

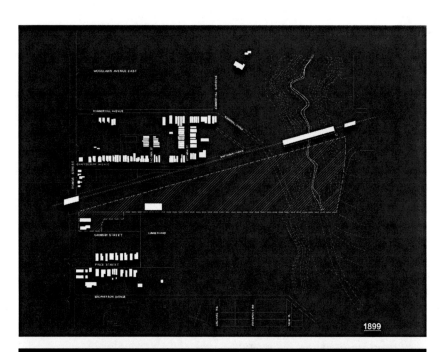

1899

This page: 1899

1910

Opposite: 1965

1996

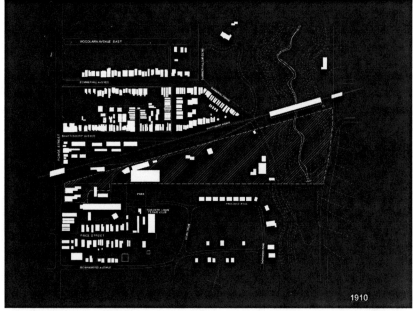

1910

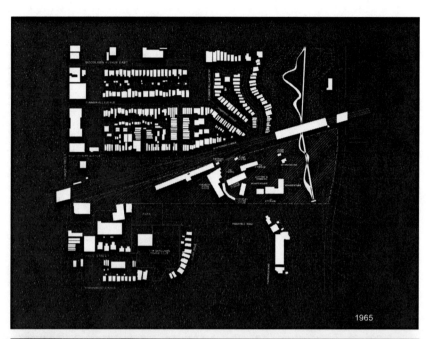

1965

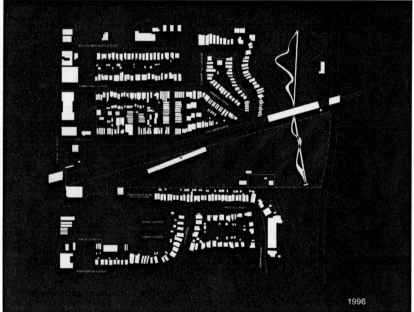

1996

123
site divine
case study
site

on-site one *interview with Dean Perry*

Monday May the 5th at 2:00 p.m., 1997

Dean Perry is a leading pendulum dowser in Canada. He is primarily a human-istic dowser, which means he reads human based energy patterns as opposed to land based energy patterns. Introduced to me by Christopher Gagosz, Dean Perry suggested that he would be able to read the residual energy patterns of human occupation on the site. Even though he understood that a site has many energy patterns, and some of those conflict, he told me that he would be able to discern dominant patterns that would indicate patterns of sickness, disease and happiness that have occurred throughout the site.

Trained throughout North America, Dean Perry is a very unassuming man, who wasn't at all interested in whether his audience believes in dowsing per se, he was more interested in what dowsing readings might add to knowledge gained through other methods of investigation. For Dean Perry humanistic dowsing is not an end result, but like a stethoscope, it is one of the many tools available to understand the human body, it's energy patterns and it's health.

Dean Perry - As we pass the electric transformers, it almost feels like a nervous negative energy, so I'm wondering if it will pass. It looks like people have been dumping stuff here for a long, long time. It is almost as if you can read the layers

of what has happened here as this has eroded away. Different structures and such, these barrels found all along the edge of the ravine. Can I have a minute on my own, I'll catch up with you later.....< *a few minutes later.>*

There is a tremendous negative energy on this site, it is not energy from pollution, but it is from people. It's been around for a while, maybe starting in the first half of the century. I can't quite get what it is. It is maybe labor related, or based upon working conditions. Or illnesses associated with predominant uses of the site, that might be working conditions. I don't know am I correct?

CL - Whether we can show historically if they are accurate or not is secondary to the fact that those are things that you are feeling. That this is what is important. For example if we were to say, in terms of Labor, this was a place where workers had significant stress or illness related to the site, we as cultural historians would have a lot of trouble showing that because all the histories of the site would be written through the owners. The history of the site that we could see would be related to ownership, and not related to working conditions. So when it comes to the actual history, I don't think that you should doubt you feelings. They are all representative of what is significant for you.

DP - Right. It just seems strange that I feel this negative energy lingering, as if it is still here in a sense.

CL - What could be other use or occupying characteristics aside from labor, that would result in the negative energy from people.

DP - Well my sense is that the negative energy came from people and it was the result of the treatment of people on this site, especially in this wooded area here. It's off a spiritual nature, though the negative spiritual energy results in illness. The illness that I sense is a derivative of the negative spiritual nature of the site.

CL - What do you mean by negative spiritual nature.

DP - Well, I mean that this is a spiritual as opposed to physical in nature.

CL - Is this illness site related, or is it brought to the site?

DP - No, it's neither. It affected peoples spirits more than physically affecting them, but it is still lingering.

CL - Do you have any idea of it's source?

DP - Not Yet, Give me a bit more space, I'll tell you in a while.

CL - Okay. <break>

DP - I was trying figure out why this negative spirituality is still affecting the energy of the site.

CL - Does it change through the site? How specific can you feel? Is it within a certain radius?

DP - Well I had a small sense that the energy originated in the wooded area when we first entered the site. It certainly got stronger as we entered the wooded area. I'll check it again to see if any of the answers in my pendulum are the same. I also get a general feel of pollution. The reading here is that it's fairly widespread, and that it is not in concentrated pockets. It needs to be cleaned up. It's from industrial sources. In running through some tests I can feel that the soil contains traces of mercury and nickel.

CL - What does that mean, what does traces of mercury and nickel mean in the soil. Are they at a level that is unacceptable. Are they hard metals which are toxic at any quantity?

DP - Any level of mercury is unacceptable, so if people were to grow foods here, mercury would enter the food system. You wouldn't want to grow vegetables here. Nickel is also considered a toxic metal for human consumption.

CL - What's interesting is that farmers have been known to test soils by eating them, but I would not eat any of this soil if my life depended on it.

DP - How true.

CL - Farmers can tell by the charge in the soil, the granularity and the moisture content whether the soil is acceptable. <examining an excavated hole in the ground>

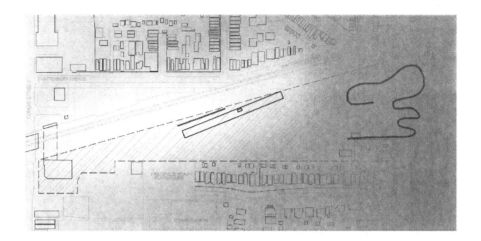

Negative energy patterns as observed by Dean Perry

DP - This excavated soil here in front of me is more toxic the further one digs down.

CL - That seems strange. Isn't that weird? I wonder why that is.

DP - If we move away from that soil and head towards this constructed enclosure, I get a more neutral reading as opposed to a mostly negative reading.

CL - What does a neutral reading mean?

DP - A neutral reading either means that the question is not clear, or that it is not an appropriate question to be asked. I was just going through a series of questions, and I was getting mostly neutral readings. I was asking if someone was living here, I was asking if someone uses this occasionally. This structures has obviously been made like this, it's been specifically constructed like this, and it is maintained to look like this. Even though it looks like it might be abandoned, it seems to be in active use.

CL - Very strange.

DP - I think that it has been used like a fort, kind of like kids using a fort, except that it is not used by kids. It still doesn't have a good feel to it, it's not like a fun fort.

CL - It doesn't look like a fun fort.

DP - There are no mass graves on the site. There is a of industrial debris. I'm getting a strong chemical reading. It seems like there is some unhealthy refuse as well as just some other stuff that needs to be cleaned up. <at the homeless mans shack>

DP - In this shack there's books and bottles and magazines. Here's a book on personal space, and here are some playboys. It almost look likes it hasn't been too long since someone has been here. There are some condoms.

CL - Cheap ones.

DP - <laughing> I hope you got that on tape. Well, hang on. Are we invading somebody's place.

CL - I don't know how active this place is.

CL - So can you summarize your experience on the site. What are some of the significant aspects of the site that are important for any designer to be aware of.

DP - I think my first reaction to the space was a negative one rather than a positive one. That negative feeling increased as we walked eastwards towards the eastern end. Then checking with the pendulum there are a number of issues, one was the level of chemicals in the soil, that seemed to be widespread rather than in concentrated pockets. These chemicals throughout the site need to be cleaned up. These would definitely affect the energy of the land and the people. The other, and probably more important one was a strong negative people energy that seemed to stretch back over the whole century. It originated at the beginning of the century, but it is still here and it still affects the space. This negative people energy would possible benefit from some kind of ritual where all the users of the site would recognize their use of the site, and also allow for some recognition of the site itself. This ritual could act as a cleansing and clearing of the negative energy. The negative sensation of the site diminished as I walked westwards along the railroad tracks, even though the amount of refuse and waste increased. Certainly the feeling in my legs and my gut disappeared and it became a more positive feeling space. I enjoyed it much more at that end. I was still getting chemical readings all over the site, but nothing compared to the readings that I was getting in the east end. The readings at the excavation suggested that the toxicity of the soil seemed to increased with the depth. There were three mounds and the earth that came from the deepest level seemed the most toxic, than the middle mound, which was more toxic than the surface soil. There was possibly some mercury and nickel in soil.

133
site divine
on-site one
interview with
Dean Perry

on-site two *interview with Sandra Yemm*

Tuesday May the 6th at 2:00 p.m., 1997

Sandra Yemm is highly representative of many of the modern practitioners of alternative sciences. Sandra's business, 'Naturally Yours Alternatives' is a one-stop shopping center, with services include dowsing, ear coning, feng shui advice, geomancing consultations, reflexology, therapeutic touch, and reiki work. Her catalogue of energy balancing devices include a ladybug energy equalizer that helps attract and redirect harmful radiation from the users of computers and televisions. The ladybug claims to help eliminate eyestrain, brain fog, and nausea. Sandra also markets crystal catalyst tabs and cellular phone tabs to neutralize harmful radiation from printers, copiers, fax machines, automobiles, and cellular phones. When placed on electric fuse boxes, her elf-pak clears away unwanted electronic pollution. It also claims to clears ants from houses and, when used while traveling, helps reduce jetlag. Finally Sandra sells vibrational cream, a cream that when worn acts as a magnet that is said to attract money. Sandra Yemm came to dowse the site and to do a traditional field dowsing survey.

Sandra Yemm - The first thing I look for when I get onto a site is to look for Hartman Grids. They are like a checkerboard of energy that radiates out on all sides. Also, you don't want to live near hydro stations or anything like that; you're getting too many electrical waves just passing through buildings. Even if you think that you have a grounded electrical system in your home, what is really happening is that the power that is not used on your electrical connection goes back to the substation, underground, and in doing so, passes under your house whether you've got the grounded system or not.

CL - Here at the transformer station, you can see that the power travels to the transformer through huge underground cables. As you notice, there is no other way besides these underground cables, that the power enters the transformers. The hydro connection actually comes from Price Street over there, it comes underground along Price Street, under the buildings, and to the transformers. To get it across the ravine, they send the hydro up and over. I don't know what the width of the affected area would be as a result of the underground hydro connection along Price Street.

SY - Have the people who work on this site now been here for a while?

CL - They have been here for a while.

SY - There has probably been a lot of illness, sickness, and death because of health problems associated with the hydro wires. Right in that neighborhood, the amount of sickness and illness would blow your mind away. It would be bad, but nobody knows what it is. They probably just think "Oh well, my father had cancer and now I have cancer." So this is the ravine. It gives me the chills.

CL - These stakes here are the end of the property. On one side of these stakes is Balfour Park, on the other side is private land.

SY - There's a man, what's he doing, just walking around here?

CL - There are many strollers who pass through this site.

SY - Who owns the park?

CL - I think the park is owned by the city, and this land is owned by a group of private individuals.

SY - And then there are these pathways. And these pathways pass between the two pieces of lands. So this side is the edge of the private land. Do the paths go all the way down? Have you followed them?

CL - It's strange, I'm not quite sure what all these paths are, you can take a look. Here you can take a look, that fence down there is supposed to be up here.

SY - Oh, that one way way down there, the one that is fallen down. It's a gorgeous area, isn't it? These men everywhere make me feel like I'm interrupting or something. They really are strange looking.

CL - Yes, there are always people throughout back here.

SY - Did you see that? There were three guys there. What were they doing there?

CL - I'm not sure.

SY - Can we get out of this part? Those guys are making me nervous.

CL - If you want, we can walk to the northeast corner of the property. So the Hartmann lines come through this end of the site in the same checkerboard gridded pattern as well?

SY - Yeah, let me check.

CL - Would the Hartmann grids be affected by the spiritual use of the place?

SY - They are affected by the electricity. When the electricity is grounded into the ground, the electricity runs along those grid lines, and that is what makes them so harmful, especially when you are sleeping on them.

CL - The transformers on the site, would they be grounded, or would they just be carrying electricity?

SY - Well, what is being used will go into the ground, and there will be electrical leakage there. And then, when they put the electricity out into the homes. There's something about the electricity, where you have the power in your home to light all you lights, but when you don't use that power, where does that electricity go? It's dumped into the ground, and then it travels back to the substation. So, if your home is between the last home on the line and the substation, all the dumping is going back underneath your home. That's not

site divine
on-site two
interview with
Sandra Yemm

only your own electrical dumping, but everybody else's dumping. It makes it very hard on the people living in those homes.

CL - What are some of the other questions that we could ask to get a better understanding of the site?

SY - Well, underground water affects where you are sleeping as well. There are probably underground streams all through here. We are talking about really deep streams. They just need to be running streams to affect people on the site. Let's see if we can find a running stream, say, within 100 feet of the surface. Let's just ask for indication of a running stream that is 100 feet or less from the surface. So, okay, we'll just ask the rods to point me to a stream, where we can find a stream that is below 100 feet. The rods say go this way. I just let the rod lead, I watch and then follow it. So it looks like right here, in this direction, so it must be right in here.

CL - So this would be a location where a stream would be coming through, or would be coming up to the surface.

SY - There will be a stream just running through the ground here. I'll just see if I can find out the direction that the stream will be taking. Yes, it's just running through here towards the ravine. So again, someone sleeping over the water would receive electromagnetic radiation which is harmful and bad for your health. If you get someone else in here, a geotechnical expert whose can pinpoint the exact location of underground water, they might be able to do a more in-depth analysis.

CL - Thanks, but even if I didn't, your help was most appreciated.

SY - In this area, away from the edge of the ravine, it feels good in here, it feels good.

CL - What do you mean by that?

SY - It just feels calm, even though the trains are not running right now, but it just feels like a very calm and protective or secure area. It just feels good.

CL - Do you feel that here specifically, or do you feel that everywhere on this site?

139

site divine
on-site two
interview with
Sandra Yemm

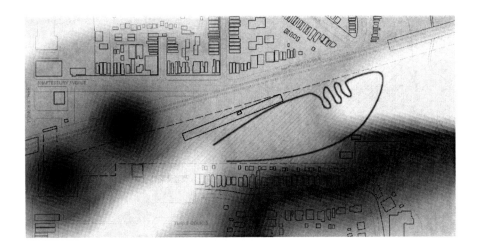

Energy patterns
and their associated
Hartman Grids as
observed by
Sandra Yemm

SY - I feel that in here, in this wooded area, not so much back there where the men were, but in this area here. This whole wooded area is a nice area. It's probably very, very old and nobody's been here for a very long time. You can see by the land that there used to be more buildings here. And then there are no old trees, if this land has not been used in such a long period of time. These trees really are very small trees, and if there haven't been any buildings for a long period of time, except for the couple of small sheds that we see, one would think that the trees would be a lot bigger.

CL - Yes, I guess you would think that.

SY - And you don't see any stumps, so it's not like the owners are cutting the big trees. The trees are more like shrubs. I think it is interesting that there are some old trees like that one there that has had the fence grow through it. That tree has been there for a quite a while, but most trees are very small. If you look at the trees on the outside of the property, there are some very large trees, and there are only a few large trees on the inside of the property, while there is much more open space. That might have something to do with the electricity and the electric magnetic radiation. If there is too much electric magnetic radiation, the trees don't grow well. Something that grows on the grid lines will lean away from the place where the grid line crosses the growing path of the tree. Do cars just back up here and throw out their garbage?

CL - Yes, that is something that the owners have
been trying to stop.

SY - That is too bad, because it's a lovely area, very beautiful, very quiet.

CL - You have the trains come through on occasion with all their rumbling.

SY - So the trains do run there? Well also then, that is bad for the natural energy. It is transporting the good and natural energy away from the site; the energy is being whipped away. So you have the electricity substation on the one corner, and then you have the energy being dragged by the train and flowing away on the train tracks. That is not good. Look, there are some more men, like you said, lots of strollers.

CL - Yes, they seem to just come out of nowhere. Those men just appear and then disappear.

SY - I would expect though that when the builders come in they will bulldoze all of this and this will be as flat as a pancake. It won't have any of the natural energy at all. It will just lose all this flavor of calmness, and become a plane of nothingness. With no energy left, it will only have the bad electric magnetic radiation from the hydroelectric transformer

CL - When a dowser looks for water, she finds it through the physical manifestations of water?

SY - No, not particularly. The dowser can find water just by using her rod.

CL - Right. What I was saying is that water is a physical manifestation of something, as opposed to a spiritual manifestation.

SY - Well, it's your muscle responses working to show you through your tools where water and energy is. That is right, it is a physical muscle response. It's nice here. Wouldn't it be great if they left those trees over there? It is interesting though that these trees are much older than the trees back there. I feel something funny over there, I'm just going to check. Yes, there is a grid line right over there. I was just wondering what was happening to this leaning tree. It looks like there is a whole series of trees that are leaning away. They are all leaning a bit. It looks like they are trying to get away from something, and sure enough, there is an energy grid line that comes right through here.

143
site divine
on-site two
interview with
Sandra Yemm

on-site three *interview with Lea Erlich*

Thursday May the 8th at 5:30 p.m., 1997

Lea Erlich has been a bioenergetic counselor for more than fifteen years. With a clinical education in psychology and an interest in metaphysics, Lea has also been a leading practitioner of biofitness. Her site-specific work has revolved around building multidimensional awareness into the use of space, emphasizing design psychosynthesis, shamanism, initiatic rituals, and astral journeying. Lea has presided over more than 80 bioenergetic management workshops throughout the Toronto area. Originally from Brazil, Lea came recommended by members of the Shamanic Institute of Toronto.

Lea Erlich - Electromagnetic fields, there are many of them here. This land is turbulent with emotions and many archetypal feelings, different kinds of thinking and happenings take place here. It is a popular refugee. When you focus your energy so much on something, you become censored, so your emotions go completely through their own channels and become lost. Because of that, those emotional energies come together in a place like this. There is a kind of barrier keeping the energy here, with trees and fences around this specific area. This emotional energy here is really strange, and it's squeezed. It's an abandoned place, like the abandoned emotions, but at the same time it's an archetypal experience. The energy here is not flowing, it is really squeezed.

Despair, I feel pain, the emotional energies here are full of despair and pain. Okay, let's walk. Because I can connect with my body to the energy around, and with the birds and the sounds and with the vibration of the site, I can understand that this is a really interesting place. Here we encounter a really interesting stage of mind. Like a window, it's like a window that opens to another dimension. And it's just in the center of the city, it's downtown, it's a kind of nothing in the center of the city. Here there is a lot of people's lost emotional energy, all the energy is really squeezed. It makes a window.

CL - This site is a window?

LE - Yes, it is very interesting. In a window, you can open or close it, but it must be opened just the right amount for energy to flow so it doesn't stay still, but not opened too much so everything flows right through, like a river. I think the trees make a fence here, and the woods, they make a fence around this energy too. There are other things. I feel a lot of children playing, so the energy here contains joy, with the imaginary thing to control. And the train, it's like a triad, with an equilibrium pressing in some ways through this window, contributing in some ways for creating the window, but at the same time offering through the nature here other possibilities, too. The energy is not flowing, it's vanishing. Do you understand what I mean by vanishing?

CL - Vanishing?

LE - You know, when something vanishes through something.

CL - So things are able to move through the site in an act of vanishing?

LE - Yes. By necessity, it's the nature of the energy here. Do you see? I've never come here before, this is the first time, and it seems like many people come here and use this place.

CL - Yes, it is used heavily, I know that every part is used very differently, and has a different history. You can see that when you move through the different parts of the site.

LE - This land is a state, specifically, in this context. Can you imagine in this multicultural culture how many different feelings, and emotions, and thinking, and reflections you could find in this place? I like to work with art, and I think when we combine art and energy it's so metamorphical. I think our energy also changes like that, and when we are just walking, sometimes people have no idea about what's going on around them just because they are so concentrated in their own thoughts. They specialize so much, they cannot spread out their minds and emotions. I was born in Brazil, it's a magical place between white and black magic, there is so much magic. I learned to walk in the earth without shoes, so for me this experience in Canada is unique because it is very cold, so I have had to learn how to use boots and cover my body. Here in Canada we need to cover our naked bodies, it is really cold. It's like putting on masks. It is so interesting, the First Nation people could teach Canadians about all the masks that they wear, the First Nation people are so bare in the streets. The rest of Canadians sure are not doing much, they just help the society to sell their masks, and contribute to hiding themselves. Well, the problems of losing all this energy will appear in our own guts, and then we can see that, unfortunately, we have lost so much. They are intellectualizing about everything, about what we need to do. They talk too much.

CL - Who are they?

LE - Here in Canada, my experience, when I arrived here, I came to do research in bioenergy, and I was so frustrated because when I arrived at the University of Toronto in the Psychology department, they had never heard about my area of research. So I decided to do my research in the streets and community centers, and hospitals. Of course in hospitals, the research follows different rules. This site and the ravine is a tunnel. It helps to flow the concentrated energy with so many different feelings through the city to . . . I don't know how to say the word in English. Where you put many things in just one place, you know how it is called? You just throw things there. Like garbage, but peculiar garbage.

CL - Dump, refuse, trash, waste, storage?

LE - No, it's like this place, for example. Artists use it a lot, because they can reform and repair and transform this old stuff.

CL - Junk?

LE - Could be for some people, it's more unusual. In Brazil there is a lot, and it's so interesting because the energy there, it's very different from the rest of the world. You can reconstruct everything there, and here, I feel that people

Lea Erlich begins
to connect with the
emotional energy
on the site

don't put too much attention to that, they just throw everything they don't need into the streets, and it's like something from the past for them. They just throw all their emotional energy away too. It's interesting, it's different, because the energy is still around and because, as I said before, people are really intellectual. They feel afraid to be in touch with their own connections, with their own emotions, and I'd like to examine this, not just in books or intellectually, but emotionally. So I appreciate that you invited me to do this, because for the first time in three years I can talk clearly about that. That's great. Now it's an exciting time, because with the opening of alternative medicine, hopefully people will understand this energy. So, on this land, we are directly in a dangerous area, it is energetic and close. It's dangerous because people are afraid to see what is under their masks, and those that aren't afraid can become addicted to the energy here. It is all a waste. It is all a cycle. Again, with the danger of the trains and the joy of children playing, the beauty of the trains, the danger of the children playing near the trains, it's like a cycle. The train is very cyclical. The train is beautiful; I like the train.

CL - It's interesting when you talk about the reuse of refuse, all along the edge of the ravine, where there is this garbage. People have created these little spaces for themselves.

LE - Yes, I saw this, it is interesting, the people who come here come to catch the energy that is on the site, the energy from those power towers, and the waste energy from people. I think for them the energy is like a drug, a high energy treat to excite the simple emotions. Do you understand that?

CL- The energy gives them excitement. . . .

LE - . . . and also because it is anesthetic.

CL - An aesthetic, the energy is?

LE - No, anesthetic, the energy here it's kind of scary. It dulls the senses a bit. Looking at physical energy is a really different approach than looking at people's muscles, bones, and joints. It's another language, but in a deep way it's the same. You see the body, the human being, is one. But maybe because here where everything is so specialized, people can't understand this energy here. You can't specialize on this energy. People ask me a lot, "how do I define myself and my understanding of energy?" and I need to wait, and, like a mosaic, to put my experiences together and only then start to describe my experiences. Because when you specialize yourself, you can't become a mosaic. It is important that you realize that you are all part of the universe, and not just one specialized thing.

CL - You can't understand this energy when you specialize a lot?

LE - Yes, but you have to study to become a mosaic, it is not simple.

CL - Why is that? You mean you should do a lot of different things to a very complex level, so you are not just doing one thing?

LE - Yes.

CL - And thereby you have your mosaic, because you have a little bit of everything. And you become more at one with the universe?

LE - Yes, I think so. For seniors and for kids, this place is important for screaming. I like to work with sound and here, people are afraid to scream, and I think we all need that, it is like oxygen. If you put your sound out, you inhale everything and it's balanced. So it's difficult for me to find a good place for work, because I like to release old energy patterns, body memories, and for that I need to use our inner expressions, sound. So this place is really a unique experience. I think that I could spread out my mind, and centuries from now, in my own belief, feel something very different here. The mosaic would become more complicated, but I would also understand more things about this place. I think here, in North America, people are afraid, scared of their own energy, so I think wherever this kind of window happens, it helps people.

CL - So this land is really important as a window then?

LE - Yes, I think so, I can feel that.

CL - So once you come through here and build, it will change the window, and it won't be there any more. So you need that window.

LE - Yes, it's a natural escape. I think this land needs trees like the ones here, because they are so important for our natural transformation, and I think the land is like a triangle, so again you're talking in cycles, because I believe the triad is a really balanced number. People live in their own life, and they don't pay attention to what is going on around. On the opposite end, other people feel everything, and they don't know, they have no idea as to why the feeling exists everywhere. This is why all people need this space; so people can go there and stay, doing whatever they need to do to look through the window.

CL - So it's not really important what they do, it's that they are there.

LE - Yes. Of course, each one will choose in some way what they need to do for themselves and to help others. I think that this land as a playground is very important, it's not a nonsense, because children can balance themselves just through their own playing, they can spread out their joy and happiness. Here, I'm not sure, but I can guess, the owner is not doing sacred uses with the land, but the energy, it's there, the patterns are there, and the history is there. This area is really different. In the middle of everything, with the sound of the playing and the train again and the machine. It's squeezing and forming the window again, it's just space. It's necessary.

CL - So the sound of the train and the industry are necessary to make the space?

LE - I think it's a combination of the sounds of the machine, and the birds, and the children. Like the machine and the human being. It's a pattern for nature, trying in parallel words to create their own realities, to survive and fix one's space, that is just here. People can come or not and you can feel that in a long distance or not, and then visit, it really depends on how many masks you are using.

CL - When you come here?

LE - No, just in life.

CL - So, if you have more masks, the less you will need a space like this, or the less you will use a space like this.

LE - I think we learn to use the masks and realize which masks we need sometimes. But we just have to learn how to take off the masks. I think you don't need masks, but we learn to fabricate them, to build them, to use them, just for our protection.

CL - How do the masks relate to the people who regularly use this site?

LE - It's like a picture, if I could draw, I would show you. When people come here they take the masks off, and realize through the energy here that they have these masks. Because then they will go back to the subway and put their masks back on. So this place or another place like it is a brief moment for breathing deep, and then, unfortunately, most will leave again and swallow their own sounds. So my goal here, and I think in life, is to work with this sound, which is not just a simple sound, it's that energy stuck like a bad memory. Sometimes I think, "why did I chose Canada, why did I chose a country where people swallow their sound, and don't understand a place like this?" Because it's a multicultural country, it's a mix. There are many different histories and energies, it's a very good place for research. And unfortunately, I couldn't find organizations to help me do this kind of research. So I'm doing it myself in the community and in the streets, in my private practice, working and talking to people.

site divine
on-site three
interview with
Lea Erlich

I feel in my own body that I can understand what a person is feeling or thinking. It doesn't matter past, present, or future, and then through my own channels, I can help rebalance the energies that I feel, and then, maybe, I'm able to help other people. In terms of research, it works like that too. I came here and I was so frustrated as I said to you because I came with so many hopes to do my research in multiculturalism. It's not what it seems to be, for me anyway, it's really important, because I suffered this changing of the weather, the different reaction from nature. I suffered this changing on my own, so I can realize better, understand better what has happened to me through my skin since I was six years old. Since then, I have always been able to feel all the feelings that people leave behind, it has always been the same, except that I was more youthful then.

on-site four *interview with Anonymous Gay Cruiser*

As gay male cruising is one of the dominant uses of the northeast corner of the site, it was my intention to interview a few of these men if possible. A majority of the cruisers that I approached would only talk to me very briefly, saying few words. Following is the transcript of one of the two cruisers that took the time to talk to me about the site. Looking at least ten years younger then I would guess his age to be, this man was lounging in the low traffic zone, away from the ravine edge that seemed to be the most active area. He was reading a John Irving book when I approached him and introduced myself as a writer who was researching the site.

CL - Tell me, how did you find this site?

Gay Cruiser - A friend told me about it.

CL - So, how did your friend tell you about it?

GC - We were just talking one day, and he happened to mention it. It wasn't particularly this part, I guess it's the whole park, across the ravine over to St. Clair. He basically mentioned the other side at Yonge and St. Clair. So one day I just came down here and sort of walked around.

CL - What is the difference between Balfour Park at Yonge and St. Clair and this particular piece of land?

GC - I guess this is much more private, like a little club. Not very many people know about, and not very many people walk through here with their dogs. It's much more private, so you can come out here and sunbathe. Even within the community, it is not that well-known, so it's mostly people in the know who come here.

CL - I understand that happens when it gets warm in the summer.

GC - On the other side, people are always walking through with their dogs and such, so I think that during the day people tend to come up here. People say that there are specific hours for this side, usually between 2 p.m. and 6 p.m. Those are usually the hours that people find themselves up here. After 6 p.m. people go home and have dinner, and then people move down into the ravine. After dark, it's difficult to navigate up here.

CL - Why? There are trees down there, I would think it gets darker down there.

GC - No, it's just that the way the trees are up here, and the tremendous drop, it gets kind of dangerous. So if you had to leave here, you would likely have to walk all the way around, across the parking lot and the railway tracks, which is dangerous. Down there it's more level, more easy to negotiate, it is more of a nature path.

CL - So all of the little constructed places in the hillside, are they mostly for gay couples? Or do they serve another use?

GC - No, they are just for an encounter.

CL - Do you live close to here? Is it an important site in that way for you? Do you think that because it is downtown, it makes this site appealing? Do you have any historic relationship with the site?

GC - Not historically, it is so natural and secluded, it's unlike all the other cruising grounds. You could just as easily cruise at High Park, but High Park is so big and there are so many people around, and you don't have this natural effect, like over there. In High Park, things are maintained; here, things are left to do what nature does, and I think that is part of the beauty of this place.

CL - Do you have any idea where this might move to, once this space changes? Will there be a migration of sorts?

GC - I haven't a clue. I guess there will be a write-up in the local gay rag, X-Tra, and things will evolve from there. From what I understand, this use as a gay cruising location really originated just after World War I. People who came back from the war and lived through the gay twenties. This is the oldest, or maybe one of the oldest gay cruising places in Toronto. People's perception of public space was so different, especially in the gay community. Places like High Park might have not been as accessible. So, as I understand it, this is the granddaddy of gay cruising in Toronto. The granddaddy of them all.

CL - Hmm. Learn something new. So how long have you been coming here?

GC - Ohh, about fifteen years. Fifteen years — that's amazing, I guess I know the site pretty well.

157

site divine
*on-site four
interview with
anonymous gay
cruiser*

CL - Are there spaces that you like better on this site, are there spaces that are safer and more comfortable? Are there spaces that you dislike?

GC - No, not particularly, most of this area is quite safe. I guess that's because nobody knows about it except parts of the gay community. The straight community really doesn't know anything about this. They know a lot more about High Park, with all the books and everything, it is written up a lot more. You know there's a lot of violence and stuff down there. That is actually the reason why I come here, because it is much safer, it is quieter, and there are no people running around, no dogs running around. And that's kind of how my friend told me about it.

CL - Are there regulars on the site? Do you recognize each other and say hi, how's it going?

GC - Oh yeah, there is a whole sub-community, but, I don't know. I guess from my perspective, and I have met so many people here, as is generally to be found in the gay community, it seems like after they meet you, they don't want to say hello, or acknowledge you, or anything like that. But within the Caucasian community there seems to be this rapport. There seems to be this line between the Caucasian community and other communities.

CL - You'd think that would lose it's significance here on site.

GC - No, it doesn't. When I see someone that I know, I try to make eye contact, and if they don't, then I just ignore them and continue like usual. I find that really odd, very odd. It permeates everything. The entire gay community, whether you see them in a restaurant, whether you see them in Church, whether you see them at the baths, whether you see them in a bookstore. You might have had sex with them the night before, and the following morning it's like, " I don't know you." Overall, even if there are regulars, there is really no constituency here where people could voice anything. Nobody comes together to say "this is such a historically important space, but it's not being regarded with any value." It has something to do with the relationship that people have to the site, people are like "well, I don't want say what I do there." So this just gets destroyed.

CL - It's very sad, isn't it?

GC - Well, in a way, yes, in a way, no. Yes, it gets destroyed and then people will have to find another place, but I think it's great that people are going to use this space for something rather than just leaving it lying here. I've seen dump trucks come in. Well, not really dump trucks, but small trucks come in and dump their garbage. It's like a dumping ground. On the other hand, if there was a constituency, it would lose it's anonymity, which is one of the most attractive features in coming here.

CL - Are there any significant occurrences here that have affected the gay cruising here?

GC - Yes, people have been hurt. People have been beaten. Actually, I don't know of this particular place, but on the other side of the ravine. I haven't heard of any bashings on this particular piece of land. I think that is because people just don't know about it. And people aren't really using this at night. Whereas they are cruising more on the other side at night where sometimes the problems take place. It might also be that people in the gay community who occupy this part have a certain amount of ownership, whereas on the other side it really is a public park.

CL - Yes, when you pass this part and you see people inside, you don't really feel like you can enter and you don't feel like you have any ownership over the land.

GC - The relationship to this land here that is very different for people passing through. In a public park, someone might say "this is a public park with kids and everything," and they might be able to rationalize violence in that way, even though it is not a correct rationalization. Here, they have no real ownership, so they can't even rationalize violence and that kind of stuff. In that way, the land belongs more to the gay people who use it.

site divine
on-site four
interview with
anonymous gay
cruiser

on-site five *interview with Mac*

Looking like an average businessman, Mac was a regular on the site who came
to the site everyday after work in the warmer summer months before going
home to his wife and children. As a regular user who tended to cruise the low
traffic areas, Mac decided to talk to me about his experiences on the site after
I approached him several days in a row. Afraid that his anonymity might be
compromised, he insisted that I take no pictures of him, and that I destroy the
tape after I finished transcribing his feelings about the site.

CL - So you're a regular here, what does that mean?

Mac - Well, when the weather gets warmer and the trees start to bud, I come
here everyday after work. I tell my wife that I'm working out, or going for a
walk, or working a little bit late, but I come here instead.

CL - Are there a lot of people here that have wives?

Mac - Oh yeah, this is one place of great denial, most people in the downtown
gay community don't even come up here. It's completely hidden, and we've
tried to keep it that way for most of the time that I've been here. When the trees

come into full green, you can't see what going on in here at all. It's like a secret place. I guess that is why it has always been here in this neighborhood. It's very different from Church and Welsley, where most of the people like me can't go, because if we're seen, then everybody will know our secret. I know a guy that happened to. He was having a business dinner, and the group decided to go to Byzantine, and all these ex-lovers recognized him. He was completely outed, because people figured that if he was there with his business partners, then he must be out to them as well. I think he managed to convince everybody that it wasn't like it appeared, and he's still married and everything, but it's for those reasons that I don't go down to the ghetto. I also happen to like the guys here a lot more, they are all like me. We can talk about our wives and our families. We can talk about the things that are important to us, and no one here wears pink stockings, if you know what I mean. Sometimes there are people, newer people, who will come through here and when you get together, they'll forget all about it, like it never happened. One time I met this guy and I said that it was good to see him, he replied that he'd never seen me before in his life. This was a guy that I was just sucking his cock the day before, and he said I was the best that he'd ever had. Anyways, he was like he'd never met me, and he was just lost and passing through. I saw him several times after that, but I never talked to him again. It's okay if you hide this from people, because them knowing it could jeopardize a lot of work that you've done. But I don't like people who are in denial to themselves, and we seem to get a lot of them here. Sometimes these guys show up and have crazy sex, and then we never see them again. I usually just assume that they are traveling through town or something.

CL - So, why is this cruising happening here, as opposed to another place where there are a lot of trees to hide behind?

Mac - Well, there have been guys having sex here since I can remember. I've been coming here for thirty or forty years, on and off. I worked in Hamilton for a couple of years, but when my wife and I decided to get married, I wanted to move back here. There have been some great stories from here, and some really sad stories too. This whole place has quite a history. I have this theory about gay cruising. To have a good place to cruise you need five things. You need running water, you need a railway bridge with an active railway, you need enough green to hide behind, and you need some garbage. This place has all of those things.

CL - That's a strange list, why do you need those things?

Mac - Well, it's only a theory, I've not given it much thought, but when I've gone traveling around America, I can find this type of place the first day that I'm there. I just look at the map for something that would indicate the presence of all those things. I've never failed. I think the water is good for cleaning your hands, keeping the trees green and giving it a lush and Eden-like quality. The bridge is a great place to hide under, and there is usually a lot of space. If there's water there, then the bridge is not going over a road, which gives you more privacy. I think the active railway line keeps people away, and it adds a bit of danger and excitement. Finally, if you're lucky and you time everything just right, you can scream all you like when the train comes by. Garbage is a good sign that the place is abandoned, and it also validates some of your internal guilt about your own dirty desires. I wonder what guys do where there are not many railroads, or where there are no trees.

CL - Do you think that the growth of this neighborhood has something to do with this cruising zone?

Mac - Absolutely. I work in investments, my job is to get people to give my company lots of money so that we can invest it for them. I specialize in high risk venture capital projects. I know that if I was known as someone who liked to have anonymous sex with men, I wouldn't be allowed to touch my job. I think that's the case with most everybody that comes here. That means everybody who's like me will want to live close to a place like this. If this place wasn't here, we wouldn't live here. I know there are other places around the city, but this one is special, because it's in the middle of a great neighborhood and I don't have to get in my car and drive there. I can go for a walk late at night, when my wife and friends are over for dinner and no one will know the difference. I don't have to say, "honey, I'm going for a drive across town for no reason, be back soon." I've never actually seen any of my neighbors here, but if I did, we would know to keep it a secret. People don't just come walking through here.

CL - So, tell me of some of the stories that you were talking about.

Mac - God, there are so many. Well, I remember there was all this crazy stuff with a guy who used to live back here. He had this farm. It wasn't really a farm, but he used to grow vegetables and stuff. I think their names were the Cowans, or something like that. Anyways, old Mr. Cowan had this son, and his son was in complete denial. People tell me that the son was really rough, he liked to be really hard, and he was always drunk. Old Mr. Cowan hired this woman to help him, she was twenty or thirty years younger than him. He got her pregnant, and then he demanded that his son marry her. Since his son wasn't much into women, he married her. I think her name was Jackie, and eventually when her husband drank himself into the grave, she took over old Mr. Cowan's business. They moved out of here a while back. I haven't heard anything about them for a while now. Then there was this time when this beautiful guy came into the woods, I was pretty young back then, and he looked like Hercules, he was really big and hot. He was wearing these tiny little swim trunks, and looked like he was in the mood for something fun. So a whole bunch of us slide up next to him and start talking to him, next thing we know he's picked up this huge stick and was swinging it all around like a wild man. He was screaming for help, until some of the workers on the other side came over and explained to him what was happening. When he left, we all laughed, walking in here with nearly nothing on. A similar thing happened on one of the first days that I was here, way back when I was just a little kid. There were all these guys lying out nude sun tanning when this secretary on her lunch break came walking in through the trees. Next thing we know she's swooned, flopped right down on the ground. So someone tried to revive her, and she starts screaming rape. I mean, she was hollering with all her might. The ambulance and police came, lights flashing. I think the owner of the storage unit explained everything. Rape? Honey, I don't think so, just wouldn't happen here. <Laughs> Once, I was talking to the owner of the storage unit and he told me the story of Gordie the Midget who used to play for money in front of the liquor store. I remembered Gordie, he was always there. "Spare a qwader, Meester." I always gave him something whenever I saw him. Anyways, Gordie stayed out one night when it got really cold and lost all his toes. A couple of years later, he was killed by a car trying to cross Yonge Street. Then, there was a homeless guy who used to show up every summer and then disappear in the winters. The strange thing was that he took a taxi cab everywhere. An older guy, he'd show up in a three piece suit and then wear it to shreds through the summer, getting very, very drunk. He'd take a taxi from his little hole in the concrete platform to the liquor store. He stuffed himself into a little hole and covered the openings with plywood to keep the rain out. He came back here to drink the beer that people had left in their bottles. Then, in the fall, when he could barely stay sober, his family would send a taxi for him, and he'd be gone for that year. Some people called him Taxi, he thought that was the funniest thing. Did you know that the old building that was over there was burned by a couple of kids? There used to be a building over there that made metal cabinets, it always smelled of solvents, if you stayed around it too long, it made you dizzy. I didn't see them myself, but some guys back here saw a couple of kids break into the office and light the whole building. It was completely burnt in a matter of minutes, the firefighters didn't have a chance. It was probably all those chemicals. I understand that the guy had no insurance. When Allison Perot was abducted and killed a couple of years ago the police came through here and tore this place up before the body was found down near the Humber, or was it the Don? I was really sad when they found her dead.

CL - What about you and the site? What are some of the stories that you can tell me about your experiences on the site?

Mac - As a cruiser?

CL - Sure, or maybe how this site is significant to you, what is the history of this place for you? More than as just a cruiser, as an occupant.

Mac - Well, I don't do much else beside cruising. Let's see, I guess I can tell you a couple of stories about me, is that going to be on that? <pointing to tape recorder>

CL - I don't think I can remember everything you say without it on.

Mac - I'm trusting you here, you're going to make sure no one gets to hear this besides you. Somebody could recognize my voice.

CL - I promise.

Mac - Well, when I was just a kid, I used to hang out with these older kids, they were about fifteen or something like that. I think one was actually eighteen. They had this gang, and I'd tag along. One day, we were in this abandoned warehouse in the west end, near King and Dufferin, and they wanted to initiate me into their group. I had to fight my way from one end of the warehouse to the other carrying this can. If I could make it across still holding the can, I'd become a member of the gang. I made it across after being tackled a whole bunch of times, so I became a member of the gang. We called ourselves The Stray Cats. When the gang wasn't around, I would hang out with the oldest guy. It started with him pulling out his penis one day and asking if I wanted to touch it. Then, one night, we walked along the railway tracks, from way down in the west end to this spot here, and he introduced me to all these guys. They all thought I was too young to know what was going on, but he pulled out his penis and told me to kiss it. With all these guys that I didn't know standing around I felt really strange, but I did what he said. That's how it all started. I've been coming back ever since. Things used to get crazy, I used to do not just one guy but a whole group. We did everything you could imagine here. In the seventies it was always a party here. Then we were all hit by AIDS. Nearly everybody I knew got sick, it was horrible. Not that you would see our pictures in X-Tra, most people said that they had cancer, or they committed suicide so that no one would know. I'm very lucky to be alive, I guess it just wasn't my time to go. Nowadays, I'm completely safe. I only do M'n'M.

CL - M'n'M?

Mac - Mutual Masturbation. Yeah, it's never been the same. Now I'm one of the older guys, and I have to watch out for hookers more than I do for any disease.

CL - Hookers?

Mac - Yeah prostitutes. They like to come around sometimes.

CL - Really? I've never seen anybody that looked like a prostitute around.

Mac - They are usually younger boys, we don't like them to come around. It makes everything feel bad. It can also bring in the cops.

CL - Oh, boys. I was thinking about girls.

Mac - Yeah, besides the hookers, sometimes we get harassed. You can always tell when a guy is dressing up as a cop to harass you.

CL - How?

Mac - Cause they are harassing you. Cops don't harass us back here. They sometimes come and warn us if we make a fire, or if there is too much noise, of if there is someone dangerous around that we should know about, but they don't harass us, they just tell us things matter of factly. Just the other day, this guy drove around to the edge and started to yell at us with one of those built in microphones that you can buy for your car. I walked up to the car and he started to talk into his radio, as if he was calling for backup. We all laughed at him.

CL - So why do you like anonymous sex here?

Mac - I knew you were going to ask that, everybody always does. Having sex out here is a declaration of my love for humanity and men in particular. I love who I am, and I love being a man. I love other men, no man in particular, men in general. I love the idea of sucking a new cock every night. I love the feeling of semen on my hand. I love being in nature, there is something raw and exciting about it, it keeps me on my toes, it makes my days bearable. When I work and I get low in energy, I just think about meeting some hot guy out here, and I can work with full steam again. I love my wife very much, but this is very different, this is not a relationship, this is not about communicating, knowing each other's name, knowing each other's faults and problems, this is not about compromising. Here, it's about connecting with all different types of men. I've had sex with every type of man that you could ever imagine, from brain surgeons to homeless men, from famous actors to people who will live their whole life in the same house. Years ago, I loved being on my back, feeling the soil on my skin and looking at the sun bounce around the leaves as they flapped in the wind. Feeling the dripping sweat of some guy run down my face. I loved being that close to God.

CL - God? Wow, God is a pretty big word.

Mac - Those were pretty big feelings.

CL - So, what do you think about the fact that the architects are not taking any of this into account in their plans for the place.

Mac - I think they probably know about this place. They are a lot of gay architects, you know. They probably know what goes on here, and there's nothing they can or should do. If I was in their place I would do the same thing. Politics can't govern the market. I would stop coming here if this was seen as some kind of cruising ground that we had to protect, cause then all our families would know about it and the ghetto gays would come up here and start hanging rainbow flags and playing dance music. I would probably fight them from coming here. I don't want anybody to come here who doesn't understand the rules. Just because we sleep with men doesn't mean that we are all gay. I can tell you about this now because it's going to be destroyed, but I would never have told you about it if nothing was happening to this place. A couple of years ago a gay columnist from the Globe and Mail wrote a story on gay cruising places in Toronto. He was retiring and it was his last piece. It was on the cover of the Arts or Life section. It traced the history of cruising here from the 1920 onwards. We were furious, I can't tell you how many papers must have disappeared that day in our neighborhood. When I went into work and people asked me about it, I answered that this seemed to be typical gay thinking. Not only did every gay person think that everybody else is gay, they were now thinking that every rubbish pile and wooded park was a gay paradise for anonymous sex. Once you tell a secret to the world, the value that it had as a secret is all lost. *<sighing>* I will probably come here until they put up the fence, and then I guess I might look for another place. It will never be the same, that's for sure.

169
site divine
on-site five
interview with
Mac

on-site six *interview with Stacey Guertin*

Saturday May the 10th at 1:00 p.m., 1997

Stacey Guertin is young witch, recently discovering the Wicca tradition. Long searching for something to explain her special awareness and belief structure, Stacey believes that the Wicca tradition might be her answer. Stacey communicates with the trees, and claims to have had this special intuitive connection with trees since she was a small girl. Stacey is very new at acting as a guide to the trees, and as of this writing, is still unaffiliated with any organization.

Stacey Guertin - This line of trees right here, you can tell have a bit of history. They are older trees that have been here for a bit. They add a bit of life and character to this area, whereas these trees here have been planted for the sake of sheltering those houses from here, from seeing this piece of land. I like looking at trees, specifically those that are in groups, because when you look at trees in groups you can see a lot of what the place might have looked like before it was built up. What are these train tracks?

CL - I don't know where these specific train tracks go; they seem to come from nowhere and disappear. Those platforms over there had train tracks on the other side, but they are not there anymore either. If we follow these tracks, they seem to turn off in that direction. You can go in any direction you want,

I don't want to direct you, so if you see anything that captures your eye, we can go in that direction.

SG - Seeing this place just reminds me of . . just the way that things have been laid out definitely reminds me of something from the twenties, when train travel was a big deal. At first, I won't have much to say, I'm just kind of feeling it out. It is interesting that all the trees are leaning away from this area, there is not a lot of growth, there is a lot of dead space right here, dead ground, to the point where even the trees are leaning away from here. There used to be more life here. The ground here is decaying. No, that's not the word I'm looking for. What is the word I'm looking for? There's an emptiness in the ground here. The root systems of these trees probably don't come very far under this ground. Something was here that was very much an abomination for the trees. There is something very negative here, just as far as maybe what it produced, maybe what it represented. The energy itself. The site here in general doesn't have a very negative feel to it. Like, as abandoned as it seems, it doesn't seem desolate, but that could be because of the neighborhood buildings around, though. This spot right here is interesting, it just feels so awkward. You have all these trees around it, and all this life around it, and this empty spot where you would think that things would have begun to overgrow. Do you know how long this spot has been empty?

CL -No, I don't.

SG - Over there on the asphalt it's really hard to take any kind of reading. The asphalt just kind of gets in the way. Here, nature is trying to take things back, life's coming back into it. But once again, it isn't dead space. When people just avoid things, and nature avoids things, you lose the energy signatures, and while the asphalt doesn't feel that way, because there are probably many people who travel through that space, this spot here feels like dead space. There is a lot of negative energy around here but it is localized, and it might be from the hydro towers and the energy they are giving off. Here's another spot where you look and you can see what nature had been, and then you turn 180 degrees and you see the absence of nature. There is still a lot of life in the soil. It's amazing how city trees are so vigorous, especially here, how they grow in practically nothing. This part is much more comfortable. The energy on this hill comes up. It's just an observation, and it's probably because it is being conducted by the hydro things, whatever you want to call them. It causes a movement, a current, and

it just so happens that it's going up the hill. That's not odd, energy does not work according to gravity necessarily.
<moving to the north-east end>

These trees here are sad. Sad not as in sorrow, but more as in pity. I can't tell you a reason why. No, it's hard to say exactly what I mean. Sad as in pathetic, apathetic, a loss, that's really all I can say. I don't know how to sum it up. There is a sense of loss. Well, I think, if anything, the trees give this place a little more of a sense of victory, in the way that the trees seem to be repossessing, but I still feel a loss.

CL - It seems as though these trees are perpetually repossessing though, don't you think?

SG - Yes, nature is always doing that. Let me just look at this for a minute. I'm feeling really negative back here, can you turn the tape off?
<tape recorder turned off for a while>

It feels like something very negative took place back there near the ravine, maybe the people that worked there, or the people that owned the land; it just had a really, really bad residual energy. It probably has something to do with the working conditions or the laborers, more than likely. People who worked there probably didn't have a high regard for life. It's odd to look at this area of the forest, or foresting, with all the human rubble in it. It really affects the feel of the forest, the purity. The rubble is like a contaminant, things just don't feel the same with all of this rubble. Even something as simple as little orange ties make things feel strange because they are so synthetic. The ground at the edge of the ravine has been falling away, eroding pretty steadily, rather quicker than usual. You can tell by the way that this tree, since these trees trunks usually grow pretty straight and close together. To have one this spread out means that this hill, which has been here for quite a while, has been eroding for quite a while, and the tree has kept trying to grow straight while the land kept pulling it down. You can also see that there is a lot of human waste here, and I think that this waste has been around for a lot longer then that railway station has. This land has a lot of history, but a lot of this erosion is the result of humans. Whatever happened here earlier really loosened this area. There is not a lot of natural cohesion in the soil anymore. It's a physical observation at the moment, but it really affects the flow of things around here. I just see a lot of decay, a

site divine
on-site six
interview with
Stacey Guertin

Stacey Guertin attempts
to communicate with
the trees on the site

lot of human decay, and a lot of natural decay that is happening very rapidly. Perhaps that was what I was feeling before in the sadness. It's not sadness, but more decay. Things are just falling apart here a lot faster than they should be. It's just because of the instability of the ground. The physical manifestation of the slope is eroding a lot faster than it should be. It all depends on the development that was here before, the land was probably lowered too much. Not necessarily recently, but some project lowered the land, and this sliding has been as a result of that. And as a result, the trees here feel very precarious. Unnaturally so. Prematurely so. Like on a slope of this incline, this type of erosion is going to happen eventually, but when a tree like this is an example, where the way that the trunks spread out, and the root system is so spread out, the tree has been falling over even as it grew, and this tree took a couple of decades to grow to this size. It's one of the few mature trees around. Yes, it feels precarious. Because even here you can see that there is some kind of building, some kind of human development, and it's fallen. The slope eroded so quickly, that whatever was here fell apart really quickly.

This tree here died within the last couple of years. It hasn't been dead that long, I'm just intrigued as to whether it was a natural death, or if the falling apart of this foundation might have crushed the root system and caused it to die. If that's so, then the roots of the tree didn't go very deep either. Either that or the foundation of the building went a lot deeper than it looks. But this tree probably grew alongside the building when it was here. It probably leaned against the building for support; as you can see it's bent, and then grew down when the building fell apart. Its interesting, I feel that the core of this tree is still alive to some degree, but the tree is dead, with no hope for growth. It makes you wonder why the core is still alive, or how it is still alive. It must be in a period of dormancy.

CL - What do you mean when you say the core is still alive?

SG - When a tree dies, it takes a while for the core to dry out. For a tree this size, maybe eight to ten years, but if the tree is still fairly moist — to the point the wood is not brittle — there is still life going through the tree, there is still moisture going through the tree. It's just that it can't do anything. It's weird, I know.

The one thing that I am surprise by is that places like this usually attract people who come here to drink, to party. The seclusion provides for a bit of wrongful doing if you will. You don't get a lot of negative energy from here from people partying with malice towards the forest. This tree here is an exception. I feel that it is mean, malicious.

CL - Which tree?

SG - That tree there.

CL - What, the small one?

SG - No, the big one. One of the odd things that I find about this site are the pockets of negative energy, it's not all over, it's not a general area of negativity, it's just specific parts of this land, as with people and creatures, all plants and trees have their own identity, and this tree seems to have a lot of malice. It seems much like an evil, crabby old man that has been malnourished, perhaps. The fence behind the tree should have fallen over a long time ago, but if you look at this tree, it has literally grown through the chain link at some points. If it wasn't for this tree, the fence, the boundary of the site would have fallen over a long time ago. It is as if this tree has wanted to keep the fence up. But if you look at how deep the exposed concrete pieces are that once supported the fences poles, if you look at how deeply set those were in the ground, it's just another indication of how quickly the slope is eroding.
You don't seem to see a lot of human movement through here, considering the well trodden path. It's less inhibition in here. I guess that has its merits. What's that steel structure over there?

CL - I don't know, there's another one over on the other side. We can go and take a look at it.

SG - Anything with rust on it I always find gives me a very confused feeling. Rust in itself, the chemical structure of rust is very simplistic, but the metal that it is on usually isn't. It usually has an very odd energy signature. I wonder what this is, I wonder what this is for? Probably some kind of access to the railway, probably for some kind of maintenance vehicles. It's kind of strange though, this place is odd, very odd. There's older wire and newer wire, probably to keep it up, to keep it from falling onto the tracks. Why they would want to do that I don't know, I don't know why this is even here. It's been here for a while. This tree here is only a few years old, but it is already growing around this. I don't know, odd.

CL - It seems that most of the understanding that you have of the site comes through the trees, is that true?

SG - Yes, yes. Because, ever since I was little, I lived in a forest near my house. I've had this tendency to listen to the trees more than anything. Most teachers have told me to base my feelings on the earth, but it's hard to base it on the earth because you don't know what is underneath. Like, if there's exposed asphalt like over there, and you don't know exactly how far that goes along the ground, and if that is getting in the way, it is hard to understand the earth. Various types of stones make it hard to read through too, and clay is hard to read through. Trees I take as the best meter, if you will, because they are life forms. They have their likes and dislikes. Like the train tracks, where the trees have grown very close to it, so it's not very heavily traveled. There are trains that go through here pretty recently, but they are not very long, or very stressful to the environment. Which is nice, the trees like that, because it gives the place a little more relaxed atmosphere, because a lot of times if you go to areas that are near train tracks, it seems to be very industrial. More stressful in the way that to me, there is a lack of nature and natural energy. But the nature here is doing fine and it doesn't seem to be to bothered by the presence of the train tracks. Oh look, there are some shoots growing out of this trunk, and the tree itself is trying again. Look at that, it's trying hard. People need to take care of the trees that are around them, it's a shame that people don't. I bet you there are a lot of monarch butterflies around here, because these look like milkweed, that the monarch feeds on. There's too much metal, there's too many non-organic things back in there. That area gives not a negative feel, but just a really dead feeling. Look, a Blue Jay. Another dead pocket right here, right here, where this old cable spool is. The train tracks used to come through here. Maybe it was just a side track to take cars off. Right here there. Maybe a couple have been ripped up. Yeah, there is something right here in this spot, there is something very negative, even though there is this beautiful tree with it's blossoms. They are beautiful blossoms. It's in the Cherry family. This feels really alive over here, it feels even more natural here than a thicker wooded part would feel, does that makes sense? It just . . . there is a lot of the human intrusion, but all the rubbish and the rail ties in this pile here has been kind of filtered out. I don't

site divine
on-site six
interview with
Stacey Guertin

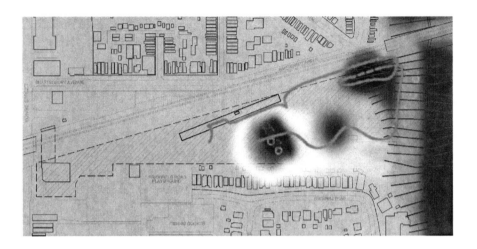

Energy and erosion
patterns as observed
by Stacey Guertin

know, it's just my feeling. Here we are back to this place. You said that this was a ceramic place, right?

CL - Right.

SG - All its wares, all that has been left in it have been smashed everywhere. Isn't that weird? Why wouldn't they have been taken somewhere and sold, why were they all broken, wasted? They are scattered throughout, everywhere. Are these big sheds next to the railway lines abandoned?

CL - Why, do they look abandoned?

SG - I guess it's hard to say that. Usually abandoned buildings have a lack of paint, but this looks like it has been upkept. I just . . . I mean, you can feel the — how you say this — the age to it, and you can feel, I don't know how to phrase what I'm trying to say. The shed has an odd, lost feeling, an abandoned feeling, which is probably a reflection of the person who might own it. Some places like this shed have a very odd effect on me like that. Some places have odd feelings, some have really bad feelings, which give me a really odd sensation in my stomach to the point where I almost feel like I am going to throw up. Literally I have to go straight to a forest and relax to reset the energy after I experience really bad energies.

CL - The trees help you? How?

SG - I just sit on a tree branch for a while, and I lean against the trunk. That, and the serenity of a forest resets my energy. I spend a lot of time with trees for the sake of resetting my internal energy. Everything vibrates, everything has a frequency, and humans obviously have their own, their individual, and to me the point of communing with the tree is because you can be out of tune with yourself. I know that sounds cliché, but it's literal. The atoms in your body can be resonating at the wrong frequency, and that offsets you and how you feel. I always find that going to a forest and meditating always helps me reset that energy a lot easier. Overall, this site, to me anyway, has a real draw to it, in the direction of that forest, and here, too. For some reason this old platform intrigues me. I don't feel anything specific for it, besides just a draw to it. When you look at the site from back to front, or front to back, however you want to call it, there's more movement towards the back. That might have something to do with the natural current that is being drawn towards the hydro poles.

CL - Before you came to the site, you mentioned something about Wicca, and how that was relevant to your connection with trees. Maybe here at the end of our tour of the site you can explain to me what exactly are your beliefs?

SG - I have developed my beliefs myself, and it was only in the last couple of years that I learned about Wicca as a religion. When I first heard about it, I was talking to a friend about my beliefs, and she said she knew a lot of women that sound very much like me. Wicca might not be as accurate, because Wicca is a religion as far as if you join a covenant, like when you become a member of the church, it's not so much a way of believing, it's a way of practicing what you believe. Each Wicca will have their own belief, whereas a Catholic will have to believe a certain way, think a certain way, and act a certain way. In Wicca, everybody is really a solitaire, and come together and acknowledge things. I haven't actually joined a convent, I've thought about it. For some reason there is just a fear. Just, what would I say when I go there, what would I do? I would feel very odd and wronged doing something wasteful with my beliefs. I'm also afraid of the fact that because there are so many different beliefs within the Wicca structure, that if I go to a specific place I'll find people who only think one way, and my beliefs won't match. I've wanted to join for curiosity's sake.

CL - Why did you tell me to shut off the tape back when those men came out of the woods?

SG -Seeing those guys there, coming out of the bushes, I just felt awkward all of a sudden, like I didn't want to talk anymore. I didn't want to let them know who I was, so I just wanted to shut down until they went away. I didn't feel any danger from their presence, just a repelling feeling, like when you want to put two magnets together, both having north polarity, and they just both push each other away, that's all.

181
site divine
on-site six
interview with
Stacey Guertin

on-site seven *interview with Katherin Potter*

Wednesday May the 7th at 11:00 am, 1997

Katherine Potter is the owner and principal of Ch'Interiors, an interior design firm located in Toronto. She is a psychic with second sight, who, due to a near death experience, is able to contact the spirits of a place. She uses a magically charged ring to focus her sight, and employs automatic speaking and writing to express the stories of the spirits that communicate with her. When Katherine first enters onto a site, she contacts a group of spirits in the hopes that they will tell her stories about the site. These spirits do not necessarily tell Katherine autobiographical stories, but rather act as guides who tell her the stories about the site as they see them. When I met Katherine, she prepared for her tour by standing perfectly still, and asking for support from the spirits that were present at the time.

Katherine Potter - There are spirits that are not helpful, and this ritual is to help them disappear. Then, the ritual asks the other spirits to understand that this is for a good purpose, and I ask that they help me.

CL- Is that how you ask, just like that, or is it an internal question?

KP - Yes, I just ask for the support like that, so that the spirits can just hang out a little bit and not make it trickier and mess the whole thing up. That's what you do.

CL - Okay, so we'll just go around the site, and if you see anything important or of notice, you can just direct the way.

KP - How far does the land go in the northern direction?

CL - See the railway tracks over there?

KP - No.

CL - See where the red and yellow markers are? It's over there. The tracks form the edge of the site on the northern side, and the ravine over there forms the edge on the easterly side of the site.

KP - So we can go over there, too?

CL - We can go anywhere. I'll follow you.

KP - Can we come back to certain spots?

CL - Sure, if that is necessary.

KP - Okay. Back in there, too?

CL - Yes, we can go in there, too, if you would like.

KP - I don't want to go to that little part over there.

CL - That is the home of someone who lives here on the site.

KP - That is his home; I don't want to go there. I don't get any feelings like that over there in the wooded area, we can go over there instead. Do you know what dowsing is?

CL - Yes, I have had two dowsers on site.

KP - Oh, have you?

CL - Yes, and it was interesting. They were each very different in their approach to the site and in what was significant about the site.

KP - What about this building?

CL- This belongs to a moving company. The owner's name is Angus Willis.

KP - What's happening to them?

CL - They are leaving.

KP - Well, I pick up that there is some sadness to them moving, they are not very happy about moving. Not as bad as back there where that little house was, I don't think they want to go. Let me get my ring off. This ring contains the power of the crystal skull. Have you heard of the crystal skull?

CL - No, I haven't.

KP - I place this ring next to the crystal skull.
Do you know anything about it?

CL - Is it a skull made out of crystal?

KP - Yes.

CL - And so you place your ring next to it to absorb energy?

KP - Yes. You've never read about it? It's incredible how it is made.

CL - How is it made?

KP - It's perfect, there are no parts to it at all, it's one piece, and it is all crystal. It's this big. <*she shows a sphere the size of a cantaloupe melon with her hands*> It's all smooth, and you have to rub it by hand. It about kinesiology, where you balance yourself, so that your left, and right brain is . . . just give

site divine
on-site seven
interview with
Katherin Potter

Katherine Potter
refers to her ring

me a second till I get . . . I wrote about this site in my automatic writing, yes, and I also saw it in my mind.

CL - You saw this location from another location?

KP - Yes. Now, what is the name of the man that works in the sheds?

CL - Gus Willis, or Angus Willis.

KP - He doesn't want to leave, this man. It has something to do with money, the move. It's not that he is attached to this place. What I usually do is read with my hands; I use my hands on something. It's easier. I trust my hands, What I do is I pick up some kind of energy, a ch'i, do you know what ch'i is? Ch'i means energy. So I pick up with my hands whatever I need. How far does the site go over there?

CL - It goes quite a ways.

KP - Are we going over there?

CL - No, we are still heading in this direction.

KP - Can we go over there?

CL - Sure. Absolutely.

KP - My sun sign is cancer, like the crab, and so I move around in circles. I feel uncomfortable when I don't go around in circles. I like to go skirting around, even when I shop, I go from left to right. Like when I'm shopping for a dress, I don't go right to it, I go around and around like this in a circle. When I see what I want, I don't go right to it; I skirt around and then I come back.

CL - That's a good point. I should remember that every person will have a different way of wanting to move through this site.

KP - Well, it's like sitting down at a table, you want to sit at a certain place, and you feel uncomfortable if you don't sit there. I am a teacher, so you know, the students might feel uncomfortable, so it's better to have the students pick their own seats. What is this? That's interesting. Where is the wind coming from? Just a second. I don't get anything here. I don't get any building here. It could be just landfill. Does this piece of land go beyond that fence, all around?

CL - Yes.

KP - Now, this is a negative vortex right here. Right here next to the fence.

CL - Does the negative vortex originate from right here, or does it just pass through here?

KP - It's really strong right here. I don't know what the heck this is, the vortex is right here in the earth, but I don't know what kind it is. Is there gas around here?

CL - I have no idea.

KP - It's very negative here, so I wouldn't want to locate anything here. Sometimes you can see that plants grow in different directions, and that means that there is a vortex in the vicinity. They grow differently around an area, but I don't see anything like that.

CL - Here, next to the railway tracks, we are coming up to the property boundary.

KP - Okay. There is something around that building over there that feels . . . that I don't . . . it's the man, it's not the place. It's the man, he is not happy, so the whole building has got something about it. That is an interesting tower at the other end there. How old is it?

CL - It was built around 1916.

KP - That tower was a guide for a lot of people in the past. People were drawn to it for a long time, it's a very positive thing for a lot of people. Now, of course, we have got skyscrapers. You can still see it, which is a very nice experience. I like driving up Yonge and passing that tower. What is it, a clock tower?

CL - Yes, it was a clock tower, and from what I understand, they are going to replace the clock in it.

KP - They are going to fix it? What is it for?

CL - It's a marker.

KP - A marker for what?

CL - A marker for the train station. It showed people where the train station was. That was the train station that was used before Union Station was used.

KP - Really, you mean before Union Station was used as a station? What would it do for the trains?

CL - This train station was the major train station in Toronto before Union Station was built. This train station was built in 1916 and Union Station was built in the 1930's, so it wasn't active that long.

KP - Oh, so it was a station. That's good. It was good. Whatever took place here was positive. I thought when you first asked me, you wanted to know if people built here, what would I say to build or not to build.

CL - The one reason I haven't asked that is that there is no program involved, so I am more interested in what is significant about this place.

KP - Oh, you want to know anything about this land. Is it possible that horses went along the tracks? Yes I feel that horses came along here. Could they come and meet the trains?

CL - I don't know. The history of transportation shows that routes develop in parallel, but I don't know.

KP - Well, I feel that there were horses along here, and there was a person called Mary. Mary, she used to come here, and something about her kids, her three kids. Mary Durham, or Mary Dowdy, or Dordee, or something like that. I don't see her husband around that much, but I see her three kids and herself. I think she is probably one of the people with the horses that used to come here. What is going on in there? Is this still part of our land? So we can get around to the other side of the tracks? Well, anyways, there was a guy over on the other side of the tracks named Joe. Whether he is dead or alive I don't know. I kind

site divine
on-site seven
interview with
Katherin Potter

of feel like he's still hanging around alive over there. The edge of the ravine is called the Catwalk.

CL - What does that mean, the Catwalk?

KP - I don't know yet. This is a path were boys play a game called catwalk. It's sort of like a follow-the-leader type of game. What they would do is follow the leader, but the leader would do something dangerous; that was the point of the game. I understand why, too. Look at this cliff, this drop off here. The end of the site here, the boys would drop off here, or just do whatever they could do to make it dangerous. This was the Catwalk. Yes, this is a play area; it looks like an exciting place to come. I think that the boys built a little shelter in there for them to play.

CL - There are a series of shelters that you will see along here, so it would be interesting for me to know what they were used for. Did the girls play too?

KP - Yes, sometimes, but it was mostly boys. The boys played with each other and did more dangerous things. Those shelters were play things, where boys would get together and play. What is this thing here? <points to a concrete slab with holes>

CL - I don't know, there are several guesses as to what it could be. What do you think it is?

KP - Ahhh, does it say 1945? Jacob, Jacob lived here, Jacob Lazeri. Lazee, or something like Lazeri. He carved those numbers, he had two children, a boy and a girl, he had a dark-haired wife. It feels good back here, it's a nice area, I don't feel any negative energy. We are not in anybody's space. In this part, there is something about Indians too, it is an Indian place, maybe they are buried here. It has something to do with food, maybe this was an Indian farm in here. Something about trading, some kind of a trade they used to do in here. Let's go look at those other structures built by the boys. Look, there are those little play places for the boys, look, they are just down there. There is something to do with dogs, something to do with animals.

CL - Well, this is Balfour Park, and so just down there where you see the path, there are always quite a few dogs.

KP - What are they doing, just running around, just pets? Oh, okay, there is something to do with that. Is this a fort down here? There is something to do with cattle over here. See there, that mess? There is a place where you can sit, and there are holes too, do you see them? They have been dug into the garbage. Did the kids do that?

CL - I don't know. I really don't know.

KP - Maybe there are homeless people.

CL - Yes, but they don't seem to be all that occupied, They don't have roofs or anything like that, and they seem a bit small for homeless houses. And I've never actually seen any kids here, every time I've been here. I've seen adults who have passed throughout here quite a bit, but the adults don't seem to be doing much, and I've never seen any kids.

KP - Let's take a look at that one over there, it looks like someone has actually dug a hole into it. They don't actually stay in them, they call this place Break-Off point. That's what they call it. There is something over here around the corner that I would like to see. Right here there was a person called Jack Mason, he was a stone mason. Did I say Jack Mason?

CL - I don't know what a Jack Mason is.

KP - That's his name. I said stone mason, didn't I? I think I said Jack Mason, stone mason. His name was Jack Mason, and he was a stone mason. I don't know if he was living here or if he just worked here. But it happened, Jack Mason came here. I get a strong feeling that he was here. This transmission tower is, of course, a negative thing. I feel that it sucks the breath out of me, sort of. But even though that other area is so close to these transmission towers, it feels so good, it has a very powerful vortex, which, now, I have never read this before, but I get the feeling that when you have such a positive area with a negative area, my science is not very good, what is that, neutral? Yes, that would seem to balance things out and make them neutral. Maybe that's the balancing effect. That was really nice over there, very relaxing. That whole area looks like it continues up in that area, and we haven't gone in there, have we?

CL - No, we haven't gone through that area.

site divine
on-site seven
interview with
Katherin Potter

KP - Oh, okay. I wonder how old this place is, it's all part of the land. I feel a little light-headed, do you feel that? After walking under the power lines, it feels like I've had a couple of drinks. Now what about there, can we go through there?

CL - Yes, we can go through the whole thing. There is another section, behind the train platforms, that we haven't been to.

KP - Can we go through there?

CL - Sure we can if you want to.

KP - There was an old shack over there, see the old sink. His name was Clarence Day, he lived here, or was here. He had a dog. What is that hole in the ground? The other one was raised up and had a date in it. He and his family were from another country, not from Canada, His relatives lived in Cliffs, which I would guess would be south of the border. I wonder what all this is? A little house and a stone path, which appears and disappears. I guess this is all part of his house, it's fairly elaborate. There's a bed spring there, so it looks like he lived around this part here. His dog had a run-in with a bear on this property. Look, there is a door turned over. Here is another fort for the boys to play here. And look, there are those cement things for parking, I wonder what they are doing here? To me, they could tether horses to these things. They connected the horses to those cement pieces, more than that, I don't know. That Mary, the one with the three kids, used to come through here to get to the train with her horse. The horse was a blonde color, and she would tie her horses there.

site divine
on-site seven
interview with
Katherin Potter

CL - After we finish coming through here, we can go to the other side of the loading docks. You'll see that on the other side it is kind of neat, too.

KP - Oh really? Over there, this is more interesting here. I just figured that there was more history here, more people and stuff, housings. I feel that the trains turned around over there. Were the trains that advanced to do a roundabout? That's what I get. How far does the use of this land go back, King George?

CL - I'm sure this land was occupied during the time of King George, I think it has had pretty constant occupation since then, and as you see there is not much remaining that was built, so it is a very fascinating piece of land.

KP - I got King George. I don't know why I get him, it's something about the onslaught of . . . and then I'm not quite sure as to what comes after that. So much about King George, and then there is a break away, and some kind of disease. I don't know.

CL - A disease from King George's time, or just generally a disease?

KP - No, not a disease from King George, it was much later than that. It was here, it was around here, it is not just this part that we are walking on. That was a concern at that time. The disease was a great concern at a time. People here became really sick with the disease. There's the house that the homeless man lives in. Is he here right now?

CL- No, I don't think he is here right now.

KP - He does live here, but he is just not here right now?

CL - I'm saying that he has occupied this house, but that he is not here right now.

KP - Do you know his age?

CL - No, I don't. There is another man that lives right around here, but I don't know his name either.

KP - I wonder if his name is George, too. One of them, maybe he is like King George. Maybe people call him King George. Here's the train station. There was a girl named Sarah who used to come to the train. Sarah had something happen in 1940-something, 1944, I don't know what. She died in 1944. There's vortex right in the middle of the tracks, I didn't even notice it.

CL - So, that being a vortex right there, you didn't recognize it because of the trains driving over it?

KP - Well, perhaps the natives would be able to notice it better. It would also be interesting to know who built that tower. Do you know anything about it? Well, let me ask the spirits to find the answer. I asked to see if the person who built that tower was aware of vortexes in that location, and I got that he did, he was aware of the vortex here under the tracks. Is that part of the train station?

site divine
on-site seven
interview with
Katherin Potter

CL- Yes, that is part of the train station, it runs under the tracks there. This is the end of the site on this, the westerly side.

KP - Was there a hospital right beside the train station here?

CL - I don't know for sure, but I don't think there was a hospital beside the train station.

KP - It's a place where there were avortments. Have you heard of the word avortment?

CL - No, I haven't

KP - It's like abort, but it's about vortexes, and it's avort. It means something like circumcised, or circumcision. There was an avortment of a vortex, a cutting away of a transaction, it was a trade that ended. The transaction got cancelled. There, that's how it relates to the circumcision. When I talk to the spirits they are very poetic. When I was doing my writing once, I asked why, in my writing I asked, "why do you give me messages that are so poetic? Why don't you make it simple for me?" and he said, " Well, you like it that way don't you?" That's the way they speak, they don't speak in simple language, because they are on a higher level, so that's what you get. Sometimes, when you get messages that are very difficult to understand, you have to sort of stretch, so if they tell me "circumcised," it meant a break in a transaction, or a trade that didn't happen. In the twenties, the lucky twenties, there was something to do with the railway station of that time. That's when the train station was closed. What about the other side, there could be something over there. Like I said, back there, it is more interesting because of the people. People lived back there. Here it's more strange versus, meeting, people meeting, a transaction between people that continues and isn't circumcised or cancelled.

I feel that I'm getting proof that what I am doing is true. By talking to the spirits, it's just reinforcing each time what I know. It's from my near death experience due to my allergies, that's when all this stuff clicked in. I had a near-death experience when I was seven, but I don't remember too many changes, I just know that I was a funny kid, I was always walking around the bush, exploring and thinking thoughts that more of an adult would think, not typical of what a child would think, anyways. Then the last time, ten years ago, that near-death experience changed everything. I became very intuitive, and I started to find all these people that were on the same wavelength. It's been an exciting ten years, I find myself drawn to strangers who have the same experiences and the same intuitive awareness. I went to Stonehenge. That was a weird experience; I started to do automatic writing when I was there, and I got a lot of information explaining why it was there. Have you read the Popcorn Report, a book by Faith Popcorn? She says that what I do is the way of future. I mean, this is the way of the past, this was common in the past, and she says that we have forgotten about it, we got sucked in by a scientific way of doing things in our machine age and we forgot that we have a brain in our head and that we can just do it. So that's the good thing about it. I think the things that we have to do are . . .

Well, we were witches at one time, the group that I get together with, we had a deep trance channeler there once. It was Halloween, so he went into his trance and he said that it was getting really hot, and we were all getting really hot. He said that we were all witches once, and everyone in the room was burned at the stake. He picked me up in France, and I insisted that he tell me what was going on because I was really getting pretty hot and upset. Well, he would draw names out of a hat to do a reading for the certain people, I said "wait a minute you're not leaving me like this. Tell me where was I, what happened." So he picked me up in France, and since I teach French, it would make sense that I was in France. I went to France last summer to find my past lives, I find myself rummaging around in a graveyard, and on this particular grave. I never found the name on it, because I ran out of time and there was no name on the stone because it was so old. So I was told that my ex-husband in that lifetime did me in. <giggle> That was a nice thing to find out.

CL - I just wanted to say that I really appreciate you coming out here to help me. Thank you so much for all your help on the site. So, do you have any last things to say about the site?

KP - Temperance. Temperance means not drinking, maybe that means that you couldn't drink around here at some time. There's something about turkeys too. Wild turkey country. There is something symbolic about the sun over the land, and the flowers that we saw in the wooded area. Something wanted to be done here, but it headed the other direction. Like you told me about the station which was here, but then it headed downtown. So that's what those symbols were all

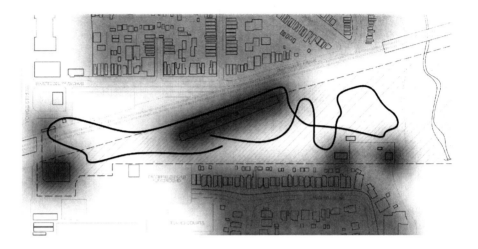

Natural and Spiritual
energy patterns as
observed by
Katherine Potter

about. It only got half used. Sometimes there are places that have a really bad feeling about them, but mostly this has a really good feeling about it. I could be wrong, but it just feels like a good space. So the fellow who thought the station should go here, and he weighed the pros and the cons, and it ended up that it worked out for a while, then it went somewhere else. I can feel this fellow's brainwaves that decided to put the station here. Somebody's life was in jeopardy here, his soul didn't die because he had back pains, and pains in his stomach, which is how he actually died. He didn't die because of that, he was a scoundrel, and that is why he died. It was his choice to come here and die that way. I don't usually call people stupid, I don't know why he said that, but he was. We are not stupid, we make choices. This being was a special spirit whose lifetime was a total write-off, but it was supposed to be that way, so that was a scoundrel lifetime. This land is a place of people, which is unusual. It is a place of history and people, and not so much a place of buildings. George was the scoundrel. Mary, like George, had a special life, a special soul. She had only one major challenge, a small challenge in her life, and it had something to do with not telling the truth, but other than that, she was supposed to be a man in this lifetime, but she was born as a woman. She used to hang around here. She liked the horses, and did manly things, but she was very feminine in appearance. I think she had dark hair though, that's not what I said before, is it? She had a very easy life, except for her death, but we all die somehow. Angus has something to do with trading-off. His family, his life, his whole background has been about trading, trading-off. Dealing, dealers, in the city he's got power. He's had to make choices between the poor and the not so poor, which he's rather cautious about things like that. Although this is Angus's land, his disappointment, not unjust, his trading, his sell-off of the land. It's his building here. Somehow, without money, he benefits from the land. I have a feeling that the homeless people here will soon find a home. Well, they are going to have to. It's a very people-oriented reading of the land, it's all the people on the land, all the people who have come through the station.

site divine
on-site seven
interview with
Katherin Potter

on-site eight *interview with Ivan Yip*

Friday May the 9th at 11:00 am, 1997

Ivan Yip is the most prominent Feng Shui master in Canada, with design consultation in over twenty major architectural projects from coast to coast and many media references, including all the major national newspaper as well as national magazines. I was very fortunate to arrange a meeting with Master Ivan Yip. Originally trained as an engineer, Master Yip worked as a forensic scientist until he retired to pursue the study of Feng Shui and the I-Ching full-time. Our discussion about the site began with an introduction to his personalized style of Feng Shui. From there, he went about taking magnetic readings and then gave me his analysis of the site. As I was very honored to have been granted an audience with Master Yip, I largely allowed him to dictate the discussion.

Ivan Yip - You would be surprised at how flexible the magnetic data on a site is. It fluctuates because the magnetic field changes quite a bit, even within an area. So many modern feng shui masters know the inside of the house, but they don't know the importance of the magnetic fields, and that they change so much. In a house, there can be magnetic fluctuation of forty degrees, at least. In an apartment it is even scarier, you can take some readings that can be 180 degrees different. In a downtown apartment that was about a thousand feet square, I measured 270 degrees difference. If you cannot determine what direction your

site divine
*on-site eight
interview with
Ivan Yip*

apartment is facing, you cannot do an accurate feng shui. This is why my technique is the most appropriate, because I can do a feng shui reading even when the degrees vary significantly. No other feng shui master in the whole world can achieve that. I'm not just doing that now, I've been doing it for the past ten years. Before we do a complete magnetic reading, let me tell you my concepts of feng shui. First, there is the I-Ching. The I-Ching is the Chinese technique parallel to geometry, but it is more senior, because it has the history of over five thousand years, ten times longer than the history of geometry. I'm challenging the whole world. Science cannot answer very simple geometrical questions that should have been asked in high school geometry classes. How many corners, and how many sides, and how many surfaces in a fourth dimension cube. I can do the parallel of I-Ching and geometry for you. I-Ching tells us this. Tai-Chi came for Wu-Chi, and split into Yin and Yang. That's the equivalent of a movement of a point making a line, and the two points making a line is the first dimension. It is the equivalent of the Yin and Yang concepts in the I-Ching. The I-Ching splits further into four, with the extreme Yin and the extreme Yang, a little bit Yin and a little bit Yang. That's four variations, and that's the second dimension in geometry. Movement of a line makes a plane, the plane has four corners. That's the second dimension right?

CL - Absolutely.

IY - Okay, the movements of a plane make a solid which has eight corners, and is the equivalent of I-Ching's eight trigrams. But if I dared the scientists to answer, the movement of a solid makes a what, they would get stuck. In I-Ching we are not stuck. We have 16 hectograms, and based on that theory I can find out the answer to how many corners and how many edges and how many surfaces in a fourth dimension cube, which is very difficult if not impossible to answer in geometry. Go back and try it out. I haven't only found the answer, I have the experiments to prove how many corners and how many edges and how many surfaces there are. I'll tell you why I-Ching can do it and science cannot do it. Because geometry has no time axis. In other words, when one plus one is equal to two, the time axis is forever. No time limit. I-Ching is based upon a different concept than geometry. Look, when you are a point, you don't know how to move. But I-Ching tells you that once upon a time, Tai-Chi moved, and split. Yin and Yang, what does it mean, two ends. If one point is heading east, then another point is heading west. In the history, the I-Ching tells us that these two points kept moving, then there came a moment and at the very end there came the new dimension. There are only one or two instants in history that a moving point makes a line. Only at those instants can a point move and make a line. It is called the exclusional of Tai-Chi. If you define light as Yang and darkness as Yin, so in a day, the noon time at exactly twelve o'clock is one hundred percent Yang, or most light, a moment after that is diminishing Yang to 99.9% to an increase of Yin. In the afternoon, the increase of Yin and the decrease of Yang continues, and then at midnight, that moment is a hundred percent Yin and zero percent Yang. Now, in a day with so many instances, there are only two instances that are absolute. In reality, I-Ching tells us that anything that exists in this world contains part of the other. In practice, there are no such things as absolutes, but you can sense them from the two instances, midday at noon, and midnight. So I-Ching has the technique to tell us the exclusional. If you find a house with 100 percent Yang, or 100 percent Yin in that environment, that is a very bad one. My version of feng shui using the I-Ching technique is based upon three laws, just like Newton's three laws used to analyze the forces in physics. Or in the engineering field, you have the three laws of thermodynamics. In feng shui, there are also three laws, which I am proud to tell you.

CL - Well thank you.

IY - The first law is the balance of Five Elements. Wood, fire, earth, metal, and the water. Of course, science through chemistry discovered that all the substances in the world are comprised of 108 elements in the world, or something like that. But Chinese philosophers described the whole world as being made up by only five elements. These five elements are a simplification and clarification of the 108 elements. These five elements have relationships that include the generating cycle. The metal genesis water, the water genesis wood, the wood genesis fire, fire genesis earth, and earth genesis metal. That is called the genesis cycle. They also have the destructive cycle, otherwise this world would expand forever. This is why they have the checking process called the destructive cycle. Metal overcomes wood, wood overcomes earth, earth overcomes water, water overcomes the fire, and fire overcomes the metal. Now this is the checking, which makes the two processes stay in check and keeps this world in balance. These five elements and the two processes can be used to analyze the environment where you're working or living. We can express anything in terms of those elements. For instance, talking about direction, we classify the east as the wood element, west is metal, south is fire, north is water, and the center is earth. The same thing is true with color: red is fire, green is wood, water is

site divine
*on-site eight
interview with
Ivan Yip*

Master Yip refers to one
of his directional tools

clear blue, earth is yellow, beige, and brown. Metal is white. Immediately we can use these rules to analyze. Like my house, the back of my house is on the north side, and it is facing south. So if my door is painted in the red color, or the yellow color, or blue color, that is no good, because the south is represented by the fire element, and you're facing it using water element, so water quenches the fire. It's in the destructive cycle, and in Feng Shui terms we don't like that. We want to harmonize the house with the outside, that means we want to use the generating cycle. So we paint with a beige color, so the outside element is generating for you. It is helping you to grow, because fire generates earth. So in designing and building a house, you use all the five elements, based on the generating cycles and the destructive cycle. If you use this law, the first law, you are already using one third of the Feng Shui laws, you fulfill one third of the feng shui laws. I give you one solid example and very useful. It took me 44 years to figure out all the information just like a puzzle, fitting all those pieces into a big puzzle. But I find that the three laws can generate prosperity. The existence of the five elements generates money, because the five elements have the generating cycles, never ending, that's why it works. But you have to put this in the right place before things really get things going. Why? This will take a lot of explanation later, but it works for sure. There are more than eight hundred feng shui masters in Hong Kong. In Asia, there are thousands, using the Five Elements to generate money, it works. So the first law is balance of five elements, the second law is the balance of Yin and Yang.

CL - And what is the third law?

IY - The third law is the conservation of the magnetic field. I know the bearing of this site based upon the survey plan, but when I measure in this corner — because of the electrical towers — they effect the value of my readings, of the magnetic field in this corner. But don't worry, if you take enough readings you will be able to take the average and find your true magnetic bearing. This is why my feng shui works, I have the three laws of Feng Shui. Many other feng shui practices are like the black magic, they are not scientific. They do not have the I-Ching as a tool to calculate the fourth dimension.

CL - The fourth dimension? Tell me more about the importance of the fourth dimension.

IY - This is very important to remember. In I-Ching, everything is based on the time axis. If a point can move, a line will result. But you know that a point cannot move. The I-Ching tells you something very important. The human sphere is three-dimensional. That's why I argue that the dying point of a person — the point when a person dies — is the time when that person is transformed from the third dimension to the fourth dimension. I give you a solid example, I will demonstrate and experiment that will prove this. I'm going to prove that ghosts have a fourth dimension, one more dimension than human beings, in the time axis. Two things to discuss while talking about ghosts. Ghosts can come from nowhere and disappear to nowhere, even when you close the door, ghosts are able to enter a room. They are not contained by length, width, and height. We know that. Ghosts enter through the fourth dimension. Secondly, they appear exactly like you. Here's an example of two-dimensional ghosts as opposed to three-dimensional ghosts. Imagine a circle, one which lives happily on a piece of paper. If this circle decides to build a house, it will use both length and width to construct an enclosure. It is quite safe for the circle, as it lives in two dimension, it never expects anybody to come from the height. So what if there is a ball, a three-dimensional sphere that crosses through the light which shines upon the house of the circle? The shadow of the sphere enters the house in the exact shape of the circle. What this experiment tells us is that the shadow of the three-dimensional object is the ghost of the two-dimensional world. In the same way, the shadows of the fourth-dimensional world are the ghosts of the three-dimensional world. In this way, the dimensions cross, though the object in the fourth dimension can never actually exist in the third dimension, it can only appear as a third-dimensional representation. Just like a ball can never exist in a two-dimensional world. This is why I help people to see the representation of the fourth dimension in our third-dimensional world.

Sometimes, when I come across houses that are said to have ghosts, and you check the magnetic fields, just as you can select a radio frequency, you can select the magnetic frequency. It is the location and orientation of the land that will select the magnetic frequency. The future task and challenge before scientists is to control the magnetic fields just like the electronic fields are presently con-trolled. Feng shui makes use of the magnetic field. It relies on magnetism much more than on electronic fields, even while they are related. This is why a house close to high voltage towers changes the magnetic fields, and changes the effect that these lands have on people. Feng shui works because magnetic fields are related directly to human health. I don't need to prove that to you, it has been proven sufficiently in science. But what I will prove to you is through hundreds of compass measurements around a place, if the deviation of magnetic readings through a constant alignment is greater than ten degrees, it is not a good place to live. If it is less than three degrees, then it is a very good place to live. So if an electrical field can influence the magnetic readings by a deviation of ten degrees, then the electrical field is negatively influencing the land. It really has a bad effect. I have records that show this to be true. As a retired forensic scientist, I want to be able to have the records to support my assertions, and I do.

In order to understand the fourth dimension fully, we must understand that the transformation towards the fourth dimension begins when we are a point, and moves through our life in the third dimension, from birth to death, and ends in the forth dimension. Time is essential in the transformation. How can I demonstrate this? You could go to the CN Tower and jump. You will find this out. <Laughs>. The scientist could do this too. Believe this or not.

When you are a point, you don't know how to move. When you become a line you can stretch up and down, backwards and forward, but you do not know how to move sideways. But the I-Ching tells us that this is not true — when you are a line you can learn to move in all directions. Keep both ends moving. One moves along the time axis for an infinite amount of time. There arrives an instance when this perpetually moving point reaches the end, it will bend and become crooked, generating the new dimension. The same thing is true with the third dimension and within the human life. Our life is ending in this world. We have to leave. The I-Ching determines that time and suggests the fourth dimension which follows.

Why did the ancient philosophers end with the eighth trigram, why not end in the sixteenth trigram? Because they know that the I-Ching was to be used only in the third dimension, and that's why the I-Ching stops with eight trigrams of broken lines and solid lines. It's the same thing as 1 and 0. While the West uses zeros and ones, ancient Chinese use solid lines and broken lines. History has proven that the ancient Chinese philosophers of five thousand years ago developed these tools already. What is amazing, and what is missing in the modern zeros, and ones is the time axis. This is why the I-Ching cannot only predict and forecast, but it can also examine the fourth dimension. An architect has geometry and can build a house, but architects know nothing about the time axis affecting the house, and the fourth dimension affecting the house. Architects are trained only in the geometry of the third dimension. They are missing the time axis of the I-Ching. We know the past already, it is the future that affects what we do. This is why architects need to be aware of the three laws of feng shui. They need to prepare for the effects of the future

CL - Let me see if I understand this. This dimension analogy is very important to your understanding of feng shui. So in the first dimension, there is only a point. The point consists of only one everything. In time, the point forces itself into a line, as there is no other way the point exerts energy over an infinite amount of time. The line then has an infinite number of points, but only one line. It has no sides. The line then stretches into infinity until it hits the end and bends, creating a plane. The plane has one side and at least three corners. When the plane takes on motion, it creates a solid in the third dimension. A rectangular plane creates a cube. The cube has six sides and eight corners. In time, the cube transforms to become a cube in motion, a cube along a time axis. This is now the fourth dimension. So how many sides and corners are there in a fourth dimensional cube?

IY - Right. This is a very simple question. We should be taught this in our basic geometry class. After I learned the I-Ching, I remarked at how familiar these ideas were and I remarked: "that's geometry." Tai-Chi comes from Vu-Chi. That means something comes from nothing. That's the same as a point. A point comes from nowhere. A point has no dimension, only position. What's that? That's Tai-Chi. When Tai-Chi splits into Yin and Yang, it's the equivalent of when a point splits to make a line. The two points define a line. It's that obvious.

CL - So what happens at the transformation from the third to the fourth dimension?

IY - That's the moment that is described in the I-Ching. You must learn more about the I-Ching to understand, then you can find out what happens in the fourth dimension. The transformation from the third dimension to the fourth dimension is not so simple. In I-Ching you can extend the concept of the tetragrams, that is based upon the four lines, to find the answer. Actually, the I-Ching has developed a way to forecast, based upon the time axis, the balances of Yin and Yang. Things cannot exist outside of the balances of Yin and Yang. Everything exists within a state between 100% Yin and 100% Yang. They cannot exist outside of this.

CL - So how many corners are there in a fourth dimensional cube?

IY - I cannot tell you, I have to keep this for myself. This answer is my certificate. This is the question that I ask my students, and only when they know the answer will I allow them to graduate from my teachings. Because after you take lessons to fully understand I-Ching tools, you may be able to find out the answer. So this answer is the certificate for a professional feng shui master. That is the exam for all my students. If someone already knows without my teachings, I will give them a certificate for professional status as a feng shui master. It took me twenty-four years to find this answer. I had to wait until the alignment of the planets in the sky was right for me to find the answer. I learned the answer to this question in 1962, when I graduated. I devoted all my time to this question. In this time I was able to study feng shui and astrology. Feng shui teaches you where to put the right thing in the right place, and astrology teaches you when the right time is to do the right thing. Palm reading and face reading are also important; they teach you how to select the right people to build in the right place. I'll tell you how to achieve everything. First, you pick the right guy, and then you select the right time and the right place. Then you will always do the right thing. All my life I've learned of many techniques world-wide. There are six techniques minimum required to use the land correctly. First, you have to select the right person. How do you know who the right person is? You use palmistry and face reading, a Western technique and a Chinese technique. Go to those experts and they will tell you quite a bit about the people you might choose. They will tell you about their health condition and other important things. I can tell you a lot about palmistry and face reading as I studied those for ten years, from 1952-62. I know how to read palms and faces, I've read thousands already. That technique will tell you within five or ten minutes whether a person is the right person, whether they are scientific or artistic, this is not hard to find out. Then, with the use of astrology and the birth data, both Western astrology and Chinese astrology, the human factor is accounted for. Western astrology is very good at detailed daily luck, but unlike Chinese astrology, they cannot do yearly luck. Western astrology is like a high-powered microscope, but it is not good for searching. Chinese astrology examines the life, but is not any good at the day to day things. They are both fast and accurate, and very important to the business people and architects who come visit me. It is just like the weather forecast for the local farmer. You can forecast, but you cannot change the readings. So, we have one factor under control by selecting the correct person to build on a site — the human factor itself and the environmental factor that is a direct result of

site divine
on-site eight
interview with
Ivan Yip

the human factor. These are the largest factors that will influence any site. One technique for determining the success of any venture is not enough, it must be confirmed by at least one other technique. We must have two techniques of different principles, one is talking about the position of the planets in the sky, and the other is the balance of both Yin and Yang from the I-Ching. Both are completely different, but they both reach towards the same conclusion. You need at least two different analytical tools before you can identify an unknown. This is the acceptable method used in court. Why should my examination of data be any different? Two techniques of different principle are very powerful, and very scientific. How dare anybody say that I'm not scientific? Come to challenge me, I will challenge you back. Give me the right answer, and don't talk behind my back. Most people talk behind my back because they don't dare take the chance to talk to me. I'd like to show these techniques to the public. I have so many things that I would like to share with the academic world, I have so much to offer because I have better tools than a scientist; that is why I can do accurate forecasting and appraisals of land and people.

So, for the last ten years, I quit my government job to begin practicing feng shui and forecasting as a permanent job. With these skills I've been able to make a billion dollars so far in the Hong Kong real estate market. Every year, more people come to me and I have never advertised my expertise. I'll tell you about one of my success stories. There were these developers who couldn't sell any homes, and for a whole year their homes remained empty. It was a feng shui problem. I went in and gave them some recommendations, and after three months all the houses were sold. It was logical; there are three steps to sell a house in any market. I will tell you what those three steps are: if you want to sell a house, the door must be oriented towards a certain direction, according to magnetic degrees. To amplify these magnetic fields, the 'For Sale' sign must be aligned along the correct magnetic degrees. Since humans are tuned to magnetic frequencies, the house must send signals that will attract people to come and buy. The door and the sign create a signal that directs the frequency of the home. In terms of magnetic fields, the frequency is 'in phase.' The first tool in feng shui is then to attract the buyer. The second tool is to add plants to the house and grounds. Prosperity spots are determined and plants are placed in those spots. This is very important. The third tool is the goldfish tank. Every prosperous place needs a goldfish tank. But North Americans don't like the goldfish tanks in their houses, they don't have room for goldfish tanks, so I invented an alternative to the goldfish tank. This is my invention, but I don't want to confine this invention to myself. Feng shui masters here already have begun to use my invention. I want this idea to circulate worldwide. This idea works and it is convenient. Using the same theory upon which the goldfish tank is based requires substitution. The hard part of finding a substitution is that the elements water and fire cannot coexist. So I use the red flower as the basis of my invention. People like carnations and roses, and these plants need water, they are put into a vase or container. Eight stones are put into the vase, and one coin. These elements substitute perfectly for what the goldfish was doing. You have the earth element, you have the metal element, the flowers are the fire element, wood is represented by the stems, you can put this anywhere. If it is put in the best feng shui spot, it works beautifully. How did I get this idea? I saw Western people who were successful but who weren't practicing feng shui, and I saw that they liked flowers. Sometimes Westerners even put their flowers in very good positions. Believe it or not, when you are lucky you do something correct. That is why these Western companies have prosperity. It can all be explained. There must be some rule in general. God has a very high IQ. It took me so long to discover these three laws. I have all the documents to prove this. I'm a forensic scientist, if you ask me for proof, I have the checks from all the companies that hired me, and the dates. My techniques are proven. I have been promoting feng shui in North America for ten years. My capacity to talk about feng shui is based upon a worldwide approach. I am not limited and local, because I am well prepared. After ten years of teaching feng shui I have seventeen students. Most of the students have gone back to Asia to make money. My students know my technique already. In my neighborhood there are four famous feng shui masters, all of them decided that this neighborhood was auspicious to live in. I was the first one to move here. I moved there in 1988.

In 1995, I went to Vancouver and I held a seminar on where the best real estate markets are. I told Hong Kong people that they should go home. The real estate market in Hong Kong would be going up and the Vancouver market would not be going up. Some people didn't believe me because that was not logical, because in 1997 was going to be the time when the last portion of people were going to move away from Hong Kong. Of course they don't believe me, but the facts prove that I'm right.

CL - So land values in Hong Kong are very high now in 1997.

IY- Oh yes, ask people how valuable Hong Kong land is. In some places, the land is ten times more valuable than it was a couple of years ago. That is why they cannot afford to misuse their lands. It is so expensive. That is why they hire feng shui masters to find out the best uses of their lands and their offices. They need the experts to tell them which places are the best, and which places are the most efficient. In Hong Kong offices, the arrangement of furniture is often crooked, sometimes this way, sometimes that way. This is because the furniture has been aligned along the suggestions of a feng shui master.

I want to have these original ideas acknowledged to me. These are concepts that I have told many people already, but I don't want to limit only to certain people. I don't want to limit my ideas to only Chinese people. I am a scientist, I have nothing to hide. Once I find something new, something useful, and I have the technique to do it, why not present it to the public? You can check my background in the forensic field. I invented a way to identify gasoline after fire. My technique was accepted as the standard by which to identify gasoline after a fire throughout the world for a whole decade. My technique is no longer used because of the use of computers. It is a very difficult problem to identify gasoline after a fire. Gasoline is a mixture only, it is a mixture of three or four hundred components. Those components can be found after a fire, through the degradation product of the debris from the fire. How can you tell the court that the original fuel of the fire was gasoline and not the other hydrocarbons found after the fire? It is a very difficult analytical problem. I solved it, because I found four components of gasoline that could not be found in other materials. After the fire, when you collect samples, you can find these four components in the same proportion as in gasoline. That is why my discovery was so valuable in the court room. I also invented how to detect nitroglycerin molecules in low doses, as used in modern bomb sniffers. I published a paper before the sniffers were developed. I have a lot of copyrights that I did not benefit from. Nitroglycerin is very hard to detect because of the low boiling of the composition and the high absorption. It is very hard to detect the whole molecule. A normal explosive detector detects the degradation product only, it is unable to detect the nitroglycerin molecule itself. I was the first to detect it at low pressure, before 100 degrees Celsius, before the molecule decomposes. Now it's accepted worldwide.

Like my discoveries with feng shui, I will not benefit from them either, I could make a lot of money with my discoveries. I also discovered a new way to teach kids. When a child is born, I can, with the use of my techniques, know what qualities this child will have. I also know what qualities he doesn't have. In order to educate him well, you need to find another child who has his missing talents. Let them play together and they will teach each other. One might have the pioneering spirit, and the other would be good at finishing projects. I have taught many older people what talents they are missing, but they are too old to use this information. This is good for the young people. This is the new way for education. Talents and skills are learned unnoticeably. The scientist cannot do this, and it will save a lot of money. This is why it is so urgent that academics studying this and present this. I am an inventor, and a feng shui master, I am not the guy to promote something. God told me through the I-Ching that I had to promise him that if I find something new, I have to tell people regardless of my ability to prosper from the ideas. Otherwise, God doesn't give me the chance to find out anything new. I'm not superstitious. I don't even go to church. God promised me that if I try hard enough and if there is only one answer I will find it. That's the contract that I signed with God. God's way is like automatic control, believe it or not, there is some creator or superpower that designed the worlds using the planets to automatically control human life. Each person is assigned a track for the whole life. God already gives each of us a talent to go through our path. That path I call 'the path of least resistance.' It is so easy to go along that path. It is like traveling where the hotel is booked and the car is rented, all you have to do is identify yourself.

I am an engineer, and you tell me to create ten thousand electrical parts, that is not hard, I can do that. I can design a system that manufactures these parts and every one is the same. God creates human beings, every one is an individual, none of them are the same. How did God do that? God makes every individual different, and then they are affected by their environment; that is where feng shui works. The planets in the sky are the energy terms. All energy emits from the sun. No sun, no light, no energy. See how clever God is? In our solar system there is one emitter, namely the sun, and different planets make up the different materials. Their position keeps moving. No matter. Independent of heredity, you will always have your relationship with the planets, which will be the same as other people who were born on the same day at the same time. This is why there is a generation gap, and this is why so many people who are educated study astrology. In 1960 there were only a few books on astrology in the library, and I had to take notes on the books by hand, because it was before the Xerox copy was invented. I still have those notes. I learned from the original books. Don't use the term bad luck; scientists don't like the term, so we use the term low efficiency. That means that luck is defined like this: normal luck is the reward is equal to the effort put into things. Bad luck is when the reward is much lower than the effort, and good luck is when the reward is much higher than the effort put into it.

CL - Master Yip, I appreciate everything you've had to say, but would it be possible to look at the site and decide what feng shui would suggest in response to this site?

IY - Yes, certainly. You understand from everything that I have said that the magnetic field is not constant, they might change a few feet away. They might change fifteen degrees or one whole direction difference. So now I'm going to stand parallel to the one point that I'm starting at. So I take some readings and then you can write them down for me, okay? In Hong Kong, the use of feng shui is everywhere, and if this land was in Hong Kong, wow, so valuable. One square inch is like an ounce of gold. Feng shui is used there where the land is so valuable. If feng shui was not valuable, then these people would be crazy to use their finances to support feng shui. It is important to look at the ancient text as I do. Okay, so I'll take readings. *<Yip begins taking readings and listing off a series of numbers as I write them down.>*

So, here are the objectives for this land as I see them: to use the land for the best commercial use, to create an environment harmonious with the surroundings, to analyze and evaluate the prosperity of properties using feng shui principles, and to forecast the future prosperity of the property. So, this feng-shui analysis focuses on existing external and internal factors, as well as future prospects. Where external factors include the location of the site, orientation of the building, neighbouring structures, and traffic flow. The internal factors consist of colour co-ordination, furniture arrangements, placement of plants and flowers, and appropriate seating arrangements for executives. So what are the favourable features of this land? Well, it's centrally located in downtown Toronto, close to public transit. According to the magnetic readings, the site is located in a prosperous feng shui location, and it is positioned in a favourable direction with respect to major structures such as City Hall and Queen's Park; this represents support from government. On the other hand, the unfavourable features of this site are that it is located in a high density and traffic area; this limits the mobility of the ch'i. The site is positioned too close to railway tracks, which represent unstable financial situations. The shape of the site is irregular, and therefore considered unstable, and access to the site is limited due to the train tracks; the only convenient access to the site is through the west side of Yonge Street. We can't look at the internal factors, because they depend on the nature of the design. So, in the final analysis, this is what I have to say: Commercial use of this property is not profitable. Even though the land is situated in a prime area, as mentioned above, access is limited to Yonge Street. This means that in feng shui terms, the ch'i is restricted to a single access, thus limiting its mobility and dynamic flow. As a result, this business will not grow and will eventually deteriorate. Using this land for residential purposes is also undesirable. Again, the single access represents limited earning potential. Furthermore, the trains operating to the north symbolize ch'i flowing out, which signifies excess spending. Thus, residents in the area experience difficulty in saving money. As well, the traffic created from a single access route prevents the flow of ch'i. The ideal use for this property is to create a cemetery. The negative aspects mentioned for commercial use is reduced to a minimum in this case. In feng shui terms, active areas, Yin areas, should be used for commercial purposes, while inactive areas, Yang areas, should be made into cemeteries. In business terms, choosing this site for a cemetery is desirable since money is made on a per unit basis. Also, maintenance fees are paid in advance, which leads to good cash flow. The need for a cemetery in this area is ideal since the Mount Pleasant Cemetery nearby is at full capacity. I also think that the future prospects for a cemetery are extremely successful, especially around 2005-2007, after a couple of years of increasing prosperity, those years would be extremely successful.

site divine
on-site eight
interview with
Ivan Yip

on-site nine *interview with Steve Topping*

Tuesday May the 13th at 10:30 am, 1997

Steve Topping is an artist and a tramp, or modern hobo, who makes art out of found objects. Well-known in the Toronto biking community, the tales of Steve's tramping are legendary. He has spent complete winters tramping in the Northern Canadian Wilds, building everything he needs to survive from found objects. A recent subject of an architectural presentation and review on his portable housing techniques at McGill University, Steve regularly uses the Summerhill Lands as a point of departure and arrival for his extended trips. For the last three years, Steve has been accompanied on his trips by Steve the Cat, who acts as Steve's alter-senses. Steve and Steve the Cat have a tremendous bond, and when not tramping, Steve the Cat can usually be found on Steve's shoulder or riding in Steve's bike basket. Having spent many nights on our site waiting for departing trains, and having an in-depth knowledge of the train system, I felt that Steve would provide a valuable perspective on the train, a major component of the site mostly ignored by the other participants of this study. Moving very quickly, Steve jogged me through the site.

Steve - I thought I remember a couple of platforms, or remnants of platforms.

CL - Yes, they are there.

Steve learns about the site
by smelling and tasting
elements in the area

Steve - This is an original building over here, I guess.

CL - Yes, it used to come all the way out to the end.

Steve - There's some siding off the main line, is that what this whole platform was for?

CL - It was for train to truck connections.

Steve - Oh yes, I remember when they put a service road over here. Let's go into these trees here, where that dug up earth is. I'm going to let Steve the Cat down around here. Steve had a great time coming here, I have a basket for my bike now. He likes baskets. Still, the only part of the site that I feel comfortable is on that platform. I can describe my feeling over the rest of the site as a kind of uneasiness, a kind of a nervous feeling when you walk on this. There was a little shanty over here.

CL - Really, recently?

Steve - Oh no, about three years ago. It wall all skids and plywood. The shanty was probably four by eight. It was only four feet high. Maybe it was too perma-nent. They were probably stopped too many times and asked to leave. Maybe we can find remains of it. I think there are all kinds of bundles of woody piles there. I like it back there, right by the valley. Look at this piano, I guess it is brass plated. Then again, that's oxidation, it must be brass.

It's such a wild thing, that transformer. The ground is so dead, there is nothing. You can see the huge cables coming up from the ground, and right into that porcelain transformer and then right out. That's all there is to it. Those things make me nervous, like, really nervous.

Let's just take a look down this trail. I've followed this trail, and it just follows the edge behind those electric ladies. It looks like a lot of landfill. Look at the asphalt just sitting there. I would probably camp in the ravine if I was going to camp here. Over on the edge feels all right, and over near the platform. It's a little different over back here. This is my original entrance to the site when I first visited it, it was from this back corner, my very first time. There is a staircase coming up on the other side of the ravine here, and you can just cross over the tracks, over the bridge, and I came back here and threw my leg over the fence.

CL - Actually, I think there is a hole in the fence over there.

Steve - Is this asparagus?

CL - No, I don't think so. The buds look very different, that would be my initial reaction.

Steve - Have you tasted the water?

CL - No.

Steve - That's a good way to learn about any piece of land.

CL - Even if it is just rain water?

Steve - It's too recent now, but yes, you could taste the water. Probably not on the road, but on this trail out here, that would be a good spot. Let's follow this trail. This feels very different from the road. Very much. The ground is softer for one, and it's cooler. We can head around back, I've just got to check and see what Steve the Cat has found. He can really get into it with me, we both try and pick stuff up from the land. Personally, especially after I exercise, I have to cool down, breathe for a while, breathe the air of the site, and then I can start to feel the site. There's Steve the Cat. Stevie . . .

CL - You have your cat trained like a dog.

Steve - Only that he is very much a cat. I often catch the trains here.

CL - From here to where?

Steve - Like from here to Winnipeg. Yep, not regularly, but sometimes. When we do, we camp out every night or every day on the way, trackside.

CL - So that's what you do, get off every night and get on every morning?

Steve - Yep, or I go straight, depends on how big of a rush I'm in. And depends on what campsites are available and what towns you are going to be stopping in. This station here is station 00. It is the first crew change. Well not the first crew change, this is the center of the Toronto subdivision. It sounds like literally a subdivision, but it is a subdivision of tracks.

As we were saying before, you can pick up feelings based on your smells and your tastes of the air and the water. *<pointing to the tape recorder>* Those things make me very nervous.

CL - I know. I can understand that, but my brain is not big enough to remember everything that you say. Besides being so fast that I can hardly keep up with you, I do notice that you are very quiet when the machine is on, and you seem to stop talking whenever I turn it on.

Steve - <Laughs>...We'll walk a bit and get my mind off that thing. I don't think the cat likes that thing either. I love that station.

CL - Why do you love it?

Steve - I love that it is all the way under the tracks. It has an old clock tower that marks the beginning and the end of most of my voyages. Mostly I love it because it is where a crew change happens. They don't use it as a crew change anymore, obviously, but I always ask trains to stop here and drop me off.

CL - And they have?

Steve - Yep.

CL - You talk to the engine driver and it's no problem?

Steve - Yep, they've offered actually, they ask "where are you going," and I say "Toronto," and they go "well, whereabouts," and I say "Summerhill will be fine." They stop the train here at Summerhill and drop me right off. Yep.

CL - How do they find out that you are on the train when you are trying to hide yourself?

Steve - I'm riding in the engines, I'm not hiding myself.

CL - How do you get to the engines, do you stick your thumb up and hitchhike?

Steve - Well, no. I catch the train at a crew change, and you tell them at crew change that I'd like a ride, or I just get on, and they discover me, and I try to be friendly.

CL - How do they discover you?

Steve - Well, there is a problem with the unit, or they are just coming back to check on things. You know, there are two or three engines on each train. The crew is only in one of them.

CL - So, those engines are actually working, pulling?

Steve - Oh yeah, full on. Always. There were three on the train that just passed. They are going full power and wired up and controlled by the lead unit.

CL - So you would get into one of the later units and that's where they would find you? I thought you usually got into the grain carts.

Steve - I do, but not in the winter. I've been riding all winter. You have to ride with the heated cabins. But I like the fact that the station continues under the track, it's like the subway, when you're on here you have this mental image of what going on underneath, what's supporting you. It's an interesting mindset. Look at this train coming in, they almost never come in here this slow unless they have to make a change. This was the other platform that I was thinking about, I just didn't place it right when I thought it was back there. This one feels good to me to. It feels very organic.

CL - How long have you had Steve the Cat?

Steve - Three years, since he was tiny, tiny. So, I was going to say about how people feel comfortable in spaces and on land, or not; what changes a person's opinion about where they are walking, and chooses trails and paths for themselves, like on an open plane. I think smell could be the most important thing. Your nose can pick up particles in the air and decide your direction for you. I'm sure the insulation of the landfill back there makes me feel not so comfortable, because of the way that it smells. Even though it might be clean fill, it has this certain scent to it. It's very different. And temperature, I like to read land in terms of what is hot and what is cold. Trains are read that way too, so you have a sense if it's warm, it's good and it could be lucky. I'm a bit superstitious about these things. If it's cool then you have to be more weary of what's going on. Like, even railway crews will tell you that they have a sense about such dangerous work.

CL - What do you feel, the heat of the air, or the heat of the thing like the locomotive or a tree?

Steve - No, it's nothing like that, it's inside yourself. I know that it is inside of myself, but some people relate to it best by thinking that it is actually coming from something, like the train or the land, whatever.

CL - Why is being on a train that dangerous?

Steve - Riding a train is not dangerous, but the minute you step outside and have to do be out in the open, it becomes dangerous. Like that train that just passed. Right there the conductor was dropped off way, way up the track, and the train pulled forward with just the engineer. The conductor got on the back of the train, or made a cut in the train, and got on the back of that, and then they backed up and switched tracks. They are probably up a car, or dropping off a string of cars. So the conductor is back there with a radio, and that's the only thing that is keeping him alive.

CL - The radio?

Steve - The radio, to tell the train and the engineer when to stop, because the engineer could just barrel and pile into a car sitting on the track side. Radio communication is not that concise. You have to have a sense of automatic instinct to have a sense of what is safe and what is not. The ideas of trains being hot and cold is a very common one within Hobo mythology and the workers. Expensive trains that are really fast are hot, too hot, sometimes. They are fast, and hard to catch, and they don't have much security. And cold is like a milk-run, which are the most dangerous trains to run.

CL - Why that?

Steve - Cause they do the most action. Back and forth, breaking up, and they have the most slack as well. You've heard of slack? Milk-runs have the most slack by far.

CL - Why do they call them milk-runs?

Steve - Because they stop everywhere. They go from door-to-door basically, they go from town-to-town, but that's door-to-door basically.

site divine
on-site nine
interview with
Steve Topping

on-site ten *interview with George*

Tuesday May the 13th at 12:00 p.m., 1997

George is a homeless man in his early thirties. Originally trained as a welder, George has been an occasional occupant of the site for over four years, and as such I thought he would have a valuable perspective on the user population of the site. After attempting to meet George at his shack for two weeks, I met him on the last day that I was on the site. I asked George to tell me about his experiences on the site.

George - Well, that blue school bus is owned by a Hari-Christna named Jeeba. He renovated it into a camper, he stays over at the Hari-Christna temple on Avenue Road, and sometimes he stays there. There was a story of some girl that was running away from her family, no one really knew much about her at the time, he allowed her to stay in the bus. Mentally, she had some kind of problem, but she was really smart, like university education. Her and I would sit here and talk and she would rhyme off all the names of birds and trees and everything. She knew all about music and all this stuff. I guess she had some kind of medical problem, and somebody found a towel with blood on it and called 9-1-1. I was lucky that day, I had made a couple of extra dollars and I went to the donut shop to buy her a hot chocolate, and I left her here. When I came back, she was long gone, and the only thing missing from the whole affair was the SWAT team. It was after dark and the police came in with their running lights on, right to the bus, scared the hell out of her, and she took off, and no one has ever seen her since. But we were to find out — from this guy who claimed to be a private detective hired from the family who came around and started asking questions about her — that she was from a rich family and she was just trying to get away. This family had total control over her, and she didn't like that, she just wanted to get away. She kept talking about heading to British Columbia someday, and so that's where I think she is. That would have been about four years. Yes, that happened four years ago, and no one has ever seen her since. I see the Hari-Christna once in a while and I ask him, but he never seen her again. This land is also used for gays. And they like to use my shelter for their practices.

CL - How can you tell?

G - I know when anything has been disturbed, someone has already been there while I've been gone.

CL - Overnight?

G - No, I was gone right over to Yonge for a while and I just got back twenty minutes ago. Nothing has ever been stolen out of there, but I don't really keep much, an extra blanket. It's just that I don't like them doing that in there, in my space. I have permission from the owners to be here, they don't. Sometimes they get quite perverted, they can get out of hand. They are scared to death of me though. I've made it that way. First, I tried to make them disgusted with me. That didn't work, that just seemed to turn them on more.

CL - So what did you do?

G - Well, I told one of them, a regular that I knew would pass the word around. I said "if you want to commit the perfect crime," I said, "you can kill me." He was a little puzzled so he kept asking the right questions, and I took out my buck knife and handed it to him closed and I said "look, I have no family, no one would even care, but there is only one catch. If you don't do it right the first time, I am going to kill you instead." So he took off like a bat out of hell, and word got around and they've never bothered me again after that. So I can walk down there at four in the morning, because I collect their old beer bottles, and they never bother me. That is just fine, and that's what I was hoping for.

See that little hole right there? There used to be an old man, I don't know how he could fit in that place, it's tiny. Have you checked that out? It's really short, but he managed, somehow. That was just before I got here, I was told about him from the storage unit owner.

CL - So, there's cruising in that place at four in the morning?

G - Oh yeah, on a warm day, it happens all day and all night.

CL - I understood that it had specific hours, like, from two until six in the afternoon.

G - No, they hang out in that park all night, all night long, they consider that their park. They definitely do. Sometimes the cops have to patrol through there to cut down on the sex and nude sunbathing. Some even come up here, on these platforms. There used to be another building right over there for trucker storage, they used to trespass at night and crawl around inside. That building was just torn down, I believe it was just this spring. You'll see where that empty space is between those two rows of trees, where you now have the porcelain pieces on the ground everywhere.

CL - Was it the same building that housed the porcelain?

G - I don't really know. There is probably all kinds of stuff, old stuff through here and the years, I'm not sure when this was all put up. I'm not sure who the original owner of this is.

CL - C.P. Rail just sold it recently, and they had owned it since the turn of the century. Before that it was parceled. From what I understand, the lease requirement was such that C.P. Rail did not want to pay property taxes on it, so you could rent it for a dollar a year if you were to pay the property taxes. So people got some really great deals. But the requirement was that once you vacated, you were responsible for destroying the buildings.

G - Someone had hired a cleanup crew the last time I stayed here, and they were about to tear this down on me, and the crew made a phone call to somebody, and they told them to leave me alone and that I was okay there. It was good, because there are not too many places where I could do this in the city. The Ravines are just too dangerous, too many people looking for trouble. There has also been a tree disease around for the last few years that is killing off all the trees. This means that there are a lot of falling trees. If you've been down in the ravine lately, you'll see a lot of the falling trees have made the erosion really bad. A lot of the trails have been fenced off. Erosion is really bad, some of the houses around here had backyards last summer, and now they are just hanging on the edge, that much has gone. So if they are going to be building, they should be building as far from the edge as possible or they are just going to lose their buildings.

There used to be a row of trees along the railroad, and that used to hide me from everybody. They just come through one day, with a machine and a big shear on it, and just sliced them all down, mulched them. Now, everybody knows, everybody that walks through here knows about this now. One time it was a secret, except for the queers down there who would walk all the way over here ever since I built it. Their main place is on the other side of the buildings, over by where the welding place was. There used to be another building over there, but it burned down. They made metal cabinets, and they used to do welding in there too. I used to hear the welding in there. I'm a welder, that's one of my trades, so I recognize the sounds and the smell of steel and everything. One day it just torched, I wasn't around when it did. Even when I had a place to live for a while and I had my bike, I used to come through here looking for bottles, for extra money to get through school. That's when I noticed it. I don't know if it was an accident or not. Kids probably, the kids do a lot of damage around here, I was asked to watch for them, they spray painted all over the trucks of the storage unit, they do a lot of damage. That's why I am more welcomed here then not, because my presence scares people off from doing that kind of stuff. The cops come in here too, every night they come here and have their coffee breaks, they never bother me. On the street they will, they will tear open my bag and throw everything all over the place, everything all over the place.

CL - Why is that?

G - Power tripping. The cops love to power trip, it's obvious. As soon as they see my tent and my sleeping bag, it's obvious that I'm homeless, and they just want to give me a hard time about it. So I call their shift supervisor and the same cop doesn't give me a hard time again. They are usually the younger cops that cause the most problems. I can just get sick of them, and living like this.

When I was seven years old, I started to become an adult. I used to hang around in a hippie hostel and get high and everything. The things that I have seen happening, it changed my perspective of life right there. I was raised by children's aid too, so I started recognizing their bullshit right away. I was told by these hippies — or what I call hippies, this was in '69 so I guess they were still called hippies — I was told that life isn't like what children's aid was. They said that life could be better than that. They proved it to me at that time. It was quite an inspiration for me. I'm usually not like this, once in while I fall into a rut.

They have their own section of town, Church and Welsley area and all that, they seem to be invading all over the place, it gets me quite riled really. Even when I lived in the east end, Main and Danforth area, they were even coming into that area. I even found out last month that the person who I thought was my only friend in the city, just because I was down and out he offers me money for services of a sexual nature. So that was really hard because I thought he was my friend. I left right away. He was the super of a building that I used to live in, and we got to be friends, and he never gave any indication when I went to go visit him. He gets drunk a lot and he breaks his appliances all the time, and I seem to have the ability to fix things. I do that for him, and so I just dropped by to see if he needed any help, and I don't drink alcohol. I quite drinking in the late eighties, but he convinced me to have a beer. And he figures that I was going to feel something off of it, and when I was about half done, that's when he started to make a pass, and I said, "No, Tom, you know that I'm not like that. Right." But he kept pressuring me. I left, I didn't even finish my beer. I never have gone back. I have nothing else to say to him. That's about all.

The wildlife seems to be disappearing around here, all the raccoons and everything. The raccoons got to know me, my scent. I wasn't allowed to reach out and touch them, but they would come up right up to my feet as long as I didn't make any sudden moves; they were just foraging for food. Sometimes they would fight, when one captures another one high up in a tree, and sometimes they go at it for hours, until I have to chase the aggressor away so I can get some sleep. I never get any appreciation for it, the other one just sits up there all night anyway. It gets really loud, it sounds like about a hundred little kids crying and whining at the same time, that's how loud it gets. Sort of the sound that they emit when they are angry. They seem to be disappearing. There used to be a fox that came across my house every night. He would run up and jump on my roof, hit the concrete, and take off from there. It was usually at night, so I couldn't tell where he was going. Foxes are beautiful, though. I haven't seen him here since I've been back, he used to come through every night. There are a couple of gophers over there, there are a few holes along the tracks. I used to have a path that went over to the gopher holes, but some guy who brought in all the garbage junk, he took care of that. There was a gopher hole right in there. It doesn't bother me, but I guess that if it's a good place for a gopher to live, it's a good place for me to build my thing. Animal instincts. We are animals, even though we are human species.

CL - So why did you chose this place to build your shack?

G - I chose this spot because of the two trees. It was shaded and camouflaged a little bit, like I said, with that row of trees that used to be there. I first discovered this spot when me and an ex-girlfriend had broken up, one of us had to leave, and she couldn't leave, she had no place to go, so I came down here from Brampton and I just slept on a piece of wood just over there. Actually, that is the same piece of wood just over there. My first night here, and then I realized that I could probably stay here for a while as long as no one knew about it, and it was sometime later that I met the storage guy and he didn't seem to mind, so that's when I built up the shelter and made it waterproof. Once I had official permission to stay here, I would just take plate numbers of people that are dumping their garbage here. It was almost like I was security. I watched the trucks over there too. Well, if anything happened, I would have been the first to get blamed for it, and I'd get kicked out of my shelter. I don't need that, I'm not a criminal, I wouldn't be living like this if I was. It might be something that I've thought about from time to time, but it's not something that I'm going to go out and look for an opportunity. I'm too busy.

233
site divine
on-site ten
interview with
George

on-site eleven *interview with*
Christopher Gagosz

Friday May the 9th at 1:00 p.m., 1997

Christopher Gagosz is a well-known cultural historian within the underground artist scene of Toronto. He is actively involved in the research of new ways to view history. His focus has been primarily on the spirit of people, both of the past and of the present. He has researched the migration of French speakers in North America, as well as the culture of the modern bank robber. Some people in the artistic community refer to Gagosz as an urban shaman, or a wise man who constantly observes the spiritual results of societal shifts. Similar to shamans of the past, Gagosz is a person whom artists regularly approach to find out what is happening in the world and what he thinks these things could mean. Although Gagosz would prefer to call himself a historian, his language and observations betray his self-imposed definition, and allude to an occupation that is very different from our accepted definition of a cultural historians. When I met Gagosz, he was frantically taking notes regarding the site as his dog Bella roamed in the distance. I asked him to tell me about his impressions of the site.

Christopher Gagosz - Well, before I came to the site, I don't know the neighborhood, so I just drove around the block, and you can see here on the North part it is a neighborhood; it's a beautiful neighborhood in fact. I think it's a

site divine
*on-site eleven
interview with
Christoapher
Gagosz*

Christopher Gagosz
documents some of
his observations

lovely neighborhood. Although you can see that the houses are slowly giving way and they are turning into businesses, law offices, and such and such. On the South side you've got, well, one of the most prestigious tennis clubs in the city. There are a few large corporate law offices abutting onto Yonge Street, and then you have the whole Yonge Street Village. Right, so it's a nice neighborhood, and then you have this place, which many people would consider a hideous waste land. So, I think what is interesting is to say . . . a lot of times you see a wealthy neighborhood being buttressed by a wasteland to protect it, and that is certainly not the case here. But I think that the question about negative spaces like this, negative spaces in the language of a developer — who considers this a waste of land — is how this negative space contributed to the atmosphere in this whole neighborhood, and I'm sure it has. I'm sure that all of these people have benefited from this being here, or maybe they have hated it here. It seems like negative space like this is often a benefit. So then the next step, I guess, is to decide what to do with it. And realizing that in doing something, you would be invading it. You're invading something.

CL - The question I would like to ask before deciding what to do with the land is to ask what would be suggested of the site, or what is significant about the site that we should incorporate into the discussion of what it was that we should do, which is why you are here. You are here to tell me what is significant about the site in the present.

CG - My approach is typically historical, cause I consider myself a historian. I consider the social history and the history of the people, so I would consider the history of the region. You know, I think that's an important thing to consider, how the dynamic of spaces evolve with people. Now, this land looks like an incredibly abused piece of land; you don't have to be a shaman to feel it in your gut, when you walk around here there is this giant electric lady here, that makes you kind of feel nauseous in your gut. You don't even need to know that it is there, you can feel it. You can look on the ground, it's seeping with toxic soil. Right. You can look around you and see the buildings, this place has been used for industry for a long time. I gather they have a policy where they would tear down the buildings after using them. So this land has been used and discarded, used and discarded, over and over again, and it's pretty obvious just walking around. What I wanted to say is that you can approach the land in steps. I think that it is important to be sensitive to the land, and consider it's various energy fields, or what human spirits have imbued the site, or whatever, and also to help understand what goes on this site. I don't know if you know this, but this is a pretty heavy cruising zone in the back here, for men to fuck each other in the park. That doesn't mean that you want to build a spa, you know. But they are all things that are probably worth considering, in being sensitive to what the site is. Well, I know that you already know this, and I know that this is what your perspective is as a designer, or you wouldn't be talking to me. So what I want to say is, you have to be honest. You have to consider that whatever you do here on the site is an act of will. That's what designing must be, right? It must be an act of will; it's an act of creation, so no matter how sensitive you are to what I say, or to the site, or to the psychic readings, or to the history, ultimately you are making an act of will to create something, and whatever you create will take on its own energy. The negative energy that I might be experiencing in this site, especially towards the back, psychically, is probably due to fifty or more years of very impersonal cruising and sex by men who are often in very serious denial, cause they live in this neighborhood with wife and children and that sort of thing. So there's a negative energy, but the minute you build something here and raze this forest, that's not going to happen anymore. You have to accept that, and not hide behind your design.

CL - Should we make any sort of recognition of those energies and such at all? I mean, in doing an analysis of this site, or any site, looking at the intangibles of the site, how should we incorporate the intangibles, how should we recognize them, what should we do with those new understandings that the site gives us? Are we going to be saying simply that the land is empty and ready for us to lay upon our meaning? When you raze all that exists here now, true, it will change all this, but is there any type of residue that we need to incorporate into designing? One of the stories that one of the gay cruisers shared with me is that cruisers are animals of instinct, animals of nature, that they continue to haunt places long after the reason that they originally went there changed. An example was that prior to the construction of Holt Renfrew in downtown Toronto, that neighborhood used to be the gay district. Holt Renfrew completely changed that, but Holt Renfrew itself became incorporated into that spatial location and became a cruising zone completely against the wishes of Holt Renfrew. They had to construct cruise-proof bathrooms. They made the bathrooms with shorter hallways, fewer urinals, smaller stalls, and the stalls where more open and less private.

CG - Well, just by walking around the neighborhood, when you are checking out a site and considering what the dynamics are around the site and in the site, it doesn't make good business sense to pretend that the outside world doesn't exist when you're building your design. This site has been a cruising site for a hell of a long time, so, on the one hand, you can say that you can't nurture that because the whole aesthetic of the cruisers here is that it's a dirty, anonymous place where you can hide, so you can't develop that into anything other than what it already is. But maybe that's not true, maybe you're looking at a market that should be fairly gay positive. I say market very intentionally, because I think that one of the big problems with idealistic new age shamans and other people who claim to be intuitive is that they think about moving towards a perfect world where we would all be sensitive to the spiritual background of lands where we would consider what is sacred, and respect those sorts of things that are not respected by the market at all. And then, when these people have to work with architects and doctors, they have to realize that the architects and doctors can't afford those same morals. It's tragic because I think that the marketplace is precisely the place where you should be bringing those ideas. If you stood here and you had all your shamans come here and your dowsers come here and tell you things, and then you incorporate those ideas with your communication with the community around here, I'm sure that they would have a powerful interest in what becomes of this site, particularly since there is a community already here.

239

site divine
*on-site eleven
interview with
Christoapher
Gagosz*

CL - The community has been very involved in determining what the actual design looks like. It has gone through twenty years of work with the community. So, community input on that level has been really important. And this is one of the reasons that the site has maintained the status it has for the last twenty years when the development pressures have been astronomical. But I don't necessarily know if the community itself brought people here who claim to have a higher degree of sensitivity to the space.

CG - Well, they must by virtue of the fact that they live here, right? They are sensitive, maybe not to this piece of land that we are standing, but in terms of this as an ecosystem. That includes their neighborhood, their social ecosystem, they must know these things. In North America it must be weird to be a designer, because modern designers are not like a Gaudi or a Michelangelo. First of all, you have a deadline within your lifetime, probably by the end of the year, and your culture is very different. A guy like Gaudi or Michelangelo, whatever they thought had to be necessarily rooted in their culture and their lands. They grew up there, their whole culture originated in that soil, like native inhabitants of the Americas whose cultures have been largely lost to themselves. As a North

American, you're looking at your land and asking, "what's the basis we have to this land?" As individuals, we may get back to nature or even encourage others to get back to nature, but as a culture that we participate in, we do nothing of the kind. There is nothing seeped in history for us. My ancestors go back one generation. There is nothing sacred to my blood about this land.

<Train Passes>
 I love trains.

CL - Why? What effect do trains have?

CG - Romance man! Oh yeah, can't you feel it? It's like an awesome sense of power. I guess romance is the wrong word, it's lust. One lusts for the throbbing that comes through the ground. It's such a visceral feel. I like to ride boxcars, and so when I see a train like that I just want to hop on and go up north. But in terms of living here it must be a really irritating thing for some people, and a really romantic thing for other people, the sound of trains going by.

CL - So, in being culturally aware and by claiming an intuitive nature that tells you about the lands that you pass, what is your intuitive nature of this site?

CG - Yeah, just a second, I don't know.

CL - You were talking a lot before about this sense of the gut, this sense of intuition and the validity of that, and I think that you can rightfully question other people's declaration of a special sensitivity when you claim to have the same sensitivity, and you claim that everyone has that intuitive sense.

CG - Well, anybody can. People who claim to have a higher degree of sensitivity are cool, because they focused on it, right? Through many various rituals, people have come to sensitize themselves to an environment. People can sensitize themselves to peoples bodies by dowsing. These guys are great, and they should be considered as having not magic, but something we all have, and they have used a structure to develop their sensitivity to things. That's great. My gut says leave this alone, leave it as a forest. That won't happen. So who cares what I might say?

CL - We are not talking about what will or will not happen, we are talking about what you suggest, what is significant for the site for you.

CG - What's significant to this site for me is the fact that there is nobody here, and that's why it is significant for the guys who cruise this place, too. That's why there are birds here. It's a toxic wasteland and it's still full of birds. Where else are they going to go? We are in the middle of the city with four million people. To be truly honest, I would want this to be a forest. Not a park, but a forest. Wild, with weeds and shit growing. And I like that there are vagabonds here. If I was God I would rip up all the concrete and turn it into a bird sanctuary, but that won't happen.

CL - We are not talking about what will happen, we are talking about you.

CG - Well, that's what I think should happen. I think they should leave the place alone, and I think that anybody who lives in this neighborhood has benefited from the fact that it has been a wasteland, even if they never come here. Totally if they have never come here.

CL - Why is that?

CG - I don't know. I don't know the neighborhood well enough, it's just something that I feel to be true. Space is like a pause. You can't understand a sentence if there are no pauses. The fact that this neighborhood is here is based integrally on this space. This space is an integral feature in this neighborhood, whether people realize it or not. So I think what is exciting for a designer who has the opportunity to look at a giant space like this, an incredible space, and then they consider the social ecosystem and the urban planning notions that they apply, and those sorts of things, then it becomes exciting because you can include these people in knowing their space, and you can teach them of the significance of a pause, and have them teach you about what the space is. I think that is beautiful. I think that is far more interesting then having Runnymede come in and do a design. Obviously, the people in the neighborhood think the same way, because they stopped them. Or whoever the development corporation is . . . Marathon. I love this notion that we have control over the land that we live in. I think that Europeans, for one, have always assumed that. They will sit there and tell you "My family has been here for a thousand years, fuck you. We've enjoyed the view of this vista for a thousand years and we are going to continue to." Maybe that feeling is disappearing now, but when I was a kid in Europe, I noticed that it was that attitude that made urban landscapes so much different there than in North America, that people felt a personal propriety over not just their own

241

site divine
*on-site eleven
interview with
Christoapher
Gagosz*

lands, but their whole lands, their neighborhood, their cities, their views and vistas. These sorts of things. *<climbs into homeless shack>*

CL - What do you think about the homeless people here on the land? You just went inside the homeless guy's house.

CG - Well, what's fun about going into a dwelling like that is that you're in a wasteland. This is a wasteland, and someone has created a sacred space. When you come up to it, it feels sacred. I'm not talking about energy fields or anything like that, it's that someone has built it and made it sacred. It's also how they built it. The door hides the occupant, and when you approach you can't tell if someone is inside. Or the fact that they have collected rainwater, or that with these pathways they've ordered it to suit their needs. They've got piles of shit — you know, garbage — in orderly places around their dwelling, and they just made it into a space that has a quiet, sacred nature to it. I think you have to see these things to be able to feel that, and I think that anybody who sees those things can probably feel that if they just stop and think about it. The thing I like about the other homeless shack over there that is not as built or ordered, is that there is a guy there right now. That's totally cool. I remember as a kid, I grew up in Athens, and where I lived I could walk across the street, up a hill, and down a valley and there were shepherds in little shepherd shacks everywhere, and I used to go there, and I used to go in shacks and they were empty and there was the smell of their leather coats and their shepherds stuff hanging around. It was very exciting and mystical for me. But it was also very important now, when I think about it in retrospect, how important it was to actually have shepherds in walking distance from my house, which was in the middle of a city, a huge city. That's all gone now, of course. It's now a suburb, there's nothing there now. There were gypsies there too, in those valleys, with houses made out of tin cans that were cut and flattened and sewn together with wire, with plastic tarps and all this kind of shit. These people were amazing, and they lived in a gigantic valley that was a wasteland, like this kind of place, that was full of garbage, and they lived this nomadic existence. Sometimes the village would be full of people, I'm talking about a village made from this kind of structure, like a shantytown. Sometimes they would be there, and sometimes they would go off. I was too young to understand what they did for money, for their survival. I know that sometimes they would be there and there would be forty people, and other times it would be almost deserted, maybe an older woman or man would be there minding the place.

CL - So, tell me what you think about the railway station here?

CG - Oh, sorry, that was a digression eh? You're very polite in your interviews. The railway station. I don't know, it's beautiful. I mean, it's not a railway station, it's a liquor store, a very beautiful liquor store with a dropped ceiling, where you can no longer see any of the architectural wonders. And you don't get the sense of connection that used to exist as people passed through this building under the railway tracks from the loading docks over to the entrance. Well, that happens. I think it's probably the most beautiful liquor store in the city, and I go there a lot. They are open late. It's hard to say, what do you want? It's not a train station and it will probably never be a train station. It would be nice if somehow the space would have been respected, but the gigantic fifty foot ceiling is a waste of heat, it's expensive, so they've made an economic decision. I don't know what to say, this is where we get into the issue that I was talking about before, and that is getting the shamans, the dowsers, and feng shui masters out into the marketplace and trying to complete one of the basic exercises of grow- ing up, which is trying to salvage as many of your values as possible before you die. It's a losing battle, for most people. Every now and then you meet someone who's actually managed it and they have that childlike enthusiasm about life, and everybody is jealous of them. I think it's all a process. Like looking at this land, and looking at these beautiful buildings both analytically and intuitively, with an acceptance that we live in a capitalist society, that the market has to be incorporated into everything else that we've talked about, the spirit of the land, the divine nature of the place, the intuitive significance of the ecosystem within which the land is located, all these sorts of things. How is it going to be paid for, what money interest can be brought to bear? This happens to be one of the wealthiest neighborhoods in the city, and you could convince, I bet, a lot of people here that have money and power and influence would agree that this site should be used for something a little more ecological. But they have a lot of park space already, don't they?

CL - Yes they do, there's a park right at the end of this property at David Balfour Ravine. Does that give pause?

CG - Yes, yes, that is a nice park. Then I guess I can't answer you about a 'what should be done' because I don't know, I really don't know.

site divine
on-site eleven
interview with
Christoapher
Gagosz

CL - That is not the question that I meant to ask. The question that I meant to ask is, what is significant now, just in the present? We can decide to invoke the market, but we can also decide not to, it is your prerogative as to what is significant about the site now.

CG - If you want to be real — and that is the most important thing to me — you have to consider what the market says, and there is a growing optimistic trend among economists for eco - economic sense, for turning the environment into a economically viable thing, using the rainforest in Brazil as an economically viable thing. Eco-tourism, all these sorts of things. Great. Whether it's going to succeed is another thing. All the shamans, feng shui masters, and dowsers can't ensure that these things succeed, the market will make that determination.

CL - So you're saying in many ways in reference to this land, is that what is significant to this land is . . .

CG - That there isn't a building. It is useless. You can't even start talking about what is significant about this land because the market will come in and trounce whatever is significant if it is economically unviable. My feelings and ideas regarding this land are not an issue of consideration because of that. I can't even go there. Whereas a lot of the other shamans that I know who are so non-market derived might be very successful in talking about the significance of the site because they don't have to invoke the market at all, in their own life and in the things that they do, which is great for themselves, but it makes them useless for others. That is why these people are great, we need them to be useless. My pendulum or my magical guide has always been my dog, Bella. Bella roams around, and she loves this place. She loves it because there are weeds growing here, because there are all kinds of smells that she doesn't get in the city. And we are in the city. She doesn't say anything specific, she says something general. She loves it. It's not like here is something different from there. That's what an ecosystem means. You know as they say, even though I don't know much about these sorts of things, but they always say that if you drive a road through a forest, you split the ecosystem in two. The fact that there is a giant parking lot there is integral to the fact that there is a rich spot there. Like birds, they need both thickets and meadows, a place to hunt and a place to fly. So yeah, the land is one space, it's all one space. So anything I say in reference to Bella is in reference to the one space, not any specific part of it. I mean, we can watch her, we could watch her and see that she may have liked certain areas more than others. She likes this kind of grass sometimes; she likes diversity really. That's why she likes abandoned fields, because they have much more diversity than a park, with their ChemLawn grasses and all that shit. <*Laughs*>

When you consider the significance of the fact that we abut onto Balfour Park, and we are in between these two amazing places, this park, Yonge Street Village, this beautiful train station, the neighborhood on the north side, and the tennis club on the south side. That whatever you do here, you have the opportunity to select a flow here. Spatial flow, traffic flow. If you open up the fence that surrounds this site, you will open up the spatial and social ecosystem of the site, literally. This site is an integral barrier between the two neighborhoods. The ecosystems are maintained because of this site. You know, I think that a community has a saturation point where they can only be so large and still be conscious of community, which is a big problem in the United States — where I went to high school — and which is why Toronto, with it's understanding of neighborhoods and their collections of spatial concepts, remains one of the most livable cities in North America. People are able to say, "I have these boundaries and I live within them." This site is such a boundary. Once you break the boundaries, people lose their sense of community. As a socially conscious designer, one would think that you would want to connect people, and that your raison d'être coming here to this site would be to create the flow of people, the exchange of ideas, the promotion of humanity and peace on earth, when in fact you could be undermining something that is very special, something that is already there.

CL - Which is why we need to do this, which is why this is so important. A designer might have the best of intentions, but that is why we need people like you, who call themselves urban shamans, to come in.

CG - Well, I think everybody has the best of intentions, it all depends on how they value different things. I totally agree with you, people do the dumbest things with the best of intentions.

CL - Can magic help us in making our intentions reflect a realistic future?

CG - I think magic is important and it should be a part of everyday life, but you have to imbue your space and make it sacred in your own way. You need to be realistic, and be comfortable in cutting out the magic in favor of realism.

245

site divine
on-site eleven
interview with
Christoapher
Gagosz

Magic was never about the unreal, it was always about becoming closer to reality. Every designer should consider that in building anything, as I said in the very beginning, it is an act of will, you are creating a space and you are imbuing it with whatever sacred nature that you want. It's not integral to the land itself oftentimes. You are changing it. You are even changing the spiritual nature of the land based upon what you feel.

CL - Should you respect in any way or even try and figure out the spiritual nature of the land prior to construction, or is that useless because you will be laying you own spiritual nature onto the land?

CG - Well, I think in North America, being spiritually bankrupt that we are, you should have to connect yourself to the spiritual history of this land, unless you were some powerful and charismatic human being. I think that anything that is believable to yourself and therefore has a chance of being sacred would have to be grounded in something that preceded you, and your will.

CL - Is there something different between the spiritual history and the social history?

CG - No, I think they are pretty connected, which is why I consider myself both an urban shaman and a social and cultural historian, more so a historian, but both of them because they are integral to one another.

CL -What would the difference be, even the slightest difference?

CG - Well, there's a huge difference in the sense that on this site, the social history would be the gay cruising area, and the spiritual history would date back to the Iroquois Indians and the Seven Nations Tribes. Balfour Park is a very important valley for natives whose culture and mysticism has evolved together over thousands of years, from human experience on this land. *<shouting>* THIS LAND, ALL OF THIS LAND. So it is far more compelling, just like the Italians, and their culture and religion derived from their land over thousands of years. My Polish-Irish background didn't evolve in that way, which is why I love this land here. I love this land because it has that tower, which is a replica of a tower in Venice. Right. I love the tower because it is a ruin. The ruins are the cultural and spiritual history of this land, and I derive my culture and spirituality from this land.

247
site divine
on-site eleven
interview with
Christoapher
Gagosz

Part Three   chapter seven *designing in the living earth*

"And the Lord God formed us of the dust of the ground and breathed into our nostrils the breath of life and we became a living soul."

Genesis II:7

The Earth is alive. Humankind's awareness of the Earth as a living being, an awareness that played an important role in our past, was dramatically revived when astronauts could, for the first time, look at our planet from outer space. The photographs of the Earth brought back by the astronauts became powerful new symbols for the modern environmental movement and forever changed our relationship with the Earth. What the astronauts and many others back on Earth before them realized intuitively is now being investigated by scientific theories as described in great detail by the Gaia theory of Dr. James Lovelock. In looking for a contemporary set of ideals to compliment divination, it is important that we examine the relatively new theory of Gaia that has been developed by Lovelock.

These theories suggest that the Earth not only teems with life, but also seems to be a living being in its own right. All life on Earth, together with the atmosphere, oceans, and soil, forms a complex system whose patterns may be characteristic of self-organization. In support of this idea, Gaia theoreticians point out that the Earth persists in a remarkable state of chemical and thermodynamic disequilibrium that through a wide variety of processes regulates the planet to maintain the optimal conditions for life. In its self regulation, theorists argue that the Earth functions not like an organism but rather seems to be an

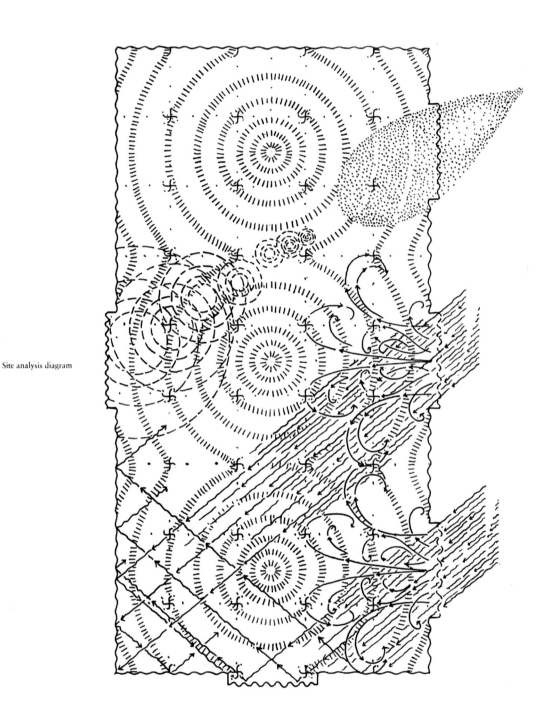

Site analysis diagram

organism — Gaia. Gaia's properties and activities cannot be predicted from the sum of her parts; each of her parts is linked to every other part and all are mutually interdependent; her many systems of communication are non-linear and highly complex; her form has evolved over billions of years and continues to evolve to this day. These observations were made within a scientific context, but go far beyond science. Similar to many other aspects of this new paradigm based on divination, these gaian observations reflect a profound awareness that is ultimately spiritual.

The Gaia theory holds that the Earth can be described as a vast, autopoietic system of many components, all of which have evolved together to enhance and regulate conditions for the perpetuation of life. Stated more precisely, all the life forms of the planet are part of Gaia. The life forms of the Earth in their diversity coevolve and contribute interactively to produce and sustain the optimal conditions for the growth of the larger whole. For example, the Earth has maintained a fairly constant surface temperature throughout the evolution from cell to complex organism, similar to the way a warm-blooded organism maintains a constant body temperature in spite of varying environmental conditions. All are regulated by intricate cooperative networks that exhibit the properties of self-organizing systems. Similar patterns of self-regulation can be observed in the chemical composition of the atmosphere and in the concentration of salt in the oceans. The Earth has regulated itself to maintain an atmospheric oxygen level at close to 20 percent for several hundred million years. If, however, this level were to fluctuate to even 25 percent, a single spark could ignite a conflagration that would sweep across the globe. If the oxygen level was 15 percent or less, lighting a match would be impossible. Geologic evidence indicates that for the same length of time that the atmospheric oxygen level has hovered at 20 percent, the salinity of the ocean has remained remarkably constant at somewhat less than 10 percent of saturation. This fact is particularly remarkable because dissolved minerals have been transported by water from land deposits towards the oceans almost since the Earth was formed. No satisfactory explanation has been advanced for this constancy, which affects all life on Earth. Lovelock is careful to note that the planet's self-regulation is not guided by a higher consciousness. In the same way divination and geomancy are intuitive frameworks to examine and investigate the processes occurring on a site, Gaia is essentially an intuitive framework used to represent the larger-scale ecological processes occurring on the planet.

The contemporary idea of Gaia was born of a question Lovelock asked himself when he looked at the planets of our solar system. That question was:

"why was the Earth different?" Research concerning the chemical analysis of the Venusian atmosphere yielded figures of 95-96% carbon dioxide, 3-4% nitrogen, with traces of oxygen, argon and methane. The atmospheric analysis results returned for Mars were similar, ranging from 95.3% carbon dioxide, 2.7% nitrogen, 1.6% argon, and only 0.15% oxygen. In comparison, the Earth's atmosphere is presently 77% nitrogen, 21% oxygen, with trace amounts of carbon dioxide, methane, and argon. Lovelock wanted to understand the complex processes at work within the terrestrial atmosphere that had occurred for many billions of years in the hopes that they would explain this uniqueness.

In the late 1960's, Lovelock began to answer these questions by considering the beginnings of life on the planet Earth. The earliest of life-forms existed in the ancient oceans and were the smallest and the simplest — less than single-celled. Contemporary microbiological research points to the fact that almost 3 billion years ago, bacteria and photosynthetic algae began extracting the carbon dioxide from the atmosphere and, in turn, releasing oxygen back into it. Gradually, over vast geological time spans, the Earth's atmospheric chemical content was altered away from the dominance of carbon dioxide and towards a mixture of nitrogen and oxygen, creating an atmosphere that would favorably support organic life that was powered by aerobic combustion. It was at that point that Lovelock began to formulate a method of explanation that argued that the Earth was a planet that had been transfigured and transformed by a self-evolving and self-regulating living system. In view of this self-evolution and self-regulation, the Earth seemed to qualify as a living being its own right. In a similar way to site divination's criticism of reductionistic modern design, Lovelock is critical of the reductionist tendencies of science, and its inability to investigate the larger systemic issues of the Earth.

Gaia theory is about the evolution of a tightly coupled system whose constituents are the biota and their material environment, which comprises the atmosphere, the oceans, and the surface rocks. Self-regulation of important properties, such as climate and chemical composition, is seen as a consequence of this evolutionary process. Like living organisms and many closed-loop self-regulating systems, it would be expected to show emergent properties; that is, the whole will be more than the sum of its parts. For more than a century students of the evolution of the living and non-living parts of the Earth have known that life influences the physical and chemical characteristic of the planet. Nevertheless, the dominant paradigm in earth sciences has been that inexorable inorganic forces, such as changing energy output from the Sun, collisions of the Earth with extraterrestrial bodies, continental drift, or other orbital element variations have been the principal driving forces behind climate twenty years ago. (Gaia: A New Look at Life on Earth, Chapter One page 30.)

To assist Lovelock with his understanding of the role that microorganisms play in the evolution of Gaia, he contacted Dr. Lynn Margulis, an expert in microbiology. As a collaborator in the development of the Gaian theory, Margulis contends that symbiosis, not chance mutation, is the driving force behind evolution, and that the cooperation between organisms and the environment rather than competition among individuals is the chief agent of natural selection. She stated that "Darwin's grand vision was not wrong, only incomplete." In accentuating the direct competition between individuals for resources as the primary selection mechanism, Darwin created the impression that the environment is simply a static arena for a series of gladiatorial combats, the victors of which are crowned fittest. In a closer approximation to reality, Margulis argues that the environment is not a static consideration in evolution, but is instead a driving and invested force. These are therefore the two fundamental components of Lovelock and Margulis's Gaia theory, the idea that the planet is, in Margulis' words, a "super organismic system," and that evolution is the result of cooperative processes rather than competitive ones.

Almost twenty years after initially considering the nature of the living systems that are in operation within the terrestrial ecosystems in the book Gaia: A New Look at Life on Earth, Lovelock published a second book, The Ages of Gaia, in which, the interconnectedness of all natural terrestrial systems, rather than simply the atmosphere, was beginning to emerge. Lovelock's evolving and refining specification of the nature of Gaia theory is presented as such:

The name of the living planet, Gaia, is not a synonym for the biosphere — that part of the Earth where living things are seen normally to exist. Still less is Gaia the same as the biota, which is simply the collection of all individual living organisms. The biota and the biosphere taken together form a part but not all of Gaia. Just as the shell is part of the snail, so the rocks, the air, and the oceans are part of Gaia. Gaia, as we shall see, has continuity with the past, back to the origins of life, and in the future as long as life persists. Gaia, as a total planetary being, has properties that are not necessarily discernible by just knowing individual species or populations of organisms living together. Specifically, the Gaia hypothesis says that the temperature, oxidation, state, acidity, and certain aspects of the rocks and waters are kept constant, and that this homeostasis is maintained by active feedback processes operated automatically and unconsciously by the biota. You may find it hard to swallow the notion that anything as large and apparently inanimate as the Earth is alive. Surely, you may say, the Earth is almost wholly rock, and nearly all incandescent with heat. The difficulty can be lessened if you let the image of a giant redwood tree enter your mind. The tree undoubtedly is alive, yet 99% of it is dead. The great tree is an ancient spire of dead wood, made of lignin and cellulose by the ancestors of the thin layer of living cells which constitute its bark. How like the Earth, and more so when we realize that many of the atoms of the rocks far down into the magma were once part of the ancestral life of which we all have come. The Ages of Gaia (pages 19-27)

Skeptics argue that this Gaia was teleological, that it supposes the evidence of some intent or purpose in the nature of the biosphere, and that this was directly contradictory to the accepted position of the Darwinian evolutionary doctrine that supported natural selection. Lovelock countered these skeptics by saying that:

When the activity of an organism favors the environment as well as the organism itself, then its spread will be assisted; eventually the organism and the environmental change associated with it will become global in extent. The reverse is also true, and any species that adversely affects the environment is doomed; but life goes on.

As such, certain claims concerning the Gaia Hypothesis could not be refuted — in particular the claim that the biota has a substantial influence over certain aspects of the abiotic world. In Slanted Truths "Gaia and Philosophy," Margulis presents an expanded understanding of a global Gaian life system:

All life on Earth is a unified spatio-temporal system with no clear-cut boundaries. Encouraging our Biophilia, preserving blocks of bio-diversity before they are converted to concrete skyscrapers and asphalt parking lots, is a way of enhancing the possibility that human beings will persist into the future. This future may be indefinite, as some few species do not become extinct but 'scale back' and become symbio-genically attenuated and reintergrated into new forms of life and patterns of living organization. By allying ourselves more closely with once distant life-forms, by affiliating ourselves biophyletically, not only with the plants and animals whose ongoing demise weighs so heavily at present on our memory, but also with the waste-recycling, air producing, and water-purifying microbes we as yet take largely for granted, we may be able to aid in the flowering of earth life into the astronomically voluminous reaches of space. (Page 157.)

The root question of Gaia's critics and a central point in the theory concerns itself with the difference between a planetary environment that might only be the aggregate result of myriad independent life forms co-evolving and sharing the same host, and one that is ultimately created by life forms whose purpose is to fulfill the requirements of the larger being. Similar to the impossibility of making an accurate distinction between the site and the planet, recent scientific work in the field of complex systems has begun to give us the impression that this opposition of terms, the larger caused by its constituents, or the constituents created by the larger, is an opposition that is a construct of our own mind, and must be removed if we are to understand the truth.

Gaia and Divination

Ancient belief and modern knowledge have fused emotionally in the awe with which astronauts with their own eyes and we by indirect vision have seen the Earth revealed in all its shining beauty against the deep darkness of space. Yet this feeling, however strong, does not prove that Mother Earth lives. Like a religious belief, it is scientifically untestable and therefore incapable in its own context of further rationalization.

Dr. James Lovelock

The ancient beliefs governing divination agree with the general principles of the Gaia Hypothesis. The records of such belief as well as the worship of deities led to the naming of the hypothesis Gaia, an ancient term suggesting the soul and living spirit of the planet. As is obvious with the practice of divination, ancient peoples were cognizant of the basic principles that are explicitly expressed in the Gaia hypothesis. Though the Gaia hypothesis is a new incarnation of the belief that the Earth is a living being, it is not a unique or new concept. The ancient recognition of the nonlinear nature of all system dynamics is the very essence of ecological awareness as expressed in the Gaia hypothesis. The essence of Gaia's 'systemic wisdom' is the foundation of both divination and geomancy. The Gaian wisdom is characteristic of the wisdom of the ancient cultures, a wisdom that is neglected in our over-rational and scientifically mechanized society. Both the understanding of Gaia and the heritage of the ancients are based on a profound respect for the wisdom of nature.

The scientific community remains divided about the Gaia Theory. Many scientists argue that since they know of no way to test Gaia scientifically, it can be seen as little more than a metaphor that can help explain phenomena that can be explained in other, more technical terms. If the Gaia theory is only a metaphor, it remains a powerful one. Any good metaphor continues to instruct. For designers, the theory of Gaia proposes new questions and new ideas. As a metaphorical approach to the world, the Gaia theory is endlessly fertile and invites constant learning and interpretation. As a metaphor, the Gaia theory can serve as the framework for a new form of intuitive understanding. The most important thing that the Gaia theory proposes to govern our passage through time, is that we are immersed in and brought into being by a living reality, without intent or manifest destiny; we are completely dependent upon Gaia. Regardless of whether or not Gaia exists, the truth remains that the earth's atmosphere could occur only as the product of living systems, for the free oxygen that makes animal life possible would not continue without the steady activity of green plants. The Earth that we think of as a lifeless mass is undeniably the product of life processes over vast stretches of geological time.

Design based upon the modernist paradigm works against seeing the unity and connections suggested by an understanding of Gaia. Focusing on the reductionistic pursuit of narrow, functionalist goals, designers pay attention to only a fraction of the whole. Most modern designers block out peripheral concerns, and design without examining the larger picture. New design theoretics will evolve into a different spiritual structure when we realize, as the Gaia theory demands, that we are totally contained in and sustained by a single living system, in which all the parts are interconnected, and in which everything we do resonates within the whole. Nothing is fully localized. The Gaia theory is a reminder that the world we live in is a biologized world, a sacred and divine process that we all share. Clearly, the new insights of global, environmental, and ecological modeling afforded by the Gaia theory proposed by Lovelock and Margulis should open up an entirely new range of design theories, experimental programs, and interdisciplinary thought, most notably between the design disciplines of architecture and landscape architecture. For under the auspices of Gaia, designers can no longer treat the Earth as an inert mass, just as they can no longer treat a tree as ornamental decoration or a meadow as a piece of wall-to-wall carpeting.

Gaia is both mysterious and constantly changing; every encounter with the environment is an opportunity for learning. Our planet is not inert, every site on the planet is alive and part of the greater network of life, for the Earth continues to be shaped by life processes. An embrace of the Gaian theory can help to make these interconnections seem intuitively obvious. The Gaia theory offers site divination a basis for creating awareness of the interconnectivity of the Earth and proposes a fundamentally new way of design based on connections that are not yet explicit. The Gaia theory offers designers the spiritual structure for a new form of site design.

chapter eight *to design the site*

"To be in error and to be cast out is part of God's design."

William Blake

Site design is a method of design that privileges the systemic nature of site and designs accordingly. The act of designing a site, as opposed to objects, recognizes the importance of a site analysis and site divination in the design process. Instead of basing design on aesthetic precedents or ideological doctrines, site design attempts to design from the site. A divinatory approach to site design is by necessity interdisciplinary. This approach towards design has been neglected in our excessively rational, reductionistic, and Procrustean society. As with ancient divination, site design is based on a profound respect for the ways of nature. By understanding the theory of Gaia, any act of site design recognizes that the earth is alive and that our natural environment is inhabited by countless organisms that have co-evolved overbillions of years, continuously using and recycling the same molecules of soil, water, and air.

In this new approach to site design, the site must be understood in terms of the systemic processes that provide organization and structure. Although the site as a whole may exhibit well-defined regularities or patterns, the relationships between its components are never rigid. Individual characteristics of the site can be so unique, and behave so irregularly that they seem irrelevant to the order of the whole site. The systemic order of a site is achieved through coordinated activities that do not rigidly constrain the parts, but instead leave room for variation and flexibility. It is an understanding of this flexibility that enables site designers the ability to envision radically new designs with unforeseen functional requirements. This understanding of the nonlinear interconnectedness of the site is an essential part of successfully embracing site oriented design over object oriented design. Moreover, the systemic nature of the site illustrates the fallacy of modernistic architectural determinism, that characteristics and elements of site designs are equal to a machine, and controlled or dictated by the limited functional requirements set out at the beginning of the design process.

Site design makes it clear that buildings and their designers do not determine the functioning of a site as the gears and springs determine the working of a clock. In the long run, the structure and function of any design cannot be imposed by a designer, but is instead established by the site itself. This may suggest that designers play no role in determining the structure of the site, and while this is true in the long term, in the short term the designers dictate the rate of a site's evolution as well as the physical confines by which the site becomes defined. Divinatory traditions exhort their practitioners to transcend the notion of both an isolated self and an isolated site, and to understand that both are inseparable parts of the earth in which they are embedded. With this understanding, designers will realize that once they begin to evaluate a site for any design, they become an integral part of the site's definition, and that any evaluation of the site is also an act of self-evaluation. The site is not only a complex ecosystem in itself, but is also imbedded in Gaia. Gaia is a dynamic and integrated whole, composed of living sites. As integral components of the harmoniously functioning Gaia, living sites exhibit boundaries that are not equal to those imposed upon them in order to function within our social structure. The actual boundary between a site's context and the environment is difficult to ascertain; it is one that is invented, falsified, and imagined. The site boundaries developed from our economic system are an inherent falsehood, and are therefore major barriers to a full understanding of site design.

The tendency of sites to consist of multilevel ecosystems whose levels differ in their complexity exists throughout nature, and must be seen as a basic principle governing the design of sites. From an evolutionary point of view it is easy to understand why stratified, or multilevel ecosystems are so widespread in nature. These ecosystems evolve much more rapidly and have a much better chance of survival than non stratified ecosystems, because in cases of severe disturbances they can be reduced into their various subsystems without being destroyed. Non stratified ecosystems, on the other hand, disintegrate and must begin evolving again from their origin. Since ecosystems encounter many disturbances during their long history of evolution, nature has sensibly favored those which exhibit stratification. Site design encourages designers to design within levels of complexity that encourage the creation of multilevel ecosystems, as opposed to the common non stratified ecosystems that dominate our modern designs.

There are three patterns of organization in sites: structure, function, and integration. Structure is the organization of space, function is the organization in time, and integration is the interweaving of structure and function at levels of complexity that go beyond space and time. This recognition has very radical implications for designs. If designers separate the site from Gaia in which they are immanent and confine it to human individuals, they will see the environment as mindless and exploit it, just as modernism has done. Designers must realize that the environment is alive, and that all sites should be designed as multilevel structures whose complexity and integration provides for their survival.

Site Divine

In interactions with the environment, there is a continual interplay and mutual influence between the outer world and a person's inner world. The patterns we perceive are based in a fundamental way on the patterns within us. In the traditional Cartesian view, it was assumed that all individuals had the same biological apparatus, and that each of us had access to the same sensory perception. Differences were assumed to arise from the subjective interpretation of the sensory data. These differences were due, in the well-known Cartesian metaphor, to the "little man looking at the screen." Neurophysiological studies have shown that this is not so. The modification of sensory perception by experience, expectation, purpose, and intent occurs not only in the interpretation, but begins at the very outset, at the "gates of perception." The psychological aspects of perception cannot be separated from the psychological aspects of interpretation. Moreover, the new view of perception also blurs the conventional distinction between sensory and extrasensory perception by showing us that all perception is, to some extent, extrasensory. Responses to the environment, then, are determined not as much by the direct effect of external stimuli on biological systems, but rather by experience, expectation, purpose, and the symbolic interpretation of perceptual experiences. Thus, the inner and outer worlds are continually interlinked in the functioning of a human organism; they act upon one another and evolve together.

Understanding the complexity and subjectivity of perception will play a very fundamental role in the new holistic world view of site design. The systems approach has shown that living organisms are intrinsically dynamic, their visible forms being stable manifestations of underlying processes. The conceptual shift from structural analysis to perceptual analysis will lead us to discover a renewed unifying description of nature, leading to a fundamentally different understanding of the site. When we use our eyes to view the world, our brain transforms the vibrations of light into rhythmic pulsations of neurons; similar transformations of rhythmic patterns occur in the processes of hearing, smelling, feeling, tasting, and in all other acts of perception. The dominant Cartesian notion of a world composed of intrinsically separate objects has led us to assume that our senses create some type of internal picture that is a faithful reproduction of reality, but this is not how sensory perception works. Pictures of separate objects exist only in our world of symbols, beliefs, and ideas. The reality around us is continually changing, and our senses translate a fraction of these vibrations into frequency patterns that are in turn processed in recognizable symbols by the brain.

Most theories about perception that involve a discussion about the nature of consciousness are variations on one of two opposing views that may, nevertheless, be both complementary and reconcilable. The scientific view of perception considers matter primary, and consciousness a property of complex material patterns that emerge at a certain stage of biological evolution. Here, consciousness is a practiced state of being, and is not a given. The divine view of perception regards consciousness as primary and as the framework for all being. In this view consciousness is a given. In its purest form, consciousness, according to the divine view, is immaterial, formless, and void of all content. This manifestation of pure consciousness is associated with the divine in ancient spiritual traditions. It is the essence of the universe and manifests itself in all matter. The divine view of consciousness, based on the experience of reality in alternate modes of perception, allows the individual mind to grasp collective patterns of energy. As with quantum physics, divination understands material structures to be considered the secondary reality, while energy is the primary reality.

The whole being contained in each of its parts may be a universal property of nature. This idea, expressed in many traditions of divination, plays an important role in this contemporary vision of reality. Two basic themes emerge repeatedly from the study of the divine view of consciousness and the Gaia theory, and are also repeatedly emphasized in the teachings of divination — the universal interconnectedness and interdependence of all phenomena, and the intrinsically dynamic nature of reality. As in quantum science, divination involves the notion of multiple levels of reality that differ in their complexities and are mutually interacting and interdependent. Although divination goes far beyond the framework of contemporary science, it is consistent with the modern scientific understanding of mind and matter. Diviners recognize the importance of subtle energies as the basis of order in their worldly observations. The mutual interdependence of all aspects of reality and the nonlinear nature of interconnections are emphasized throughout divination. These ideas of process, change, and fluctuation are emphasized in the spiritual basis of site design.

For a comprehensive method of site design, two complementary approaches are needed: a reductionist approach to understand the detailed mechanisms, and an approach rooted in divination to understand the systemic integration of these mechanisms into the functioning of the entire system. Since the beginning of time, humans have intuitively sensed the existence of another phenomenon, a hidden world whose presence underlies the one we experience each day. The principle vehicles through which we explore our notions of this hidden world are religion, philosophy, and the arts. Religion is perhaps the most travelled path to this hidden world, but it is not the only one. For this reason great artists such as Picasso, Matisse, and Stravinsky constantly pursued the primitive in an attempt to find the divine. Ironically, this is also why Le Corbusier, the father of modernism in architecture, began his creed with a pictogram of the diurnal pathway of the sun. In the ultimate analysis, and with deep respect, it was this profound understanding of the divine that compelled Le Corbusier to create the chapel at Ronchamp. In site design, rationality, science, and the divine should act like the transparent layers of a palimpsest, with each element influencing both the layer above and the layer below. To disregard any layer of this palimpsest is to fail in creating designs that approach the world of the non-manifest, and as such diminishes life.

The impoverished architecture and landscape architecture designers create today is not simply due to the banality of the forms they construct, but is also due to the prosaic and mundane concepts they address. To try to understand the non-manifest, the hidden, the unseen, is to look deeply into our own selves. It is this that concerns the divine, which is what site design is ultimately concerned with. Otherwise designers are in danger of making only a mere superficial transfer and placement of forms, as the majority of them have done for the last century. The distinction between transfer and transformation is of fundamental importance. Understanding this distinction bears the wisdom of divination and suggests what site design can be. Transfer involves the simple creation and placement of forms. Transformation, on the other hand, involves an absorption, an internalization, and ultimately a reinvention of the site. For design is not created in a vacuum, it is created on a site, and it is the compulsive expression of beliefs central to our lives. Each is a transparent overlay that must affect any proposed design. The complete act of site design should recognize the explicit nature of these overlays and understand their relationships to one another.

Designers must reinvent themselves. All designers, architects, and landscape architects must regain that special position in society in which they serve as the role of the mediator between the mundane and the sublime, creating and activating form and space that is imbued with meaning and hope. Designers must insist that their essential role is to project a vision of life's special potentialities, giving wholeness to fragmented space. Designers must connect people to the divine, to time, to nature, and to other people in the spaces and places they build. That designers engage people imaginatively in the environment through their designs is a sacred and special task. Designers must become the modern diviners of place and time. To propagate the role of the architect or landscape architect as a "problem solver" is to disable their fundamental role, which is the creation of space. Designer's unique roles are to be the poets of space, form, and process. No line shall be drawn until the totality of the site is thoroughly defined and understood. Understanding this totality includes the task of divination. This understanding must flow from the internal reality of the designer to the external reality as expressed through his or her designs.

Every site has its own ingredients for magic, and the designer's task is to discover these ingredients. Designers should be prepared to handle the mental shifts required in divination, to achieving a thought process wherein a new balance between intention and a response to Gaia is possible. A dialogue between the intellectual traditions of scientism, spiritualism, and primitivism will do a great deal to inform and enrich designer's intellectual lives and therefore influence their designs. Uncertainty need not mean license or the lack of purpose or intent. To be alive, the process must continuously change so that preferred ideas of the past, present, and future do not freeze into formulas for mindless reproduction. The credo of site design must constantly change, otherwise its reproduction will spell its death. Site design must be based on a dialectic process of constant conceptual renewal. The ancients claimed that to search was to discover the divine; in actuality they may have meant that to search, err, and search again is to embody the divine.

Designers must continually strive to make something from the site. Designers must also understand that site design is the creation of life. Whereas architects have been traditionally critiqued as they strive to create structures that exist independent of any system, site designers create entire systems that are wholly dependent on the site that exists within Gaia. In the gestation of site, the future site designer will work within new frontiers where Gaia becomes the fundamental initiator of design. By relying upon Gaia and its ways, designers are being challenged to develop new techniques of design — solutions that are based on the site, and no longer based upon imposed ideologies and historic aesthetic precedents. It will rest with the designers, the diviners, and the scientists together to develop new and alternative processes of design.

chapter nine *to design eternally*

Design without religion is lame, design without science is blind.

anonymous

The contemporary codified body of site analysis emphasizes the scientific analytical methodologies of site analysis, continuing to uphold the modernistic heritage of privileging the object over the site. As explained throughout this book, modernism and the beliefs upon which modernism is founded repudiates the site and intuition as valuable parts of the design process. These beliefs, rationalism, scientism, and utility, should no longer be the sole spiritual underpinnings of design. The ancient values of spiritual integration through enlightened manifestation are values that need to be incorporated into the site and its design.

The critique of modernism is based upon a belief that modernism has grown beyond its theoretical foundation in design. Although the structure of scientific site analysis is extremely valuable under modernism, it does not represent the varied spectrum of site analysis tools and techniques developed by different cultures in different times. Time has shown us the value of divination. Used for thousands of years, divination is a system of distributing a spiritual land ethic. It is time to reappraise divination, in an attempt to reunite the intuitive and analytical understandings of the site. Geomancy as site based divination is the key to understanding and embracing that reappraisal.

The examination of augury, vastu, feng shui, and dowsing as forms of geomancy allow contemporary designers the ability to envision ritualistic methodologies that may assist them in the examination of a site. Although each form of geomancy is different, such that feng shui may be seen an analytical approach to site analysis based upon spiritual foundations and dowsing as a sensory approach to site analysis based upon scientific explanations, each form can provide ritualistic methodologies that can be incorporated into the design process. Throughout this investigation, it is important to remember that many of the traditional forms of divination are poorly served in their modern interpretations, which tend to be both inaccurate and inappropriate tools to instruct design. Traditional geomancy provides for a better philosophical understanding of humans' place in nature. Fundamental to this understanding is an awareness of the planet as a living being.

The survey of methods of site divination provides us with an alternative to design based upon programmatic constraints and requirements, sociotheological beliefs, and aesthetical precedents. Such an investigation is valuable because it provides both professionals and students with a wider range of tools to use when attempting site design, and an examination of site divination will likely encourage designs that are more site aware. In attempting to look at the site using various forms of site analysis, a more comprehensive understanding of the site is achieved. Allowing the site to speak through its various interpreters and realizing the value of the different voices is the primary motive of this investigation of site divination.

This book is not a discussion of the viability, applicability, successes or weakness of the different tools of site analysis. This book instead serves to illustrate the fact that each method of divination and its representative participant, as illustrated in the following section, has something unique to say about the site, and that, in time, with practice, rituals, and perseverance, designers can return to a process of design where they, too, will be able to elicit reactions from the site, and have something meaningful to say in return. Successfully presented, divination, with an understanding of the Gaian principle, will articulate the need for a new, broader perspective in site analysis and subsequent design work.

In the analysis of the Summerhill Lands, it is important for the reader rather than the author to undertake the task of evaluating the participants and their various perspectives. The reader must decide for his or herself which perspectives are valuable and which are not. The author will refrain from passing judgment on the participants, not because the author agrees with or believes everything that was said, but because in part, this book requires that the reader engages herself with the participants claims and passes any judgment on her own.

In the end, regarding the evaluation of the words of the participating diviners and users, it is important to understand that at some level, every designer is a diviner. This book is not an informal accreditation of the work of diviners worldwide, nor is it an endorsement for designers to hire diviners as part of their everyday process of design. This investigation proposes that site divination is a learned experience, one that predates the scientific analysis of site, and one that was passed through the generations as an orally based ritualistic tradition. Site divination is learned through experience, and cannot be taught through textbooks and the like. Once the basic forms of site divination are understood, the onus is on the designer to take the time to enter the site and search for the clues that, over time, will provide a greater insight into their conscious act of design. In time, and through their own ritualistic divination methods designers can create a continuum in their design process, along which the divine nature of the site is both sought and experienced.

To fully grasp design and site analysis in a spiritual structure where divination and the search for the divine hold an esteemed place, a more holistic approach towards design is needed: An approach that is based upon divination as brought to us through modern physics and its changing understanding of the world. The time has come to privilege the site in conjunction with the object. In the end, this holistic approach will be based upon a new view of the site, one that views the site as full and in action, not as empty and motionless. For the sake of a new form of design, one that recognizes the potential of Gaia, design must participate in the investigation of the divine, through the act of divination, on the site that is privileged instead of neglected. The act of investigating, the process of discovery, and the experience of the site, must each play a fundamentally important role in site designing. In the end, it is the role of the designer to divine.

The Final Tenets of Systemic Design

The more designers believe in the mandate of modernity and the ordered regularity of all events, the firmer their conviction that there is no room left by the side of this methodological regularity for a different nature of design. Designers must learn that neither the rational nor the rule of divine exist as independent causes of nature. All designs must be able to maintain itself not only in the clear light of rationalism, but also in the dark corners of the unknowable.

It is in the unification of the rational and the divine that design will encounter its greatest success. As presented in this book, it is through this design that we can experience the spiritualization of our understanding of life.

Since the days of Darwin, scientific and religious views have often been in opposition, the latter assuming that there was some general blueprint designed by a divine creator, the former reducing evolution to a cosmic game of dice. A gaian foundation to site design can bridge that opposition, and from that bridge create the understanding that religion, design, and science are all elements of the same act of discovery. All human beings are part of the universe. Even though we experience ourselves, our thoughts, and our feelings as something separate from the rest, this idea is a delusion of consciousness that imprisons us, restricting our personal desires and affections. Designer must free themselves from this prison by embracing all living creatures and the whole of nature in its beauty. To engender this design with which to govern the gestation of site, following are some proposed tenets. These tenets are the organizing principles and underpinnings for designs that stem from the site. Henceforth, that form of site design shall be called 'systemic design.' Though these are not the only tenets needed to create, these tenets are meant to provide broad generalities as foundations to ideas about design and its role in the creation process.

The Seven Tenets to Systemic Design

1. Create Complexity and Diversity

To create complex designs, begin simply and allow for incremental growth. Complex and diverse designs cannot be created instantly; they are structures of various independent modules that change and evolve over time. Time is an essential factor in all design.

2. Mandate Creation

Distribute interacting units over smaller units. Mandate that the sum of the parts adds up to more than the parts, thereby creating something from nothing.

3. Design from the Bottom.

Create designs based upon interdependent acts built at fundamental levels, not based upon acts enforced by centralized hierarchies.

4. Denounce Optimization.

Challenge efficiency. Complex structures do not optimize any single function, but instead satisfy a multitude of functions, and thereby are able to adapt. Complex systems are not precise. They are imprecise, and therein lies their survival.

5. Seek Disequilibrium

Stabilize towards persistent disequilibrium. Understand the dynamic nature of life.

6. Accept Change.

Over time the methods for change must be changed themselves. As change strengthens, and reinforces successful methods, it is essential to embrace change.

7. Nullius in verba.

site divine
to design eternally

appendix one *an explanation of dowsing instruments*

The Rods

The rods are the most popular of field dowsing tools. To make dowsing rods, the new dowser will need two metal rods, each measuring about 50 cm, or 20 inches in length. Old clothing hangers can be used as a source of wire. Bend the wire to obtain two identical rods with 'handles,' with a straight angle (90 degrees) between the handle and the main part of the rod. The handle should be 10 cm, or 4 inches long. Some rods contain witness chambers, which is a small container that can be attached to the rear of a dowsing instrument. Many dowsers believe that by placing a sample in the chamber of what is sought, whether it be water, gold, or oil, it will help focus the subconscious mind on the vibrations of that particular object. Prospectors and rock hounds use the witness chamber most often. It is crucial to hold the rods properly. Place the handle of the dowsing rod in the middle of your palm, then close your hand. Do not squeeze the rods too tightly for they need to be able to move. Hold the handles so that the main part of the rod is parallel to the ground and always keep the rods in that position. Hold the rods at waist level, pointing forward like you would hold two pistols.

Practice holding the points of the rods facing forward, with the tips pointed slightly downwards so the rods do not spin around uncontrollably. Standing straight with both feet flat on the floor, adjust the rods forward and backward until a spot is found where they are balanced. Gripping the ends of the rod firmly with both elbows close to the

273

site divine
appendix one
an explanation of
dowsing
instruments

chest and the forearms level and straight ahead, stay relaxed but alert. Point the rod at an object and rotate your body back and forth from the hips, while keeping the rod tip pointed at the target. Practice this technique until the rod remains fixed on the target without consciously thinking about it.

Next, point the rod to the right of the target and rotate to the left until the tip of the rod is pointed directly at the target. Make the rod 'lock-on' as the tip moves across the target. Once again, practice this until it no longer requires a conscious effort on your part to make the rods lock onto the target. Walk slowly forward with the rod pointed straight ahead. Now, focus on any straight line on the floor and walk slowly across it, crossing the line perpendicularly. Force the rods to swing away from one another when crossing the line. Practice this until the rod swings back without thinking about it. Now that your subconscious mind is getting the idea, it can be programmed to lock onto a known but unseen target. Think of an unseen tree or some other fixed object. Practice focusing the mind on the object and, slowly rotating the body, move the rod back and forth across the object. Make the rod lock onto where the unseen object is located. Finally, attempt to locate the unknown. Walking forward, mentally ask for whatever it is being sought. Follow the direction of the rods as they swivel, but be aware that as one passes over the target the rods will either cross together or open outward. Beyond the target, the rods should resume their original search position, pointing in parallel. This fundamental method of dowsing is the same as with other dowsing tools, the differences are simply in how the device reacts to one's individual muscular contractions.

Forked Stick

As stated before, the forked stick, also called the Y - Rod, has an age-old connection to dowsing. To make a forked stick, simply cut a fork about 50 cm or 20 inches long from a tree or bush. Take care that the stick is limber enough to respond to the twitchings of the hands, yet stiff enough to resist all but a definite pull from the vertical, or search position. Hold the two ends of the stick in a palms-up position, with your thumbs pointing outwards. The two ends of the stick should be held between the third and fourth fingers and the palm. The searching end of the stick is held parallel to the ground, with the tip pointing slightly upwards. Proceed as with the angle rods, mentally holding the desired target until the forked stick reacts over it by creating a pulling motion. This pulling may be either towards or away from the body, although many dowsers find the latter response more common. Once the dowser has progressed beyond the target, the stick should return to its search position.

The Pendulum

The pendulum is favored by beginning dowsers. Using a six inch string or chain, suspend a weight from one end, such as a ring or a nut. Hold the string or chain between the thumb and forefinger. To fully understand how to work with the pendulum, it is best to first practice with the pendulum and to become acquainted with the tool. Instead of deciding which motions will represent which answers, concentrate on a definite answer and let the pendulum swing the way it will. Start by maintaining a neutral position, by concentrating on the word "neutral," "pause," or "wait." Then focus on "yes," "positive," or "affirmative'" and wait to see how the pendulum swings. Then, concentrate on "no," or "negative," and again let the pendulum decide how it will swing. Remember these results, as they are articulating the subconscious mind. Every so often, repeat this procedure to ensure that the pendulum is still in sync with your subconscious. Always remember that different people with different pendulums will have different results. If after repeated trials the modes appear differently, do not attempt to change them, but instead use the pattern that is the most consistent. Begin a search by setting the weight swinging in motion in the neutral mode. Ask simple questions that have yes or no answers such as "Should I go forward?," or "Should I stop here?" After some practice, the pendulum dowser will not need to ask questions in the search mode, for the dowser will understand that for them, 'no' means stop and 'yes' means go forward.

The Bobber

The most uncommon of all dowsing devices is the wand, or bobber. A bobbert can be made from a four foot tree branch that is 1/2 to 1/4 inch in diameter. A similar length of rigid wire or the plastic tip of a fishing rod can also make a fine bobber. The best bobbers are thicker at one end, and taper down into a smaller diameter at the other end. Using a fist, grasp the wand at the smaller end. You will see that in holding the bobber parallel to the ground, the search position causes the bobber to move in a horizontal direction, bobbing back and forth. The bobber will nudge in the direction that it wants the dowser to follow. Walking over the target area, the opposite motion or a vertical motion will prevail, and the up and down motion will signal that the tip of the bobber is over the target.

275

site divine
appendix one
an explanation of
dowsing
instruments

glossary

anesthetic: (an + aisthesis) Being in a state of physical awareness lacking perceptive sensitiveness. Not feeling, insensibility. Feeling without sense, unfelt, imperceptible.

augurs: A member of the highest class of official diviners of ancient Rome, whose purpose was to promise and to give direction through indirect evidence, signs, or omens.

augury: Divination through the interpretation of omens or portents. The rite or ceremony of divination followed by an augur.

automatic writing: A spontaneous act of forming letter to record in visual form words, that is unpremeditated and performed without conscious awareness.

autopoietic: Capable of self-making or self-creating. A being's internal formative process that results in its further production.

avoca: a+ from away, and vocare + to call, from vox - voice. A calling away.

avort, avortment: (These words are non-existent words that do not mean anything.)

aya: A single governing mathematical computation used in Indian design. Traditionally, the entire series of computations consist of six calculations. 6 X (Aya) = the Remainder Aya = the prime unit of design.

brahman, brahmanical: A member of the highest or sacerdotal caste among Hindus having as chief duty the study and teachings of the Vedas and the performance of religious rituals. A class of Hindu sacred writing devoted chiefly to the instruction of the Brahmins in the performance of Vedi rituals (Brahmani or brahmanee refers to a woman brahman).

chan hou: The ancient Chinese science investigating the atmosphere. The study of the clouds.

ch'i: The sacred life force of the universe that drives all universal cycles. The breath of life, the cosmic breath, the vibrating energy which the Chinese believe permeates all living things. Its beneficial qualities are enhanced when yin and yang are in harmony, hindered when they are imbalanced.

ch'ih yin: The ancient Chinese science investigating sounds, including tones, pitches, and harmony. The foundation of Chinese musical theory.
chu-shr: The part of the universe encompassing everything irrational, illogical, and beyond understanding.

CN Tower: The Canadian National Tower located in downtown Toronto, Ontario, and owned by the Canadian National Railway. Completed on June 26, 1976, and, at 1,815.5 feet or 553.33 meters, the tallest freestanding structure in the world to date.

Compass School from the Sacred Book of Rites: The ancient Chinese methodological structure of divination based upon the magnetic orientation of the Earth. One of two founding schools of feng shui.

Le Corbusier: Architect who was fundamental in refining thoughts of modernism in design. The designer of the Notre-Dame du Haut, a religious sanctuary in Ronchamp, France.

cosmic: As relating to the cosmos, or the extraterrestrial vastness. A characteristic of the cosmos. Something of a magnitude universally transcending or subsuming.

Daedalus: Mythical Greek craftsman or inventor, noted especially for the construction of a labyrinth to contain the Minotaur and for the invention of wings with which he escaped imprisonment.

Darwin: English naturalist who developed the theory of the origin and perpetuation of new species of plants and animals. Darwin believed that organisms tend to produce offspring that varying slightly from their parents and that the process of natural selection tends to favor the survival of individuals whose peculiarities render them better adapted to their environment. This is how new species not only have been but still are produced. As such, widely different groups may have risen from common ancestors.

Delphi: The location of the ancient Greek oracle.

Descartes, René: A French philosopher and mathematician from the mid seventeenth century. Founding proponent of methodological doubt, and the distinction between objective and subjective knowledge.

design: To conceive and plan out in the mind. To indicate with a distinctive mark or sign. To plan, plot, and indicate function, shape, and disposition of the parts. To originate, draft, and work out, set up, or set forth. Deliberate, purposive planning.

designer: One who conceives plans. One whose work is creating.

Devil: The personal supreme spirit of evil and unrighteousness. The tempter. The spiritual enemy of God. Also called Apollyon, Beelxebub, Lucifer, and Satan.

dili: Ancient Chinese word for landforms. The Form School is based upon a specialist who divinates by observing the dili, or geographical features of a site.

disbelieve: To hold not to be true or real. To reject.

divination: The art or practice that seeks to discover hidden knowledge. The act of unusual insight or intuitive perception.

divine - adj. : Relating to God. Proceeding from God. Supremely good or admirable. To have a sublime or inspired character.

divine - vb. : To discover or make known. To discover or locate. To perceive, make out, or discover intuitively or through keenness of insight. To indicate something unknown. To portend. To use or practice divination. To perceive, recognize, or acquire understanding concerning some fact or circumstance by insight or intuition.

diviner: One that seeks to discover. One that practices divination.

divining rod: A rod believed to divine in the presence of water or minerals by dipping sharply downwards when held over a vein.

doodlebug: One professing skill with an unscientific device for locating underground gas, water, minerals, or ores. One professing skill with a seismograph, gravimeter, or other scientific device for the purpose of locating mineral ores.

dowse: To use a diving rod. To seek something with meticulous care. To find by dowsing.

dowser: A person who uses a divining rod for dowsing.

dragon: A huge serpent. A fabulous animal represented as a winged and scaly serpent or saurian with a crested head and enormous claws. A monster with a griffin's head, a scaly winged body with four legs, and a long barbed tail.

Earth: The sphere of mortal life comprising the world and its lands and seas as distinguishable from the spheres of spirit life. The planet upon which we live, being approximately 93 million miles from the sun and the third planet in order of distance from the sun. The Earth has a diameter at its equator of 7927 miles and is fifth in size among the planets of our solar system.

ecstasy: A state of being beyond reason and self-control through intense emotional excitement, pain, or other sensation. A state of exaltation or rapturous delight manifested either demonstratively, in a profound calm, or in abstraction of mind. A trance state of intense absorption in divine or cosmic matters.

ecstatic: As relating to ecstasy.

Einstein, Albert: Physicist and mathematician who developed the theory of relativity, leading to the assertion of the equivalence of mass and energy and of the increase of the mass of a body with increased velocity. Additionally he postulates that if two systems are in relative motion with uniform linear velocity it is impossible for observers in either system by observation and measurements of a phenomena in the other to learn more about the motion that the fact that it is in motion.

electromagnetism: Magnetism developed by a current of electricity.

Emperor Yu: Ruler of the Hsia Dynasty, the first dynasty in China, who is said to have practiced dowsing.

enlightened manifestation: To be freed from ignorance and misinformation, often based on full comprehension of all elements involved by being capable of readily and instantly perceiving by the senses. To understand or recognize at once by the mind.

err: To deviate from a standard. To wander aimlessly. To turn aside from the proper path. To make a mistake. To violate an accepted standard of conduct. To be inaccurate.

exorcise: To drive out or away. To get rid of. To relieve of the presence or influence of an evil spirit. To address or summon by adjuration.

exorcism: The act, ritual, or practice of exorcising.
extispicy: To examine the entrails of slaughtered animals for divinatory purposes.

feng ch'iao: The ancient Chinese science of climatology, investigating winds and related effects.

feng shui: A system of geomancy employed in China to bring into practice harmony with natural forces.

Form School: An ancient Chinese methodology that uses land forms to unveil the flow, direction, and patterns of ch'i in an area. One of the two founding schools of feng shui.

fusion ecstasy: A union by or as if by melting into a state of ecstasy. A merging of diverse elements into a unified state of ecstasy. A blending of sensations, perceptions, ideas, or attitudes such that the component elements can seldom be identified by introspective analysis.

Gaia: The goddess of Ge. The goddess of all the earth. An understanding that the goddess and the Earth are inseparable. Later used under the suggestion from the novelist William Golding as the name for Dr. James Lovelock's theory that the Earth is a living organism.

gallbladder: A membranous muscular sac present in most vertebrates in which the bile from the liver is stored until required for digestion.

garbhagriha: Basic three-dimensional cubic unit of measurement in traditional Indian architecture. Thought to contain the energy necessary to originate the construction of a building. All proportions become derived from this cubic unit.
6 X (Aya) = Remainder = prime unit of design. Prime unit cubed = garbhagriha.

gastric-enteritis: Inflammation of the lining membrane of the stomach and the intestine.

Ge: Earth, ground, soil.

geomancer: One that practices geomancy.

geomancy: Divination by means of figures or patterns of natural or artificial configuration of the Earth.

Georgius, Agricola: Writer who in 1556 wrote 'De Re Metallica' with a biographical introduction, annotations, and appendices upon the development of mining methods, metallurgical processes, geology, mineralogy and mining law from the earliest times to the sixteenth century

gestalt: A structure or configuration of physical, biological, or psychological phenomena so integrated as to constitute a functional unit with properties not derivable from its parts in summation.

gnomon: An object that by the position and length of its shadow serves as an indicator. A column or shaft erected perpendicular to the horizon used to find the sun's meridian altitude.

God: The supreme or ultimate reality conceived. The holy, infinite, and eternal spiritual reality presented in the Bible as the creator, sustainer, judge, righteous sovereign, and redeemer of the universe who acts with power in history carrying out his purpose. The eternal, invisible, arbitrarily omnipotent Lord of the worlds and final judge of all. The Being that is all knowing, just, compassionate, merciful, and unchangeable. The unchangeably perfect Being that is the first and final cause of the universe. The whole of the universe and its unity. The one infinite reality that is pure existence, consciousness, and bliss without distinction. The infinite mind.

harmony: A fit, mediation, or correspondence resulting in a combination creating a consistent whole. Internal calm.

haruspex: A diviner in ancient Rome basing his observations on inspections of the entrails of sacrificial animals.

hydro: Hydroelectric power, hydroelectric power plant, or relating to hydroelectricity. (Chiefly used in Canada.)

I Ching: The Chinese Book of Changes that has been used for three thousand years as a means of divining the future and as a source of wisdom.

inductive, induction: To conclude or infer from particulars. To reason from the part to the whole, from particulars to general, or from the individual to the universal.

interpretative, interpret: Explanation of actions, events, or statements by pointing out or suggesting inner relationships, or by relating particulars to general principles. To translate into audible or familiar language.

lituus: The curved staff used by an augur.

Lo P'an: The Chinese geomancer's compass, an instrument used to divine based upon varying magnetic orientation. Contrary to Western compasses, the Lo P'an points to the south, not the north. Translated as 'net plate.'

magos: The Greek word for knowledge, beyond wisdom and experience.

mandala: A graphic mystic symbol of the universe that is typically in the form of a circle enclosing a square and often bears symmetrically arranged representations of deities.

manteia: The Greek word derived from magos, which means knowledge from wisdom and experience. Translated as divination.

mason: A skilled worker who builds in stone or similar materials, such as brick or concrete. Someone who builds stonework or brickwork.

materialism: A doctrine, theory or principle according to which the only or the highest values or objectives of living life are material wellbeing, pleasure, and in the furtherance of material progress. A preoccupation with or tendency to seek or stress material things rather than intellectual or spiritual things.

metaphor: One kind of object or idea in place of another to suggest a likeness or analogy between them.

Michelangelo, Buonarotti: Italian sculptor, painter, architect and poet whose work is preeminent for grandeur of conception, dramatic action, and technical mastery of execution. Died 1564.

modernism: The philosophy and practice of a self-conscious and deliberate break with the past and a search for new forms of expression in an assertion of the superiority of modern time.

Mongolians: Natives or inhabitants of a vast territory with indefinite boundaries in east-central Asia.

mosaic: A structure in which each visual facet receives independently a small portion of the image and the total visual impression is a composite of the various unit images.

Moses in Exodus (17:1-6) and Numbers (20:1 -12): Biblical prophet and law giver who led the Israelites from Egypt to Cannan in twelve hundred B.C. Receiver of God's Ten Commandments.

mysticism: The experience of mystical union or direct communion with ultimate reality. The doctrine or belief that direct knowledge of God, of spiritual truth, of ultimate reality, or comparable matters is attainable through immediate intuition, insight, or illumination and in a way differing from ordinary sensory perception. Any theory postulating or based on the possibility of direct and intuitive acquisition of ineffable knowledge or power.

objective: Existing independent of the mind, relating to an object as it is in itself or as distinguished from consciousness. Belonging to the sensible world, observable or verifiable by scientific methods. Independent of what is personal and private. Emphasizing or expressing the nature of reality as it is without distortions by personal feelings or prejudices.

omphalos: The center of the earth, the earthly part resembling or dealing with the navel, or the umbilicus.

palimpsest: a manuscript (usually written on papyrus or parchment) on which more than one text has been written with the earlier writing incompletely erased and still visible

paradigm: A model, example, or pattern.

perception, perceive: To become conscious of. To recognize or identify as a basis for or as verified by action. To become aware of through the senses.

Platonists: Related to the Greek philosophy of Plato, stressing that ultimate reality consists of transcendent eternal universals which are the true objects of knowledge, that knowledge consists of reminiscence of these universals under the stimulus of sense perception, and that objects of the sense are not completely real but participate in the reality of ideas.

pneuma: An ethereal fiery stuff or universal spirit held by ancient stoics to be a cosmic principle. The soul of God. The life-giving principle of humankind. A spirit superior to both the body and the soul.

processus pyramidalis: The scientific name given to the gall bladder.

Procrustean: As relating to Procrustes, the villain in Greek mythology who forced travelers to fit into his bed by stretching their bodies or cutting off their legs. A social structure that has ruthless disregard for individual differences.

Progressivism: The principles or belief in continuous improvement, advancement, and progress in order to improve the conditions of the majority of people.

Purushna: The soul that constitutes the primary cause of phenomenal existence. An individual soul that is created from an infinite number of like, discrete, and eternal souls merged into one.

quantum: A tiny subdivision of a quantity or amount. One of very small increments which forms the aggregate, gross, or bulk quantity.

ravine: A small, narrow, steep-sided valley that is larger than a gully and smaller than a canyon, usually created by running water.

reductionism: The transformation into an objective form, representations of reality. The translation of all the physical world into the perspectives of science. The principle or belief of domination by force. The determination of truth through observation.

ru-shr: The part of the universe that contains everything that is rational and logical.

sacred: To dedicate, or to set apart. Being holy or hallowed by association with the divine or the consecrated. Worthy of religious veneration. Entitled to reverence and respect. Religious in nature, association, or use.

scientific method: The principles and procedures used in the systematic pursuit of inter-subjectively accessible knowledge and involving as necessary conditions the recognition and formulation of a problem, the collection of data through observation, and, if possible, experimentation, the formulation of a hypothesis, and the testing and confirmation of the formulated hypotheses.

scientism: A thesis that the methods of the natural sciences should be used in all areas of investigation, including philosophy, humanities, and social sciences. A belief that only such methods can fruitfully be used in the pursuit of knowledge.

Sh'a: The breath that hurts, where evil influences prevail.

shaman: A wise person who divines the hidden in order to understand events that affect the welfare of the people.
sin: To commit offense against God.

site: The local position of a space of ground. The original or fixed position of a place.

site analysis: The separation or breaking up of a site into its fundamental elements, or component parts. A detailed examination of the land made in order to understand its nature to determine its essential features. A thorough study of a place. The presentation in visual and written form of such an analysis. The resolution of knowledge of the

Earth into its fundamental factors or original principles and the tracing or reduction of physical phenomenal or abstract entities to their source or element.

site divination: To discover or make known about a site. To discover or locate the animate and inanimate characteristics of the land. To perceive, make out, or discover intuitively or through keenness of insight. Knowledge about a place. To use or practice divination in investigating the site. To perceive, recognize, or acquire understanding concerning some fact or circumstance regarding the earth by insight or intuition.

spiritual: Ecclesiastical rather than lay or temporal. Relating to the moral feelings or states of the soul as distinguished from the external actions.

spiritual structure: The moral feelings or values as relating to the sacred, supporting a belief.

spiritus: The breath of the soul or the spirit.

subjective: Belonging to the real that is based on qualities, attributes, or relations. Determined by the mind or consciousness of the experience and knowledge. Knowledge conditioned by merely personal characteristics of minds or by particular states of mind as opposed to what is determined by the universal conditions of human experience and knowledge. Knowledge arising from within or belonging strictly to the individual often as contrasted with something modified by an interpreter. Peculiar to a particular individual bias and limitation. Arising from conditions within the brain and not directly caused by external stimuli. Lacking in reality or substance, existing in the mind alone. Modified or affected by personal views, mental, and emotional backgrounds.

systemic design: Organized for the collection and distribution of knowledge. The component units of an aggregate exist and operate in unison or concord according to a coherent plan for smooth functioning. Stressing overall design for the interrelation of components, a carefully calculated design. Suggesting a network of interconnections or intercrossings at salient points. Design stressing an elaborate interweaving, interconnection and interrelationships of components. Suggests analogies to biological systems.

tabula rasa: A smooth tablet or blank stare, especially before the mind receives outside impressions.

Tai Ji: The great extreme. The state of existence before the creation of the universe.

teleological: The belief that the existence is being directed towards an end or shaped by a purpose. The argument that natural processes or nature as a whole is determined by a final cause or by the design of a divine providence, as opposed to purely mechanical determinism. The use of design, purpose, or utility as an explanation of any natural event.

theory: A metaphor between a model and the observed.

Thoth: An Egyptian god.

trigrams: Figure made by three lines or elements.

vale: The earth, world, or earthly life in contrast to heaven or eternity.

Vale of Avoca: The place on Earth where heaven and eternity calls.

vanish: To disappear entirely, to pass altogether out of sight, to become invisible. To disappear by departing. To disappear by passing out of existence, and cease to be.

vastu: Ancient Indian geomancy.

vastuvidya: Ancient Indian text outlining methods of scientific inquiry and sacred rituals fundamental to the geomantic standards of ancient Indian architecture.

vidyas: The ancient Indian scientific disciplines.

Vitruvius: Roman civil servant whose task was to record the architectural standards to be used throughout the Roman Empire.

Wicca: An ancient pagan religion, ancestors of the Vicar.

Wu - Hsing: The Five Elements. Conceived as the five forces of nature by the Chinese as early as the fourth century B.C. The Five Elements are comprised of Wood, Fire, Earth, Metal, and Water.

X-Tra: Weekly Toronto newspaper focusing on lesbian and gay issues.

Yang: The bright, masculine, and positive principle in nature (such as activity, height, heat and dryness) that combines and interacts with yin to produce all that comes to be.

Yin: The dark, feminine, and negative principle in nature (such as passivity, depth, cold, and wetness) that combines and interacts with yang to produce all that comes to be.

Zeus: The king of the gods in Greek mythology who ruled from his throne on Mount Olympus.

bibliography

Geomancy, Augury, and Extispicy Bibliography:

Ankerberg, John and Weldon, John. *The Facts on the Occult..* Eugene: Harvest House, 1991.

Benes, Peter. *Wonders of the Invisible World: 1600-1900.* Dublin Seminar for New England Folklife (17th: 1992: Dublin,) Boston: Boston University, 1995.

Cicero, Marcus Tullius. Brutus. *On The Nature of the Gods. On Divination. On Duties.* translated by Hubert M. Poteat, with an introd. by Richard McKeon. Chicago: University of Chicago Press, 1950.

Halliday, William Reginald, Sir. *Greek Divination; A Study Of Its Methods and Principles.* London: Macmillan, 1913.

Hitching, Francis. *Earth Magic.* London: Cassell, 1976

Hopman, Ellen Evert. T*ree Magic. Custer : Phoenix* Publishing Inc. 1991.

Jeyes, Ulla. *Old Babylonian Extispicy: Omen Texts In The British Museum*. Nederlands Historisch-Archaeologisch Instituut te ÁIstanbul, 1989.

Koch, Kurt. *Occult ABC*. Grand Rapids: Kregel, 1980.

Pennick, Nigel. *The Ancient Science Of Geomancy: Man In Harmony With The Earth*. London: Thames and Hudson, 1979.

Poddar, Prabhat "The Mysterious Energies Within and Around Us" *Architecture + design* 1991 July-Aug: 22-25,27,29-31.

Regell, P. *Roman Augury and Etruscan Divination*. New York: Arno Press, 1975.

Sarton, George. *Ancient Science and Modern Civilization*. Lincoln: University of Nebraska Press, 1954.

Screeton, Paul. *The Mystic Leys: Their Legacy of Ancient Wisdom*. London: Thorsons, 1974.

Starr, Ivan. *The Rituals of the Diviner. Malibu: Undena*, 1983.

Feng Shui Bibliography:

Albertson, Edward. I *Ching for the Millions*. Los Angeles: Sherbourne Press, 1969.

Bloomfield, Frena. *The Book of Chinese Beliefs: A Journey into the Chinese Inner World*. London: Arrow Books, 1983.

Boyd, Andrew, and Hugh, Charles . *Chinese Architecture and Town Planning, 1500 BC - AD 1911*. London: A. Tiranti, 1962

Chua-Eoan, Howard G. "How to Keep the Dragons Happy." *Time*, 22 June, 1987.

Chu, W.K, and Sherrill, W.A. *An Anthology of I Ching*. London: Routledge & Kegan Paul, 1983.

Dennys, N.B. *The Folklore of China*. 1876. Reprint. New York: Benjamin Blom, 1972.

Dore, Henry. *Researches Into Chinese Superstitions*. 1917. Reprint. Ten volumes. Taipei: Ch'eng-Wen, 1966.

DeGroot, J.J.M. *The Religious System of China*. 1897. Reprint. Six volumes. Taipei: Southern Materials Center, 1982.

DeWoskin, Kenneth J. *Doctors, Diviners and Magicians of Ancient China: Biographies of Fang-shih*. New York: Columbia University Press, 1983.

Eberhard, Wolfram. *Studies in Chinese Folklore and Related Essays. Indiana University Folklore Institute Monograph, Vol. 23*. Bloomington: Indiana University, 1970.

Eitel, Ernest J. *Feng Shui: Or the Rudiments of Natural Science in China*. 1873. Reprint. Cambridge: Cokaygne, 1973.

Ernst Eitel. *Feng Shui: The Science of Sacred Landscape in Old China*. 1873. Reprint London: Synergetic Press, 1984.

Feuchtwang, Stephan D.R. *An Anthropological Analysis of Chinese Geomancy*. Vientiane: Vithagna, 1974.

Freedman, Maurice. *Geomancy*. Proceedings, Royal Anthropological Institute of Great Britain and Ireland, 1968.

Galen, Michele. "The Chinese Art for Changing your Fortune." *Business Week*, 6 Aug. 1990

Goh Yeang Choo. "Feng Shui: Its Impact on the Design of Buildings in Hong Kong" *Architecture + Design* July-Aug 1991:39,41-47.

Govinda, Anagarika. *The Inner Structure of the I Ching: The Book of Transformations*. San Francisco: Wheelwright Press,1981.

Hook, Diana. *The I Ching and Mankind*. London, Boston: Routledge and Kegan Paul, 1975.

Hook, Diana. *The I Ching and You*. London, Boston: Routledge and Kegan Paul, 1973.

Knapp, Ronald G. *China's Traditional Rural Architecture*. Hawaii, 1966.

Lagatree, Karen M.; forward by Angi Ma Wong; illustrations by Frank Paine. *Feng Shui: Arranging Your Home to Change Your Life*. New York: Villard Books, 1996.

Lam, Kam Chuen. *Feng Shui Handbook: How To Create A Healthier Living And Working Environment*. New York: Henry Holt, 1996.

Langdon, Philip. "Lucky Houses." *Atlantic* Nov 1991.

Lee, Chin & Wong, Kay. *I Ching. Book of Change*. Tujunga: K. King C, 1971.

Lip, Evelyn. *Feng Shui: Environments Of Power: A Study Of Chinese Architecture*. London: Academy Editions, 1995.

Lip, Evelyn. *Wind & Water*. Singapore: Times Books Int., 1993.

Lip, Evelyn and Har, Mong. "Designing with Feng Shui." *Architecture + Design* July-Aug.1991: 33-35,37.

Lip, Evelyn. *Feng Shui: A Layman's Guide to Chinese Geomancy*. Union City: Heian International, 1987.

Lip, Evelyn & Mong Har. *Chinese Geomancy*. Singapore: Times Books International, 1979.

Mathews, R.H. *A Chinese-English Dictionary*. 1931. Reprint. Revised American Edition. Taipei: Caves, 1975.

Needham, Joseph and Colin, Ronan, A. *The Shorter Science and Civilization in China*. Two volumes. Cambridge: Cambridge University Press, 1978.

Picker, Lauren. "Well Placed" *House Beautiful* Mar.1996: 26.

Rasch & Au Architects. "Fong Shoi Philosophy: Toronto Complex Shows Respect for Chinese Tradition." *Buildings Design Journal* Feb, 1985: 8.

Reifler, Sam. [Oracles rephrased as poetry with the help of Alan Ravage].*I Ching, A New Interpretation for Modern Times*. New York: Bantam Books, 1974.

Rossbach, Sarah. *Feng Shui: The Chinese Art of Placement*. London: Hutchinson, New York: E.P. Dutton, 1983.

Skinner, Stephen. **The Living Earth Manual of Feng Shui: Chinese Geomancy.** London: Routledge & Kegan Paul, 1982.

Smith, Richard J. *Fortune-Tellers & Philosophers: Divination in Traditional Chinese Society.* Boulder: Westview Press, 1991.

Tankha, Brij. "Techniques of Destiny: Principles of Orientation in Japan according to Feng Shui" *Architecture + design* July-Aug, 1991: 49-55.

Tarthang Tulku. *Time, Space and Knowledge: A New Vision of Reality*. Oakland, Dharma Press, 1977.

Teh Tien Yong. "Fengshui: Its Application in Contemporary Architecture" *Mimar: Architecture in Development* Mar 1988, no.27, p.27-33

Tyndall, Kate. "In the Chinese Art of Placement, We Are How We Live" *Museum & Arts* Nov.-Dec, 1988, v.4, no.6, p.66-68,

Wagner, Michael. "Feng Shui." *Interiors* Aug, 1991: 92-93.

Walters, Derek. *Feng Shui: The Chinese Art of Designing a Harmonious Environment.* New York: Simon & Schuster, Inc. 1988.

Xu, Zhihua. F*engshui : Its Theory and Application On Landscape Architectural Design.* 1994

Yoffe, Emily. "Ancient Art, Modern Fad." *Newsweek*, 23 Dec, 1991.

Yoke, Ho Peng. *Li, Qi and Shu: An Introduction to Science and Civilization in China.* Hong Kong: Hong Kong University Press, 1985.

Dowsing Bibliography:

Agricola, Georgius. *De Re Metallica*, Book 12. 1556 English translation 1912, Mining Magazine, London. Also translated by Hoover, H.C. and L.H,Hoover, Dover Publications: New York,1950.

Bachler, Kathe. *Earth Radiation*. New York: Wordmasters Ltd. 1989.

Bailey, R.N.,E. Cambridge, D.H. and Briggs. *Dowsing and Church Archaeology*. Wimborne: Intercept Ltd, 1988.

Baum, Joseph. *The Beginner's Handbook of Dowsing; The Ancient Art of Divining Underground Water Sources*. New York: Crown Publishers, 1974.

Bell, A. H.,eds. *Practical Dowsing; A Symposium*.London: G. Bell, 1965

Baker, R.R. *Human Navigation and the Sixth Sense*. Hodder & Stoughton, London, 1981.

Bentov, Itzhak.. *Stalking the Wild Pendulum: On the Mechanics of Consciousness*. New York: E.P. Dutton, 1977.

Bird, Christopher. T*he Divining Hand.*, Atglen: Whitford Press/Schiffer Publishing, 1993.

C.Coalson, "Dowsing: The Eternal Paradox," *Psychic* March/April 1974: 13.

Coddington, Mary. *Seekers of the Healing Energy*. Rochester: Healing Arts Press, 1990.

Doczi, György. *The Power of Limits: Proportional Harmonies in Nature, Art and Architecture*. Boulder, London: Shambhala, 1981.

Ellis, A.J. "The Divining Rod: a History of Water Witching." *U.S. Geol. Survey Water-Supply Paper* 416, Washington, 1917.

Graves, Tom. *The Diviner's Handbook*. Wellingborough: The Aquarian Press, 1986.

Graves, Tom, Editor. *Dowsing and Archaeology, Selected writings from the Journal of the British Society of Dowsers*. Wellingborough, Northamptonshore, UK: Turnstone Books, 1980.

Graves, Tom. *Needles of Stone Revisited*. Glastonbury: Gothic Image Publications, 1986.

Graves, Tom. *Dowsing: Techniques and Applications*. London : Turnstone Books, 1976.

Hansen, G.P. "Dowsing: A Review of Experimental Research." *Social Psychical Research* 51(792), 343 367, 1982.

Hester, Ben G. Dowsing: *An Expose of Hidden Occult Forces..* Arlington, rev. ed. 1984.

Joffre, Michael J. and Robert T. McKusick. *Alive and Well, Neutralizing Environmental Radiations*. Globe: Biomagnetic Research, 1991.

Lawlor, Robert. *Sacred Geometry*. New York: Crossroads, 1982.

Lethbridge, T.C. *Ghosts and Divining-Rod*. London: Routledge & Kegan, 1967.

Lonegren, Sig. *Spiritual Dowsing: History of the Earth Energies and Geomancy*. Glastonbury: Gothic Image Publications, 1986.

Lonegren, Sig. *The Dowsing Rod Kit*. Boston: Charles E. Tuttle. London: Virgin. Victoria: Lothian, 1995.

Maby, J.C. and T.B.Franklin. *The Physics of the Divining Rod*. London: George Bell, 1939.

MacLean, Gordon. A *Field Guide to Dowsing*. Danville: American Society of Dowsers, 1976.

McKusick, Robert T. *Practical Dowsing*. Globe: The Association of Universal Philosophy, 1979.

Michell, John. *The Earth Spirit: Its Ways, Shrines and Mysteries*. New York: Avon Books, 1975.

Michell, John. *The New View Over Atlantis*. London: Thames & Hudson, 1983.

Miller, Hamish, and Paul Broadhurst. *The Sun and the Serpent*. Launceston: Pendragon Press, 1989.

Mullins, J. and Sons *The Divining Rod; Is history, Truthfulness and Practicability*. Wiltshire: Colerne Box, 1894.

Naylor, P. *Discovering Dowsing and Divining*. Princes Risborough,Shire Publications Ltd, 1980.

Nielsen, Greg, and Joseph Polansky. *Pendulum Power*. Rochester: Destiny Books, 1987.

Lucas Pat. "Living Water" *Traditional Homes* Aug,1989: 95-97.

Perry, Maria, Editor. *The Water Dowsers Manual*. Danville: The American Society of Dowsers, 1990.

Roberts, Kennith. *Henry Gross and His Dowsing Rod*. Garden City: Doubleday & Company, 1951.

Roberts, Kenneth Lewis. *The Seventh Sense*. Garden City: Doubleday, 1953.

Roney-Dougal, Serena.. *Where Science and Magic Meet*. Shaftsbury; Rockport; Brisbane, 1993.

Ross, Terry. Edward and Richard D. Wright. *The Divining Mind: A Guide to Dowsing and Self Awareness*. Rochester: Destiny Books, 1990.

Stark, Erwin E. *A History of Dowsing and Energy Relationships*. North Hollywood: BAC, 1978.

Underwood, Guy. *The Pattern of the Past*. New York: Abelard-Schuman, Ltd, 1973.

Vogt, E.Z. and R, Hyman. *Water Witching USA*. University of Chicago: Chicago Press, 1959.

Von Franz, Marie-Louise. *On Divination and Synchronicity: The Psychology of Meaningful Chance*. Toronto: Inner City Books, 1980.

Watkins, Alfred. *The Old Straight Track*. London: Abacus, 1974.

Willey, Ray. *Modern Dowsing: The Dowser's Handbook*. Sedona: Esoteric Press, 1976.

Wright, Patricia C. & Richard D.Wright. *The Divining Heart: Dowsing and Spiritual Unfoldment*. Rochester: Destiny Books, 1994.

Wyman, Walker D. *Witching For Water, Oil, Pipes, And Precious Minerals* . Madison: University of Wisconsin Press, 1977.

THE AMERICAN SOCIETY OF DOWSERS
P.O. Box 24
Danville, VT 05828
(802) 684-3417
A.S.D. Book Store
101 Railroad St.
St. Johnsbury, VT 05819
(802) 748-8565 (800) 711-9497

Gaia Bibliography:

Abraham, Ralph; Terence McKenna; Rupert Sheldrake; foreword by Jean Houston Trialogues at the *Edge of the west : Chaos, Creativity, and the Resacralization of the World*. Santa Fe: Bear and Co, 1992.

Allaby, Michael. *A Guide To Gaia A Survey of the New Science of Our Living Earth*. New York: Dutton, 1990.

Arguelles Jose A. *Earth Ascending : An Illustrated Treatise on the Law Governing Whole Systems*. Boulder: Shambhala, distr. by Random House, 1984.

Bunyard, Peter. eds. Gaia In Action : *Science of the Living Earth*. Edinburgh: Floris Books, 1996.

Devereux, Paul. and John Steele, David, Kubrin; foreword, Lyall Watson. *Earthmind: A Modern Adventure in Ancient Wisdom*. New York: Harper & Row, 1989.

Goddess of the Earth. NOVA program from WGBH, Boston. 60 minutes. 1986.

Goldsmith, Edward. *The Way—An Ecological World-View*. Totnes: Themis, 1996.

Lawrence, E. Joseph. *Gaia : The Growth of an Idea*. New York: St. Martin's Press, 1990

Lovelock, James. *The Ages of Gaia : A Biography Of Our Living Earth*. New York: Norton, 1995.

Lovelock, James. *Healing Gaia : Practical Medicine for the Planet*. New York, Harmony Books, 1991.

Lovelock, James. *Gaia: A New Look at Life on Earth*. Oxford: Oxford University Press, 1972, 1979.

Mann, Charles. " Lynn Margulis: Science's Unruly Earth Mother." *Science*, Vol. 252, April 19, 1991: 378-381.

Margulis, Lynn and Dorion Sagan. *Slanted Truths: Essays on Gaia, Symbiosis and Evolution*. New York: Copernicus, 1997.

Margulis, Lynn and Dorion Sagan. *What is Life*. New York: Simon and Schuster, 1995

Nicholson, Shirley and Brenda Rosen. *Gaia's Hidden Life: The Unseen Intelligence Of Nature*. Wheaton: Quest Books, 1992.

Sahtouris, Elisabet. *Gaia: The Human Journey From Chaos To Cosmos*. New York: Pocket Books, 1989

Schneider, Stephen H. and Penelope J. Boston, eds. *Scientists on Gaia*. Cambridge: MIT Press, 1991.

Thompson, William Irwin. eds. *Gaia 2 : Emergence : The New Science Of Becoming*. Hudson N.Y.: Lindisfarne Press, 1991.

Thompson, William Irwin. eds. Gaia, *A Way Of Knowing : Political Implications of the New Biology*. Great Barrington: Lindiefarne Press, 1987.

Zoeteman, Kees; [translated by Tony Langham and Plym Peters]. *Gaiasophy: The Wisdom Of The Living Earth : An Approach To Ecology*. Hudson: Lindisfarne Press, 1991.

Site Analysis Bibliography:

Alberti, Leon Battista. *Ten Books on Architecture*. Translated into English by James Leoni, and edited by Joseph Rykweert. London 1755.

Brooks, Gene. *Site Planning: Environment, Process, and Development*. Englewoods Cliffs: Prentice-Hall, 1988.

Chiara, Joseph De and Lee E.Koppelman. *Time-Saver Standards for Site Planning*. New York: McGraw-Hill, 1984.

Clayton, C.R.I., N.E. Simons, and M.C.Matthews, *Site Investigation*. New York: Halsted Press, 1982.

Itten, Johannes. *Design and Form: The Basic Course at the Bauhaus*. New York: Van Nostrand Reinhold, 1975.

Jarvis, Frederick D. *Site Planning and Community Design for Great Neighborhoods*. Washington DC: Home Builder Press, 1993.

Joyce, Michael D. *Site Investigation Practice*. London; New York: E. &F. N Spon, 1982.
Lampert, Dan and Douglas R. Woodley, eds. *Site Selection and Investigation : A Practical Handbook*. Aldeshot, Hants; Brookfield: Gower, 1991.

Lynch, Kevin and Gary, Hack. *Site Planning*. Cambridge: MIT Press, 1984.

McAvin, Margaret. *Site Planning for Energy Conservation*. Monticello: Vance Bibliographies, 1981.

McHarg, Ian L. *Design with Nature*. New York: J. Wiley, 1992

Rubenstein, Harvey M. *A Guide to Site and Environmental Planning*. New York: J. Wiley, 1987

Russell, James E. *Site Planning*. Reston: Reston, 1980.

Teague, Edward and Mary Vance. *Site Planning: A Bibliography*. Monticello: Vance Bibliographies, 1986.

Torre, L. Azeo ; edited by William Lake Douglas ; foreword by William Turnbull. *Site Perspectives*. New York: Van Nostrand Reinhold, 1986.

Vitruvius. *De architectura*. Translated by Caesare Caesariano. Como, 1572. On Architecture. Translated by Frank Granger. 2 vols. London, 1920.

White, Edward T. *Site Analysis : Diagramming Information for Architectural Design* Tuscon, Arizona: Architectural Media, 1983.

New Scientific Paradigm, and Skeptics Bibliography:

Capra, Fritjof. T*ao of Physics: An Exploration of the Parallels Between Modern Physics and Eastern Mysticism*. Boston: Shambhala Publications, 1991.

Capra, Fritjof. *Belonging to the Universe: Explorations on the Frontiers of Science and Spirituality*. San Francisco: Harper, 1991.

Capra, Fritjof. *Uncommon Wisdom: Conversations With Remarkable People*. New York: Bantam Books, 1989.

Gleik, James. *Chaos: Making a New Science*. New York: Viking Penguin, 1987.

Hanen M.P., M.J. Mosler, R.G. Weyant Science, *Pseudi-Science and Society*. Waterloo: Wilfrid Laurier University Press, 1980.

Harper's Magazine. "Dowsing is Nonsense" New York, *Harper's Magazine Co.* July 1951.

Kuhn, T.S. *The Structure of Scientific Revolutions.* Chicago: Univesity of Chicago Press, 1970.

Martin, Michael. "A New Controlled Dowsing Experiment: Putting the President of the American Society of Dowsers to the Test." *The Skeptical Inquirer* Winter 1983-84: 139.

Mazumba, Asit. " Ripple Effects". *The Sciences.* November/December. 1990: 38-42.

McClain, Ernest G. *The Myth of Invariance.* Boulder, London: Shambhala Publications, 1978.

Nash S. Science and Uncertainty. *London: Science Reviews* Ltd, 1985.
Pecujlic M.,G. Blue and A.Abdel-Mahlek *Science and Technology in the Transformation of the World.* London: MacMillan Press Ltd, 1982.
Randi, James. "The Great $10,000 Dowsing Challenge." *The Skeptical Inquirer* Summer 1984: 329-33.

Randi, James. "A Controlled Test of Dowsing Abilities." *The Skeptical Inquirer* Fall 1978: 16-20.

Russell, Peter. *The Awakening Earth: The Global Brain.* London: Routledge & Kegan Paul, 1982

Schneider, Michael S. *A Beginner's Guide to Constructing the Universe: The Mathematical Archetypes of Nature, Art, and Science.* New York: Harper Perennial, 1995.

Schwenk, Theodor. *Sensitive Chaos: The Creation of Flowing Forms in Water.* New York: Schocken Books, 1976.

Smith, Dick. "Two Tests of Divining in Australia." *The Skeptical Inquirer,* Summer 1982: 34-37.

Starr C.and P.C. Ritterbush. *Science, Technology and the Human Prospect.* New York: Pergamon Press, 1980.

CPSIA information can be obtained at www.ICGtesting.com
Printed in the USA
244870LV00010B/21/P

9 780982 280904